Streetlights and Shadows

Streetlights and Shadows

Searching for the Keys to Adaptive Decision Making

Gary Klein

A Bradford Book
The MIT Press
Cambridge, Massachusetts
London, England

First MIT Press paperback edition, 2011
© 2009 Massachusetts Institute of Technology

MIT Press books may be purchased at special quantity discounts for business or sales
promotional use. For information, email special_sales@mitpress.mit.edu or write to
Special Sales Department, MIT Press, 55 Hayward Street, Cambridge, MA 02142.

Set in Palatino on 3B2 by Asco Typesetters, Hong Kong. Printed and bound in the United
States of America.

Library of Congress Cataloging-in-Publication Data

Klein, Gary
Streetlights and shadows : searching for the keys to adaptive decision making / Gary
Klein.
    p.   cm.
"A Bradford Book."
Includes bibliographical references and index.
ISBN 978-0-262-01339-0 (hardcover : alk. paper)—978-0-262-51672-3 (pb.)
1. Decision making. 2. Problem solving. I. Title.
BF448.K54   2009
153.8'3—dc22   2009007501

10   9   8   7   6   5   4   3

to Helen, Devorah, and Rebecca

Contents

List of Examples

A policeman saw a drunk searching for something under a streetlight. "What have you lost, my friend?" the policeman asked. "My keys, said the drunk. The policeman then helped the drunk look and finally asked him: "Where exactly did you drop them?" "Over there," responded the drunk, pointing toward a dark alley. The policeman then asked: "Why are you looking here?" The drunk immediately replied: "Because the light is so much brighter here."

Ten Surprises about How We Handle Ambiguous Situations

A commercial airliner isn't supposed to run out of fuel at 41,000 feet. There are too many safeguards, too many redundant systems, too many regulations and checklists. So when that happened to Captain Bob Pearson on July 23, 1983, flying a twin-engine Boeing 767 from Ottawa to Edmonton with 61 passengers, he didn't have any standard flight procedures to fall back on.

First the fuel pumps for the left engine quit. Pearson could work around that problem by turning off the pumps, figuring that gravity would feed the engine. The computer showed that he had plenty of fuel for the flight.

Then the left engine itself quit. Down to one engine, Pearson made the obvious decision to divert from Edmonton to Winnipeg, only 128 miles away. Next, the fuel pumps on the right engine went.

Shortly after that, the cockpit warning system emitted a warning sound that neither Pearson nor the first officer had ever heard before. It meant that both the engines had failed.

And then the cockpit went dark. When the engines stopped, Pearson lost all electrical power, and his advanced cockpit instruments went blank, leaving him only with a few battery-powered emergency instruments that were barely enough to land; he could read the instruments because it was still early evening.

Even if Pearson did manage to come in for a landing, he didn't have any way to slow the airplane down. The engines powered the hydraulic system that controlled the flaps used in taking off and in landing. Fortunately, the designers had provided a backup generator that used wind power from the forward momentum of the airplane. With effort, Pearson could use this generator to manipulate some of his controls to change the direction and pitch of the airplane, but he couldn't lower the flaps and slats, activate the speed brakes, or use normal braking to slow down when landing. He couldn't use reverse thrust to slow the airplane, because the engines weren't providing any thrust. None of the procedures or flight checklists covered the situation Pearson was facing.

Pearson, a highly experienced pilot, had been flying B-767s for only three months—almost as long as the airplane had been in the Air Canada fleet. Somehow, he had to fly the plane to Winnipeg. However, "fly" is the wrong term. The airplane wasn't flying. It was gliding, and poorly. Airliners aren't designed to glide very well—they are too heavy, their wings are too short, they can't take advantage of thermal currents. Pearson's airplane was dropping more than 20 feet per second.

Pearson guessed that the best glide ratio speed would be 220 knots, and maintained that speed in order to keep the airplane going for the longest amount of time. Maurice Quintal, the first officer, calculated that they wouldn't make it to Winnipeg. He suggested instead a former Royal Canadian Air Force base that he had used years earlier. It was only 12 miles away, in Gimli, a tiny community originally settled by Icelanders in 1875.[1] So Pearson changed course once again.

Pearson had never been to Gimli but he accepted Quintal's advice and headed for the Gimli runway. He steered by the texture of the clouds underneath him. He would ask Winnipeg Central for corrections in his heading, turn by about the amount requested, then ask the air traffic controllers whether he had made the correct turn. Near the end of the flight he thought he spotted the Gimli runway, but Quintal corrected him.

As Pearson got closer to the runway, he knew that the airplane was coming in too high and too fast. Normally he would try to slow to 130 knots when the wheels touched down, but that was not possible now and he was likely to crash.

Luckily, Pearson was also a skilled glider pilot. (So was Chesley Sullenberger, the pilot who landed a US Airways jetliner in the Hudson River in January of 2009. We will examine the Hudson River landing in chapter 6.) Pearson drew on some techniques that aren't taught to commercial pilots. In desperation, he tried a maneuver called a slide-slip, skidding the airplane forward in the way ice skaters twist their skates to skid to a stop. He pushed the yoke to the left, as if he was going to turn, but pressed hard on the right rudder pedal to counter the turn. That kept the airplane on course toward the runway. Pearson used the ailerons and the rudder to create more drag. Pilots use this maneuver with gliders and light aircraft to produce a rapid drop in altitude and airspeed, but it had never been tried with a commercial jet. The slide-slip maneuver was Pearson's only hope, and it worked.

When the plane was only 40 feet off the ground, Pearson eased up on the controls, straightened out the airplane, and brought it in at 175 knots, almost precisely on the normal runway landing point. All the passengers and the crewmembers were safe, although a few had been injured in the scramble to exit the plane after it rolled to a stop.

The plane was repaired at Gimli and was flown out two days later. It returned to the Air Canada fleet and stayed in service another 25 years, until 2008.[2] It was affectionately called "the Gimli Glider."

The story had a reasonably happy ending, but a mysterious beginning. How had the plane run out of fuel? Four breakdowns, four strokes of bad luck, contributed to the crisis.

Ironically, safety features built into the instruments had caused the first breakdown. The Boeing 767, like all sophisticated airplanes, monitors fuel flow very carefully. It has two parallel systems measuring fuel, just to be safe. If either channel 1 or channel 2 fails, the other serves as a backup. However, when you have independent systems, you also have to reconcile any differences between them. Therefore, the 767 has a separate computer system to figure out which of the two systems is more trustworthy. Investigators later found that a small drop of solder in Pearson's airplane had created a partial connection in channel 2. The partial connection allowed just a small amount of current to flow—not enough for channel 2 to operate correctly, but just enough to keep the default mode from kicking in and shifting to channel 1. The partial connection confused the computer, which gave up. This problem had been detected when the airplane had landed in Edmonton the night before. The Edmonton mechanic, Conrad Yaremko, wasn't able to diagnose what caused the fault, nor did he have a spare fuel-quantity processor. But he had figured out a workaround. If he turned channel 2 off, that circumvented the problem; channel 1 worked fine as long as the computer let it. The airplane could fly acceptably using just one fuel-quantity processor channel. Yaremko therefore pulled the circuit breaker to channel 2 and put tape over it, marking it as inoperative. The next morning, July 23, a crew flew the plane from Edmonton to Montreal without any trouble.

The second breakdown was a Montreal mechanic's misguided attempt to fix the problem. The Montreal mechanic, Jean Ouellet, took note of the problem and, out of curiosity, decided to investigate further. Ouellet had just completed a two-month training course for the 767 but had never worked on one before. He tinkered a bit with the faulty Fuel Quantity Indicator System without success. He re-enabled channel 2; as before, the fuel gauges in the cockpit went blank. Then he got distracted by another task and failed to pull the circuit breaker for channel 2, even though he left the tape in place showing the channel as inoperative. As a result, the automatic fuel-monitoring system stopped working and the fuel gauges stayed blank.

A third breakdown was confusion about the nature of the fuel gauge problem. When Pearson saw the blank fuel gauges and consulted a list of minimum requirements, he knew that the airplane couldn't be flown in that condition. He also knew that the 767 was still very new—it had first entered into airline service in 1982. The minimum requirements list had already been changed 55 times in the four months that Air Canada had been flying 767s. Therefore, pilots depended more on the maintenance crew to guide their judgment than on the lists and manuals. Pearson saw that the maintenance crews had approved this airplane to keep flying despite the problem with the fuel gauges. Pearson didn't understand that the crew had approved the airplane to fly using only channel 1. In talking with the pilot who had flown the previous legs, Pearson had gotten the mistaken impression that the airplane had just flown from Edmonton to Ottawa to Montreal with blank fuel gauges. That pilot had mentioned a "fuel gauge problem." When Pearson climbed into the cockpit and saw that the fuel gauges were blank, he assumed that was the problem the previous pilot had encountered, which implied that it was somehow acceptable to continue to operate that way.

The mechanics had another way to provide the pilots with fuel information. They could use a drip-stick mechanism to measure the amount of fuel currently stored in each of the tanks, and they could manually enter that information into the computer. The computer system could then calculate, fairly accurately, how much fuel was remaining all through the flight.

In this case, the mechanics carefully determined the amount of fuel in the tanks. But they made an error when they converted that to weight. This error was the fourth breakdown.

Canada had converted to the metric system only a few years earlier, in 1979. The government had pressed Air Canada to direct Boeing to build the new 767s using metric measurements of liters and kilograms instead of gallons and pounds—the first, and at that time the only, airplane in the Air Canada fleet to use the metric system. The mechanics in Montreal weren't sure about how to make the conversion (on other airplanes the flight engineer did that job, but the 767 didn't use a flight engineer), and they got it wrong. In using the drip-stick measurements, the mechanics plugged in the weight in pounds instead of kilograms. No one caught the error. Because of the error, everyone believed they had 22,300 kg of fuel on board, the amount needed to get them to Edmonton, but in fact they had only a little more than 10,000 kg—less than half the amount they needed.

Pearson was understandably distressed by the thought of not being able to monitor the fuel flow directly. Still, the figures had been checked repeatedly, showing that the airplane had more fuel than was necessary. The drip test had been repeated several times, just to be sure. That morning, the airplane had gotten approval to fly from Edmonton to Montreal despite having fuel gauges that were blank. (In this Pearson was mistaken; the airplane used channel 1 and did have working fuel gauges.) Pearson had been told that maintenance control had cleared the airplane. The burden of proof had shifted, and Pearson would have to justify a decision to cancel this flight. On the basis of what he knew, or believed he knew, he couldn't justify that decision. Thus, he took off, and everything went well until he ran out of fuel and both his engines stopped.

Mental gears

The Gimli Glider incident illustrates an extreme case in which plans and intentions fall apart, the typical procedures and routines don't work, and people have to draw on experience. Few of us will ever experience such an emergency, but we all face smaller disturbances and dislocations. Flights get cancelled and we have to find alternative routes. New projects get started and we have to juggle them into our schedules. A child becomes ill and all our priorities change.

We can't treat every situation as an emergency; that's why we depend on standard strategies to let us reach our everyday goals. However, we can become vulnerable if we are too rigid, too locked into our routines to adjust to changing conditions.

We need both mental "gears": one for using the standard procedures and the other for improvising when situations become unsettled.

Our eyes are built for two perspectives. During the daytime we rely on our cone cells, which depend on lots of light and let us see details. At night the cone cells become useless and we depend on rod cells, which are much more sensitive. The rod cells in our eyes are connected together to detect stray light; as a result they don't register fine details. If we want to see something in bright light, we focus the image on the center of our retina (the fovea), where the cone cells are tightly packed. To see something at night, we must look off to the side of it, because staring directly at it will focus the object on the useless cone cells in the fovea.

The way we see in bright light differs from the way we see in shadows. Neither is the "right" way. We need both.

This dual viewpoint of light and shadow affects how we make decisions and how we make sense of situations. It affects how we plan and how we manage risks and uncertainty. It guides how we develop expertise and how we use our intuition.

Most of the research on thinking and decision making takes place in bright and clear conditions. Most of the advice offered is about how to think and decide when the issues are straightforward. That isn't what I'm interested in. In this book, I will explore how we think and decide in the world of shadows, the world of ambiguity.

The Gimli Glider incident shows crew members intensely trying to think their way through a crisis that was unexpected and unfamiliar. It illustrates different aspects of thinking. Despite all their checklists, Pearson and Quintal found themselves in a situation that none of the procedures covered. They made tough decisions, starting with the misguided decision to take off without fuel gauges and continuing with the decision to divert from Winnipeg to Gimli. They had to make sense of what had happened to them, diagnosing that the engines had failed because they had run out of fuel and then sorting out the impact on their ability to control the airplane. And they had to adapt—they had to work out ways to keep flying the airplane and ways to slow it in order to land safely.

These aspects of thinking—making decisions, making sense of events, and adapting—are the primary themes of parts I, II, and III of this book. They are related to each other, but they create different demands on us. Making decisions, choosing what to do, is the most direct and visible challenge; it is the theme of part I. Yet the choices we make depend on how we size up the situation (the topic of part II). Adapting to events (the focus of part III) builds on the way we understand those events and reflects our decisions and our ability to learn. These three cognitive functions appear over and over in many kinds of human activities.[3] (See figure 1.1.)

In the past 30 years my colleagues and I have done hundreds of studies, working with firefighters, military commanders, housewives,

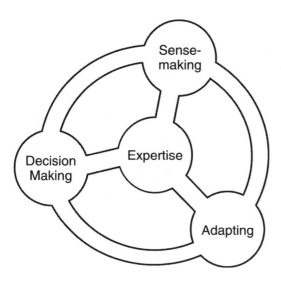

Figure 1.1
Three strands of thinking.

pilots, chess masters, process controllers, and everything in between. We conducted our studies in natural settings, rather than in laboratories, because we wanted to understand how people think under shadowy conditions, such as ambiguity, vague goals, and situations that keep changing.[4] In my book *Sources of Power* (1998), I described the initial studies that showed us how people actually make tough decisions. Since then, researchers working in natural settings have learned much more about how decision makers think under pressure. I have written *Streetlights and Shadows* to help readers understand what these discoveries imply about the way they work and the way they carry out their daily pursuits.

Most people have arrived at a set of beliefs about how to perform each of these three functions shown in figure 1.1. I have identified ten typical claims about how to think more effectively. In ambiguous and shadowy situations, I believe the claims are misleading. Let us examine them one by one.

Ten claims about how to think more effectively

Table 1.1 lists the claims that will be examined in the following chapters. If you like, record your opinions about each one. I am going to

Table 1.1
Claims about the ways to improve performance.

Claim	Scale						
	1 Completely disagree for any situation	2 Strongly disagree for almost all situations	3 Tend to disagree for most situations	4 Hard to tell	5 Tend to agree for most situations	6 Strongly agree for almost all situations	7 Completely agree for any situation
1. Teaching people procedures helps them perform tasks more skillfully.							
2. Decision biases distort our thinking.							
2a. Successful decision makers rely on logic and statistics instead of intuition.							
3. To make a decision, generate several options and compare them to pick the best one.							
4. We can reduce uncertainty by gathering more information.							
5. It's bad to jump to conclusions—wait to see all the evidence.							
6. To get people to learn, give them feedback on the consequences of their actions.							
7. To make sense of a situation, we draw inferences from the data.							
8. The starting point for any project is to get a clear description of the goal.							
9. Our plans will succeed more often if we ID the biggest risks and find ways to eliminate them.							
10. Leaders can create common ground by assigning roles and setting ground rules in advance.							

present this same survey at the end of the book in case you want to see if your beliefs have changed.

I compiled these claims by collecting examples of the advice given by researchers, organizational developers, and management specialists. Then I trimmed my collection down to the claims that worried me the most.[5] I began running workshops and giving talks about these claims to a wide range of groups—from the top echelon of Fortune 50–size companies, to military leadership programs for Army generals, as well as to graduate seminars in universities. I have probably talked about these claims with several thousand people. The reaction by audience members is usually the same: Disbelief that anyone would challenge the claims, followed by a grudging appreciation of what is wrong with the claims, and ending with disbelief that they had ever fully accepted the claims.

Now it is time for an admission: I used to believe all the claims described in the survey. No, that's too soft. These claims seemed so self-evident that I couldn't imagine not believing them. So I'm not in a position to criticize anyone who strongly subscribes to them, who assigns a 6 or a 7 to any of them. You are not alone.

How strongly do people agree with these claims? I worried that in criticizing them I was beating a dead horse. To find out if the claims were widely accepted, I collected data from more than 160 people. Some were graduate and undergraduate students enrolled in business classes. Others were military officers and process managers. Each of them filled out the survey, rating the same set of statements.[6]

I started with sixteen claims. Then I threw out any claim for which the average agreement rating was lower than 5: Tend to agree for most situations. That got the number of claims down to ten. Some of the claims listed above got average ratings as high as 5.89, one just squeaked by at 5.06, but none was lower than 5.0. The average rating for all ten was 5.44. People really do accept these claims. Very few people marked any disagreement at all—there were very few ratings below 4.[7]

Sharp-eyed readers will have noticed that I have listed eleven statements above, not ten. The reason is that claim 2a ("Successful decision makers follow logic and statistics instead of intuition") didn't make the cut. The average agreement rating for this statement was 4.05, just on the border between agreement and disagreement. That result frustrated me. Here I was ready to refute it, only to find out that people don't believe it. I decided to include a chapter on this statement anyway because most textbooks and decision researchers still make this claim. But I can't count it as one of the ten surprises—the ten claims that people believe in.

For many readers, the surprise is going to be that you cannot count on these claims. I am going to try to convince you to reduce your confidence in them. I'm not going to argue that any of the claims is wrong. Each of them is sometimes right.

In fact, there is a correct answer for filling out the survey: It depends, it depends, it depends. What does it depend on? Primarily, it depends on how complex and unpredictable the situation is.

Complex and unpredictable

The claims work best in well-ordered situations. Well-ordered domains are structured and stable. We know what causes the effects we want to achieve. We can think systematically about well-ordered domains because we know how they work. We can calculate what decisions to make and how to predict the future.

However, we don't usually live in that world of clarity. Much of the time we find ourselves in a different world—a world of shadows where we don't know all the causes or how they work, we can't pin down all the knowledge we need in order to be successful, and we aren't sure we understand the goals.

Complex domains aren't as structured or stable as well-ordered ones. These situations may change rapidly and unexpectedly. We have to keep track of more factors, and they link to each other in lots of different ways. We may also have the feeling that we don't know some of the important linkages. We aren't entirely sure what causes events to happen. We can't make good predictions about what will happen next. And we rely a lot on stories and examples instead of rules.[8]

How does the Gimli Glider incident stack up against the ten claims?

Captain Pearson would have liked to follow procedures for gliding a 767 with both engines out but the emergency checklist didn't provide him with any. His intuition about using the side-slip maneuver wasn't a bias—it prevented the crash. Pearson was trying to make sense of events but he wasn't gathering every scrap of information, waiting to see all the evidence, and deriving new inferences. He focused on the most useful data points. He didn't waste time and mental energy trying to diagnose why the airplane had run out of fuel. His job was to improvise a landing. He needed to quickly learn how to control the

Gimli Glider before there were any consequences, not after. He certainly didn't try to get a clear description of the goal. He didn't know exactly where he was going to land, or at what precise speed. He figured that out as he went along, first diverting to Winnipeg, then to Gimli. If necessary, he would have attempted to land on a highway or even in an open field. He would have preferred landing at the Winnipeg airport to cut the risks. He would have liked having emergency equipment on hand to help passengers escape, but he didn't systematically trace all the possible risks because the primary risk—crashing his airplane—dominated his thinking.

Pearson didn't work carefully with his co-pilot to ensure common ground. Quintal knew where to take initiative, warning Pearson that they wouldn't reach Winnipeg and suggesting that they land in Gimli. Besides, it was a breakdown in common ground that got Pearson into this mess. He believed the previous pilot had been flying the airplane without any fuel gauges. Assigning roles and setting ground rules can't prevent this kind of confusion; that's why common ground breakdowns are so insidious, and why they cause so many accidents.

Why correcting the ten claims matters

Our decision making takes on different forms when we are facing ambiguous, complex, and unpredictable situations. The advice that is so beneficial in well-ordered situations may not work as well. It may not work at all. In fact, that advice may sometimes work against us. These are the conditions for which we need the most guidance. Yet conventional wisdom doesn't apply as well—it can send us in the wrong direction. If that's true, then I think we better re-examine the ten claims, and re-examine our confidence in them. I'm not denying their attractiveness. The ten claims in the survey appeal to our eagerness to treat complex problems as if they were orderly and manageable. How many times have we heard "Look, this is simple. All you need to do is. . . . "

And we want to believe. We want to think it is simple. However, bitter experience tells us that an approach to decision making or planning that seems so easy to follow can just as easily fall apart.

As I have stated, the ten claims aren't wrong. They work fine in well-structured situations. They even have some value in complex situations because any given situation has both ordered and complex aspects simultaneously. There is light even in shadows. We can see it with night vision goggles. In the Gimli incident, many procedural aspects of the situation continued to persist and in fact everybody depended on them (e.g., procedures for evacuation of passengers during emergency landings). No situation is purely complex.

Conversely, few situations are entirely well-ordered. The darkest shadows are closest to the source of light. The things we take for granted can turn out to be more complicated than we appreciate.

The goal of this book is to explore the boundary conditions where the ten claims apply well, where they aren't really relevant, and where they work against us. I want to open a dialogue about these issues, rather than assume that the claims hold in all situations. This dialogue may unsettle some readers, particularly when I explore the strengths and limitations of a favorite claim. Be assured, I am not trying to convince anyone to reject any of the claims.

We make progress when we find regularities in situations that appeared to be highly complex. We should encourage those researchers who look for order in complex situations. Many hygiene and public health procedures are examples of initially complex domains which, after painstaking study, analysis, data gathering, and assessments, evolved over many years to orderly understandings. SARS was complex and initially required complex responses, but over time we have figured out how it works and now have a repertoire of very structured responses to it. The boundaries between the streetlight and the shadows aren't sharp—there are many gradations.

We can make blunders when we use intuition in cases in which we should be relying on scientific analysis. We can also blunder when we rely too heavily on scientific analyses. The statistical analyses that seem so impressive under stable conditions often turn out to be brittle and insensitive to surprises.

If we can't rely on systems analysis to tame the complex domains, how are people able to work successfully in these domains? One answer is that they can rapidly build expertise in adapting to unexpected events. After all, experts have little difficulty in mastering situations that may seem hopelessly complex and unpredictable to most of us.

That's another reason why revising the ten claims matters. Most of the claims, rooted in well-ordered situations, try to substitute analysis for experience. The claims discourage us from using intuitions based on experience. They seek to replace insights with structured techniques for thinking. But in complex and ambiguous situations, there is no substitute for experience.

I   Making Decisions

The claims that I will review in this part of the book are about decision making. I will explain why we can't rely on procedures to make decisions in complex situations, and why tacit knowledge plays a more important role in decision making than is acknowledged by the claims surveyed in chapter 1. I will also show why biases aren't always bad, why logic doesn't always help, and why generating multiple options doesn't always make sense. We put too much emphasis on reducing errors and not enough on building expertise. The last chapter in this part will describe why people often reject methods or computer programs designed to support analytical decision making.

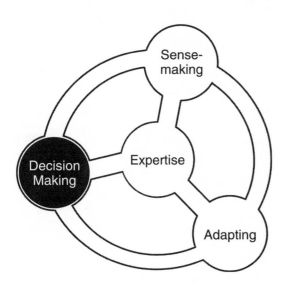

2   A Passion for Procedures

The first claim reflects our enthusiasm for taking the guesswork out of decisions by providing procedures to follow and clear criteria for how to move on to each step. It reflects our desire to break complex tasks into step-by-step procedures. I ran into this attitude in my initial research with firefighters. I asked them how they made decisions and they explained that they rarely, if ever, had to decide anything. "We just follow the standard procedures," they explained. But when I asked to see these procedures they told me they weren't written down. Firefighters just knew what to do. We'll get back to the firefighter research in chapter 6. This chapter examines the conditions under which procedures work for us and the conditions under which they aren't so helpful. Let us begin by considering the arguments in favor of claim 1.

Claim 1: Teaching people procedures helps them perform tasks more skillfully.

The process of transforming skills into procedures is irresistible. All we have to do is break a complex task down into steps and provide some tips about when to start and finish each step. Then we hand the procedures out so that workers can perform this task even without years of practice. Much of our progress in fields such as training, coaching, and safety management comes from this strategy.

Pilots rely on flight checklists to carry out many kinds of actions, including taking off, landing, and handling a whole range of malfunctions and emergencies. These checklists consist of the current wisdom about how to get the job done. Procedural checklists seem particularly useful when pilots are stressed, overloaded, or not particularly experienced. They are a shield against interruptions, reducing the chance that a radio call from an air traffic controller or a dispatcher might distract the pilot into omitting an essential step in a routine.

Procedures also help us evaluate performance. We can see if someone knows the procedures, and is following them.

Flight checklists are just one example of procedures that have successfully captured a task and have improved performance and safety. Procedures are also relevant to health care. Peter Pronovost, at the Johns Hopkins University, developed a procedural checklist approach for a specific and common problem in intensive care units: infections from catheter lines inserted into patients' bodies. Pronovost identified five simple steps for handling patients in an ICU whenever a line is to be inserted: (1) Wash your hands with soap. (2) Clean the patient's skin with antiseptic. (3) Cover the patient with sterile drapes. (4) Wear a sterile mask and gloves. (5) Put a sterile dressing over the line once it is inserted. Pronovost didn't make these steps up; they are standard knowledge. All he did was codify them. Next he arranged for nurses to assess if the surgeons followed the steps. Not always, as Pronovost knew. Pronovost then took more aggressive action. He convinced the hospital administration to authorize nurses to intervene if they saw any steps being omitted. The nurses also had to assess if any of the lines could come out even if the physician was prepared to leave it in. The results were clear: line infections dropped to zero for the next year (from a baseline of 11 percent), and the hospital saved several million dollars.[1,2] A larger program in the state of Michigan, using three of Pronovost's checklists in intensive care units, reduced infections by 66 percent and saved an estimated $175 million.[3]

Obviously, there are good reasons why people in my sample bought into the value of procedures. They gave an average rating of 5.57 to the statement "Teaching people procedures helps them perform tasks more skillfully." Only six out of 160 expressed any disagreement (that is, gave it a rating of 1, 2, or 3).

Disclaimer

I believed claim 1 until I started working as a research psychologist at Wright-Patterson Air Force Base in Ohio in 1974. One of my projects was to compile a procedural guide for a radar system on the F-106 air defense interceptor. I worked with several pilots at Tyndall Air Force Base in Panama City, Florida.

One day after work, at the Officers Club, two of the pilots on the project, Scotty and Mad Dog (I no longer remember their actual names), confided in me about a problem they were having on a different project. They had been assigned to come up with a procedure for air-to-air combat when flying their F-106s against invading airplanes. "That seems like a hard assignment," I commiserated. They agreed. It was hard, but they had just finished writing a draft of the procedures. "Great," I said. "What's the problem?"

Scotty and Mad Dog hesitated, looked around to see if anyone was listening, and admitted that they didn't follow any of the procedures in their guide. "Well, why not just write down the procedures you do follow?" I asked. That was the problem. They didn't think they followed any procedures. They believed that a new pilot, following the procedures they had documented, could get the job done. But not very well. They wondered why they couldn't capture the task in procedures. By the end of the conversation, we concluded that the aviation skills needed for this mission couldn't be proceduralized. Their story got me interested in the topic of procedures. The Air Force was introducing Instructional Systems Design, a way to decompose complex tasks into procedures that could be readily taught. If the basic assumption was flawed—if tasks couldn't be broken down into procedures—the whole training concept was going to run into trouble.

In his 1974 book *The Inner Game of Tennis*, Timothy Gallwey argued that in tennis following procedures is the opposite of skill. Instead of engaging in the sport, players worry about their form—whether their feet are too far apart, if one elbow is bent at the correct angle, and so forth. Those kinds of rules and procedures are more likely to interfere with performance than to improve it.

Putting Gallwey's ideas together with my discussion with Scotty and Mad Dog, I began to wonder about the notion of breaking complex tasks into steps. I documented some examples in which the procedures that trainee pilots were being taught didn't match how skilled pilots performed the same tasks.[4]

I also enlisted the help of Hubert and Stuart Dreyfus to provide an alternative view. Both of them were Berkeley professors, Bert in philosophy and Stuart in operations research.[5] Bert and Stuart described the inherent limits of procedural accounts and offered a model of how people develop expertise. According to their model, novices are given

simple procedures that don't depend on context—on what else might
be going on. Thus, beginning chess players might be taught numerical
values of the pieces and advised to be careful not to lose exchanges.
For example, it's a bad idea to trade a queen for a pawn.[6] Of course,
these numerical values are fictions; the real value of a chess piece
depends on what is happening in a position, and will change as the
game changes. But that's too complicated for novices; they are grateful
to know the point values. By the time people become proficient, they
are seeing situations instead of calculating procedures. Experts rely on
their immediate intuitive responses. That is how chess grandmasters
can play so skillfully under blitz conditions where they only have 5–10
seconds per move. It's also how skilled drivers maneuver through traffic while conversing with their passengers.

The Dreyfus model of expertise emphasizes intuition and tacit
knowledge that can't be captured in rules and procedures. People
might need some rules in order to get started, but they have to move
beyond rules in order to achieve mastery.[7]

Procedures, including checklists, are tools. Every tool has limitations, and I am not arguing that we should do away with procedures.
For example, I admire Peter Pronovost, who advocated for Intensive
Care Unit checklists, and others who have made similarly impressive
contributions. Pronovost appreciated how to focus checklists on the
right kinds of problems—ones like line infections that were costly and
life-threatening, where safety was degraded because people were too
rushed or careless to take normal precautions. Pronovost isn't suggesting that putting checklists in the hands of nurses eliminates the need
for skilled physicians. He understands the boundary conditions for
using checklists and procedures.

But organizations often overstate the importance of procedures. During an accident investigation, if someone finds that a procedure wasn't
followed, even if it didn't directly cause the accident, there is a good
chance that "procedural violation" will be trumpeted as one of the contributing factors. I once participated in an aviation accident investigation. The flight data recordings showed pretty clearly that the pilots
hadn't done everything exactly by the book. The senior pilot next to
me pointed out that pilots violate some procedures on almost every
flight. There are so many procedures that pilots are bound to violate
some minor ones. No one pays attention to that unless there is an accident; then "procedural violations" become part of the story.

By appreciating the limitations of procedures and checklists, we'll be able to make better use of them. What are those limitations?

Procedures alone aren't sufficient.
In complex settings in which we have to take the context into account, we can't codify all the work in a set of procedures. No matter how comprehensive the procedures, people probably will run into something unexpected and will have to use their judgment. It often takes government regulation to force organizations to compile reasonably comprehensive sets of procedures, and those procedures usually have some gaps.

Even the routine task of flying an airplane can move beyond procedures. And in emergencies, procedures may be cast aside. Not in *all* emergencies—checklists have saved the lives of many pilots. But we also have stories such as that of Bob Pearson, who landed the Gimli Glider despite running out of fuel (as described in chapter 1), and Chesley Sullenberger who landed in the Hudson River after both of his engines failed soon after takeoff. Here is another example.

Example 2.1: A flying brick   The Douglas DC-10 commercial airliner is equipped with three hydraulic systems to provide redundancy. Risk analysts estimated that there was a billion-in-one chance of losing all three hydraulic systems. Yet it happened.[8] Unfortunately, in the DC-10's tail section the three hydraulic lines converged for a stretch of 10 inches.

On July 19, 1989, during United Airlines' flight 232 from Denver to Philadelphia, when the airplane was at 37,000 feet, the fan disk of its tail-mounted engine broke in two. Pieces of shrapnel severed the lines for all three hydraulic systems and the hydraulic fluid drained away. At that point, the pilot, Al Haynes, lost the use of his cockpit controls. That should have been the end of the story, and the end of Haynes and his passengers. But it wasn't.

Haynes and his crew found that they could still achieve some control by varying the thrust of the two wing engines to steer the plane. Almost like a stroke victim re-learning basic functions of speech and movement, the crew rapidly re-learned how to fly the airplane. Haynes was able to crash land it on the runway at Sioux City, Iowa. Although 111 passengers and one crew member perished, 185 people survived because Haynes and his crew adapted to a crisis that never appeared in the flight checklists. They were able to fly an airplane that didn't have any hydraulic controls—a feat that had previously seemed impossible to everyone in the aviation industry.

There aren't procedures for flying commercial airplanes that have lost all of their hydraulic fluid. There aren't procedures for lots of other kinds of anomalies that pilots have to overcome.

One way to ensure that a set of procedures is sufficient is to take every eventuality into account. However, this strategy can result in the opposite problem: procedural guides that are over-sufficient and sometimes incomprehensible.

Example 2.2 was related by a senior air traffic controller in a country that will remain anonymous.

Example 2.2: The hijack procedures   A call came in from an inbound passenger aircraft from the country's national airline that the plane had been hijacked and the hijackers were demanding to have a meeting with a visiting head of state. The plane was scheduled to land in 20 minutes. This was the first time the country had encountered a hijacking, but it had developed a secret procedure for handling such events. The procedure involved coordination with security agencies, communications centers, and government ministers.

The senior air traffic controller on duty had not seen the procedure, but he had the key to the safe in which it was kept. He went to the safe and opened it. At this point in recounting the story, he held his hands about six inches apart. "It was this thick—I had less than twenty minutes to put something together, and there was no way I was going to read through this document. So I dumped it, called my contacts in the security agencies, and started to improvise. I basically lied to the hijackers until we were able to get the special forces unit onto the plane. After the incident, I was reprimanded for not following the procedure, and commended for handling it with no civilian casualties. Then I was asked to re-write the procedure. It's still too thick."

The hijack procedures may have been perfect for this case, but they were so voluminous that the senior air traffic controller didn't have time to review them. This appears to be a common problem and a consequence of trying to make procedures sufficiently comprehensive. The more comprehensive the procedures, the more voluminous they become. And the more voluminous, the more forbidding they appear, the more work to find what is needed, and the lower the chances that anyone will try.

Procedures are difficult to keep updated.
Procedures are often out of date because work practices keep evolving. Neil Johnston, a retired airline pilot, training officer, and aviation researcher with Aer Lingus, calls the evolution of procedures "procedural drift."[9] In commercial aviation, procedures are written when a new aircraft is being designed. These original procedures aren't particularly sensitive to the everyday demands of keeping those airplanes flying. Once the plane goes into service, new management teams start tinkering with the procedures and assume that their changes will be obvious to everyone. The history of the changes and the rationale for them aren't necessarily clear to subsequent teams, who make up their own interpretation for the reasons behind the changes.

Remember the example of the Gimli Glider. Captain Pearson relied more on the maintenance crews than on the procedure manuals. In its first four months with 767s, Air Canada had changed the minimum requirements list 55 times.

Furthermore, the procedural changes that get made are often excessive. The changes, though imposed to reduce the chance of adverse consequences, may create inefficiencies in working with the new type of airplane. People create workarounds to cope with the inefficiencies. Each airport or depot may evolve its own daily work practice for maintaining that kind of airplane. Personnel turnover adds to the problem of procedural drift as new employees make their own adaptations to the procedures. The result is a continual and confusing evolution of procedures during the lifetime of the airplane.

Because procedures keep evolving, procedural guides are rarely complete. Greg Jamieson and Chris Miller (2000) studied four petrochemical refineries in the United States and Canada to see how they managed their procedures. In none of the four cases did the workers ever completely trust the procedural guides and checklists, because they never knew how updated these guides were. Over time, some procedures became obsolete or even counterproductive. The people doing the job learned workarounds. They used their experience to adapt, just as we would expect in a complex domain. But how often could the managers revise the procedural manuals? How often could they retrain all the staff members? How could a worker track the updates in the current manuals? How could a worker predict whether other team members were familiar with the latest updates?

Inevitably, the procedures lagged behind the actual way people did their work. Up-to-date procedures had to be interpreted and carried out by workers using their judgment and experience, and obsolete procedures created even more headaches.

But there is a bigger problem than the fact that procedures are rarely sufficient and often out of date. In many cases, procedures can make performance worse, not better. They can lull us into mindlessness and complacency, and an erosion of expertise. In some cases, procedures can mislead us.

Procedures can lead to mindlessness and complacency.
Procedures can lull people into a passive mindset of just following the steps and not really thinking about what they are doing. When we become passive, we don't try to improve our skills. Why bother, if all we are doing is following the procedures? So the checklists and procedural guides can reduce our motivation to become highly skilled at a job.[10]

Example 2.3: The high road and the low road   In 1996 my colleagues Rebecca Pliske, Beth Crandall, Rob Hutton, and David Klinger conducted a study of weather forecasters. They traveled around the United States to interview some of the top forecasters working for the Air Force, then they visited Atlanta just after the Olympic Games to talk to the weather forecasting team that had provided advisories and guidance for the various events. One of their findings was that the mediocre forecasters relied on procedural guides when collecting data, and also when turning the data into forecasts. They took the "low road" illustrated in figure 2.1.

In contrast, the highly skilled forecasters tried to understand what was going on. They foraged for data that helped them build a better understanding, and used their understanding to make predictions.

When I presented figure 2.1 at the 21st American Meteorological Society Conference on Weather Analysis and Forecasting, in Washington, in 2005, an executive from the national forecasting service Accuweather commented that his company was increasingly reliant on the procedures its forecasters needed to take the low road in figure 2.1. The senior staff referred to these procedural guidelines as "the great equalizer." They permitted the mediocre forecasters to just follow some rules and still put out adequate forecasts. But they tied the hands

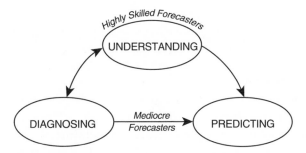

Figure 2.1
Forecasting processes used by mediocre and skilled weather forecasters.

of the skilled meteorologists and degraded their performance to the point that they were just putting out adequate forecasts, no better than that. The procedures mandated which data to collect and what types of analyses to perform, leaving no room for expert forecasters to follow their hunches and detect unusual weather conditions.

Accurate weather forecasts can affect lives—not just those of people who are disappointed when it rains on a picnic or dampens a golf outing, but also those of fishermen (who might get hit with an unexpected storm), hikers (who might get stranded on a mountaintop without enough food or clothes to survive very long), or pilots (who might be forced to divert when an unexpected thunderstorm closes an airport). It might be cheaper to hire inexperienced forecasters and give them enough procedures to get the job done, but those who depend on accurate forecasts might pay the costs.

Procedures can erode expertise.
When we get comfortable with procedures, we may stop trying to develop more skills. Why bother, if the procedures usually get the job done? The result may be an erosion of expertise in organizations that rely too heavily on procedures. That's what the Accuweather executive was finding.

Research supports this idea of eroding expertise. A number of studies have shown that procedures help people handle typical tasks, but people do best in novel situations when they understand the system they need to control.[11] People taught to understand the system develop richer mental models than people taught to follow procedures.[12]

Procedures can mislead us.

The biggest worry is that following procedures can lead us in the wrong direction and that we won't notice because the reliance on procedures has made us so complacent. Kelley and Littman (2005) gave an example of how the Parisian subway system was extended to Charles de Gaulle Airport. The architects and designers followed their standard template for putting in subway stations. After all, you don't want to waste time and energy re-designing every new addition if you already have a template that works well. Unfortunately, the Charles de Gaulle station wasn't like all the others. The passengers coming into the station were different—they tended to carry luggage. Lots of luggage. The turnstiles that worked so well elsewhere in the metro were too small. Some passengers had to toss suitcases over the barriers in order to get through. Perhaps the developers should have spent a few minutes wondering if their templates were suited to this new station.

Kim Vicente, a Canadian authority on cognitive engineering, described an example of procedural breakdown in a nuclear power plant with highly experienced control-room operators.[13] When they had been tested for their response to simulated emergencies, the operators had always performed very well, but they hadn't always followed every step of the official procedures. In the previous tests, the inspectors had criticized the operators for each departure from the standard procedures. Therefore, as they awaited an upcoming exercise, the operators made a pact to follow all the procedures completely. And they did so. By chance, the emergency conditions sent them into a loop: one operator carried out his responsibility, then the next operator performed his step, then the next operator followed in turn but restored the plant to the earlier status. They looked at one another, knowing how easy it was to get out of the loop, but they remembered their pact, so they kept going round and round until the inspectors intervened and moved them forward. But they still got written up for "malicious procedural compliance." This incident has an amusing punch line, but the message is very serious. Skilled performers need latitude to depart from procedures.

Lia DiBello found the same thing in her observations of maintenance technicians. Experts may claim to follow procedures, but when DiBello watched them she saw them deviate from the procedures when they needed to. Here is a transcript from an interview with a maintenance technician about how he performed a periodic inspection of a bus—surely a straightforward and routine activity[14]:

Ed: Well, there is not much to this. We just go down the checklist. Nothing to it really.

Lia: So we start at the top and just go down.

Ed: No, I don't do that. I mean, I skip around the list.

Lia: Why is that?

Ed: Well, the order doesn't make sense. See that guy back there (points to rear of bus). I'll be in his way if I start back there. And if I follow the list exactly, I'll be running around the bus all day, literally. So I begin with the things in front. And since I have it up on the lift, I begin with the things underneath first.

Lia: Okay.

Ed: (looking at steering arm bushing under bus). Here, hold this flashlight for me (picks at dirt and rust around bushing).

Lia: What's that?

Ed: That's the bushing. What's bothering me here is that it looks like some rust here. That's not good. Shows me there's a problem. Let's look and see when this is due back in (looks at schedule of inspections and picks more at the dirt and rust around bushing).

Lia: What's up?

Ed: Well, see this bushing over here. Shine the light right here. This is good. See, no rust mixed in with the dirt. Now look at this one. There is some rust in here. But not too much. Not very red. See that?

Lia: (researcher sees no difference).

Ed: That bushing really needs to be changed. But given that this is coming in in 3000 miles for an A inspection, we can take care of it then. It's got at least that much time on it left. And they need this bus this afternoon. It's gotta wait. So we will make a note of it.

Lia: How do you know it has another 3000 miles left on it?

Ed: Well, it's obvious. By the color of the dirt. The amount of rust in there.

Typically, experts like Ed don't compulsively follow the procedures. If they did, they wouldn't be doing their job.

In example 2.4, a manager also faced a conflict between procedures and judgment. Fortunately that manager rejected the procedures.

Example 2.4: The bubble   The manager of an offshore oil drilling rig was awakened at 1:30 a.m. by a telephone call reporting a blocked pipe. A bubble of natural gas had somehow gotten trapped and was rising through the pipe. This posed a risk to operations. Fortunately, the company had a standard procedure for these cases: inject heavy mud into the pipe to counterbalance the pressure. The night crew was ready, just waiting for him to give the order. But he didn't give it. Something didn't feel right. He tried to imagine what might go wrong, and couldn't find anything. Still, it didn't feel right. He couldn't come up with anything. It was just a gut feeling. So he got dressed and helicoptered over to the rig. By that time it was daylight. They searched for ignition sources, leaks, anything that might pose a problem for the procedure. And then they found it. The relatively small amount of natural gas at a depth of 4,500 meters was under 15,000 psi of pressure. As it rose, and the pressure diminished, it would expand to 100,000 cubic feet by the time it reached sea level. It would flow through the pipes and processors in the oil rig until it finally reached the separator. But the 100,000 cubic feet was far too great for the limited capacity of the separator, which would undoubtedly explode, blowing up the rig and killing everyone on board. The manager's intuition avoided a disaster.

The manager called his supervisor to explain the problem. He said that he was not using the standard procedure, to which his supervisor replied "Are you crazy?" But when the manager explained his rationale, the supervisor agreed it was the right decision. The manager then turned to an alternate strategy and resolved the problem.

When we questioned him years later, the manager first insisted that he had no idea of why he felt uneasy about initiating the standard procedure. As we probed, he remembered that what was bothering him was the size and depth of the bubble. At the time, he didn't know how it might go wrong, but he didn't have confidence in simply following the prescribed method. Like most experts using their intuition, he couldn't articulate what he was noticing.

In summary, we can see that procedures are insufficient, can get in the way, can interfere with developing and applying expertise, and can erode over time. Procedures work best in well-ordered situations in which we don't have to worry about changing conditions and we don't have to take context into account to figure out how to apply the procedures, or when to jettison them, like the oil rig manager who felt that something wasn't right.

Unintended consequences

If we took claim 1 seriously, we might create the following unintended consequences.

We would establish "adequate" performance as the new ideal. It is too difficult and inefficient to continually fiddle with better procedures, which creates an endless cycle of updating. By signing onto a procedural strategy, we would live with ineffective designs such as the metro station servicing Charles de Gaulle airport. We wouldn't mind workers who settle for an "adequate" level of performance, like the Accuweather forecasters.

We would discourage people from using their judgment. We wouldn't want them to overrule the procedures. Standardization is more important than the occasional explosion of oil rigs. If someone did overrule a judgment, as in the bubble incident, we would try to keep it quiet. Instead, in every accident or error we would find some violations of procedures and publicize them. That way we could give early retirement to senior workers—their tacit knowledge wouldn't be useful, and they are the ones least likely to refer to procedures when they perform their jobs. We wouldn't worry about all the nuances of context. We would accept the inefficiency of transit mechanics who follow their inspection checklists regardless of what else is happening around them. We would expect military pilots to follow checklists for aerial combat just as for taking off.

We would generate massive volumes of procedures because it is too expensive to go back and cull procedures we don't need anymore. The only changes we'd be able to envision would be to add more and more procedures.

We would save money by retaining our current ways of doing the work. Anyone who proposed a different business or work strategy would have to ensure that it was consistent with all the existing procedures. Or else we would just let the paperwork discourage anyone from suggesting improvements. Consider the international ISO 9000 standards. ISO 9000 refers to a family of international standards that documents the procedures covering the business processes a company uses. A friend of mine proudly told me that his factory was officially recognized as ISO 9000 compliant. But a few months later he admitted that when he and his co-workers found a better way to get the job done they debated whether rewriting all the procedural manuals was worthwhile. Usually they decided it wasn't. They had grown less enthusiastic about improving their practices because of the cost of keeping their standardized practices current. ISO 9000 was making the company less adaptive.

We would issue procedures as a way to change behavior even though there may be simpler and more effective strategies. For example, public officials in Taiwan grew frustrated by merchants who failed to pay sales taxes. The merchants handled cash transactions off the cash registers, leaving no trail for inspectors to follow. Instead of increasing penalties and warnings, Taiwan set up a lottery in which every entry was required to be accompanied by a sales slip. Suddenly, in that lottery-crazed country, people were demanding sales slips from their merchants. Thus the problem was solved without any need for new regulations.

Replacement

By now it should be understandable why claim 1 (that teaching people procedures helps them perform tasks more skillfully) doesn't always apply. Procedures are most useful in well-ordered situations when they can substitute for skill, not augment it. In complex situations—in the shadows—procedures are less likely to substitute for expertise and may even stifle its development.

Here is a different statement that I think works better: *In complex situations, people will need judgment skills to follow procedures effectively and to go beyond them when necessary.*

For stable and well-structured tasks we should be able to construct comprehensive procedure guides. Even for complex tasks we might try to identify the procedures because that is one road to progress. But we also have to discover the kinds of expertise that come into play for difficult jobs.

Like all tools, procedures have strengths and weaknesses. Although I have been describing their limitations, we certainly shouldn't discard them. Here is what they buy us:

• They are training tools. They help novices get started in learning a task.

• They are memory aids. In many jobs they help workers overcome memory slips.

• They can safeguard against interruptions. For example, pilots following a flight checklist often get interrupted; the checklist helps them carry out all the steps.

• They reduce workload and make it easier to attend to critical aspects of the task.

• They are a way to compile experience and historical information. Procedures are useful when there is a lot of turnover and few workers ever develop much skill. They help less-experienced workers do a reasonably acceptable job. They can walk a skilled pilot through the steps of handling an unfamiliar malfunction. They can help automobile mechanics troubleshoot a tricky electrical problem. (Diagnostic procedures differ from memory aids.)

• They can help teams coordinate by imposing consistency. If the people on the team know the same procedures, they can predict one another's next moves.

The last advantage is particularly important for *ad hoc* teams that don't have a chance to practice together regularly. These include flight crews and surgical teams—the two examples given at the beginning of this chapter. Both flight crews and surgical teams work in complex settings, and yet procedures effectively reduce errors. The value of procedures in these settings isn't to substitute for experience. Flight crews and the surgical teams know what to do. But they sometimes get distracted or they forget.

Flight crews accept procedures because they know the checklists work. Further, the procedures aren't intended to substitute for expertise—they aren't "aviation for dummies." The aviation community accepts that senior pilots can override the procedures when appropriate. Aviation illustrates the ideal arrangement: skilled decision makers living in harmony with procedures.

The downside of procedures is that they usually aren't sensitive to context. In complex situations we may not know when to start and end each step. The people making up procedures usually try to substitute precision and detail for tacit knowledge. People sometimes make up procedural guides to capture what they think experts are doing. That's a noble intent, but procedural guides really can't explain the tacit knowledge that people acquire over decades of experience.

Procedures help when you need people to reliably follow the same steps. However, that's different from needing reliable *outcomes*. For example, a blacksmith must bring the hammer down to the same point stroke after stroke, yet we don't care if the arc of the hammer is the same each time. And it isn't the same. Even highly experienced blacksmiths alter the arc in order to get precision at the strike point (Bernstein 1996; Latash 1996).

Getting procedures "right" is not just a matter of getting them to be accurate or efficient or updated or covering all needed contexts, which may well be both impossible and prohibitively expensive. It is also a matter of getting the organization to have the right attitude toward procedures.

In a study of petrochemical plants that I mentioned earlier in this chapter, Jamieson and Miller explored the culture of procedures. Some places and companies regarded procedures as requirements— behaviors that *had* to be followed for organizational or even legal reasons. Others regarded procedures as recommendations: "Here is the normal way of doing things, and what people will expect, but there may well be reasons to deviate....Just make sure everyone knows you're going to do so." And still others treated procedures as suggestions, an organizational repository of experience and lessons learned: "This procedure has worked in other circumstances. Use it as a starting point, but don't ever assume that it's necessarily going to work this time around." Jamieson and Miller advised the plants to explicitly distinguish which of these three attitudes they were using, to avoid confusion.

To put procedures into perspective, consider the difference between directions and maps (Vicente 2002). When we have to travel to an unfamiliar destination, we sometimes get directions—a sequence of actions (e.g., turn right, go straight for two blocks, then turn left). Other times we get a map showing where we are, where we want to be, and the terrain in between. The directions are easier to follow, but if anything goes wrong (say, a street is blocked off) we are stuck. A map demands more of us but makes it easier for us to adapt and can be used for other routes in the same area.

For many types of complex work we need both procedures and the judgment to interpret and work around the procedures. Hockey, Sauer, and Wastell (2007) used a laboratory process control task to compare the value of training rules and procedures against the value of training people to understand the system they had to control. As was expected, people trained to understand the way the system worked were more flexible, and did a better job of spotting and fixing unfamiliar and complex malfunctions, than people trained to follow rules and procedures. However, they also took longer to do the work, and they were more affected by a stressor—noise—than people who had merely been trained to follow procedures.

Teaching procedures

When we do want to teach some procedures, the typical way is to present the standard procedures and make everyone memorize them.

Here is another way to teach procedures: Set up scenarios for various kinds of challenges and let the new workers go through the scenarios. If the procedures make sense, then workers should get to see what happens when they depart from the optimal procedures. When procedures are taught in a scenario format, people can appreciate why the procedures were put into place and can also gain a sense of the limitations of the procedures. This scenario format seems to work better than having people memorize the details of each step. The scenarios provide a good counterpoint for learning the steps of complicated tasks. Moreover, the scenarios can help people acquire some of the tacit knowledge they need in order to apply procedures effectively. (The topic of tacit knowledge will be taken up in the next chapter.)

Why claim 1 matters

Claim 1 (that teaching people procedures helps them perform tasks more skillfully) matters because it creates a dilemma for workers. Too often supervisors insist that workers follow some shallow rules that never were validated, some of which may be obsolete. Workers then face the dilemma of whether to do the job right or to stick to the procedures. If they use their judgment and then run into trouble, they may get penalized for not following the guidelines. If they stick to the guidelines and run into trouble, they may be penalized for failing to get the job done. They lose either way.

It matters because when we emphasize procedures over skills we set a standard of mediocre performance. The standard procedures become a basis for evaluating job performance, making people even less likely to adapt or improvise and more careful to comply with the rules. In some mature industries, such as aviation and nuclear power, decision makers should follow the rules, as long as those rules make sense. In unpredictable settings, the standard procedures can impede progress because workers may have to experiment and not be told what to do every step of the way.

It matters because too often we issue procedures in order to change behavior even though there may be simpler and more effective ways to do that.

3 Seeing the Invisible

How do we recognize a person's face? How do we suspect that someone didn't understand or agree with what we just said? How can sports announcers on TV watch a diving competition[1] and notice slight imperfections in the way the diver's legs are aligned, or in the splash the diver made on entering the water? The commentators tell us about the anomalies as the dive happens, then we get to confirm their statements during the slow-motion replay. All these are examples of tacit knowledge as opposed to explicit knowledge—facts and rules. Explicit knowledge is easy to write down, easy to communicate, easy to teach, and easy to learn.

However, we also know a lot of important things that don't boil down to facts and rules. Tacit knowledge is being able to do things without being able to explain how. We can't learn tacit knowledge from a textbook.[2] We know more than we can tell.[3]

Think about how to decide whether to make a left turn in traffic.[4] We face this life-and-death decision on almost every trip.[5,6] If we get the decision wrong, we risk a head-on collision.

Fortunately, there is a simple rule to keep us safe. All we have to do is calculate how much time we need to make a left turn, estimate the amount of time free between the gaps in the oncoming traffic, and subtract the time needed from the time available. If the number is positive, we can make the turn. If it's negative, we should wait.

Warning: Do not try this procedure in an actual traffic situation. No one would or should ever follow this rule. No one would teach it to a teenager learning how to drive. Even though the rule seems foolproof, it just won't work. We don't have the time to do the calculations. And we need not do them. With practice, we have learned to recognize when to turn and when to wait.

We wouldn't use this rule even if we had plenty of time. When we see a large gap between oncoming cars, we don't calculate time differences. Some people might argue that we do these calculations unconsciously, but that doesn't make sense. Few of us know how long it usually takes us to make a left turn; few of us could estimate the number of seconds between pairs of oncoming cars. If we can't do these calculations consciously, it seems unlikely that we are doing them unconsciously.

How do we judge when to turn? We just draw on our experience to recognize when it looks safe and when it doesn't. We gauge whether the car in front of which we will be turning seems to be slowing down or speeding up. We also notice complications such as a pedestrian who could be getting ready to cross the street we are about to enter, because complications may slow us down. We compare the situation against our experiences and judge whether the situation feels safe or whether it matches earlier situations in which we cut it too close and got honked at.

We do this pattern matching in less than a second. For example, if the oncoming car unexpectedly turns into a driveway, thus opening a sufficient gap, we immediately decide to make our left turn. We don't have to calculate.

Tacit knowledge[7] plays a prominent part in our ability to cope with complex conditions.[8,9] Every day we entrust our lives to our tacit knowledge, and not only for making left turns. We rely on it to carry out rules—to know which rules to use, to modify them as needed, and to recognize when to break them. We rely on tacit knowledge to interpret facts, to judge their credibility, to fit them together, and to judge what counts as a relevant fact in the first place. We rely on tacit knowledge in walking, in throwing a baseball, and in riding a bicycle. We can't learn these skills by reading an instruction manual or by getting directions over the telephone.

Tacit knowledge isn't just about actions like making a left turn or riding a bicycle. I recently had the pleasure of watching an experienced lawyer scrutinize a contract, and I realized that I was seeing tacit knowledge in action. Good lawyers have mastered all the relevant laws in order to pass the law exams and get certified. That's the explicit knowledge. However, in scrutinizing the contract, my lawyer wasn't just trying to remember the statutes. He was also imagining what could happen to create headaches for me. He looked at each clause and statement and mentally rotated it to see where it could go wrong. He was trying to conjure up events that could leave me unprotected and spot risks that weren't specifically called out. He was drawing on his experience with how the world works to anticipate what could go wrong. You don't find that in law books.

The claims surveyed in chapter 1 downplay tacit knowledge. In trying to convince us that the world is simple and responsive to rules and procedures, the claims either dismiss tacit knowledge or encourage us to distrust it. That seems like a mistake; tacit knowledge is the basis for our skills and the reflection of our experience. The claims in the survey depend heavily on explicit knowledge and also fit best into well-ordered situations. When we move to complex situations in which success depends on tacit knowledge, the claims become less trustworthy.

Explicit knowledge is important, but it isn't the entire story. Tacit knowledge is like the part of an iceberg that is below sea level (figure 3.1). We don't notice it, and we can't easily describe it. Therefore, we are usually oblivious to the tacit knowledge we use in applying our explicit knowledge of facts, rules, and procedures. Expertise depends heavily on tacit knowledge, as do many of our everyday skills. Some procedures can be carried out directly, as when we follow the steps in a checklist. But others depend on tacit knowledge to adapt a given procedure to fit the circumstances. That's why even the entry for routines and procedures is partially submerged in the figure.

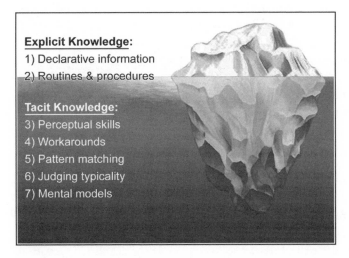

Figure 3.1
Explicit and tacit knowledge.

It is easy to ignore tacit knowledge, which is hard to articulate or even to notice. We depend on unconscious processes to carry out tasks. That's how our experience gets translated into our actions. Because most of the time we don't think about this background knowledge, it stays hidden under the surface of our lives.

To make tacit knowledge more visible, I'm going to describe different aspects of it: its roles in making perceptual discriminations, in performing workarounds, in recognizing patterns, in judging typicality, and in using mental models. These are the aspects that are below water in figure 3.1. I'll also cover the use of tacit knowledge to follow procedures, because, as we saw in chapter 2, procedures aren't always straightforward.

However, please don't expect these aspects to be clearly distinct from one another. Our ability to make perceptual discriminations will affect how we perform workarounds and recognize patterns. Our mental models will affect how we carry out procedures and perform workarounds. The aspects are just that—different ways that we can use tacit knowledge.

Further, these different aspects can include conscious thinking. When we perform workarounds, when we use our mental models, we are usually deliberating about the tasks at hand. Tacit knowledge is critical for these activities but we are also thinking critically, relying on our memory, consciously imagining how things might play out, and so forth. I am not arguing that all our important skills are unconscious. Rather, I just want to illustrate the ways that tacit knowledge comes into play.

Perceptual skills

With experience we learn to see things that others don't notice. I have already mentioned the examples of making a left turn against traffic. Making left turns or merging onto an expressway separates the experienced drivers from the 16-year-olds. In his 2005 book *Blink*, Malcolm Gladwell described many examples of skilled performance, including the ability to tell by tasting foods what the ingredients are and how they were prepared and the ability to predict which physicians will be sued for malpractice by examining thin slices of their interactions with patients. In each case, the experts can see or notice or taste things that are invisible to the rest of us.

Consider again how sports commentators describe diving competitions. One cue they notice is the amount of splash a diver makes upon entering the water. This cue relates to how vertical the diver is when entering the water. The splash lasts less than a second. The commentator distinguishes large from small splashes, in relation to the type of dive and the amount of last-minute rotation. Afterward, in slow motion, we can see it too. But we don't see it at the time.

With experience we learn where to look as well as how to make discriminations and recognize connections. We learn how to direct our attention.

Here is a fictional example that describes how tacit knowledge depends on years of experience.

Example 3.1: Sailsmanship   Patrick O'Brian's *Master and Commander* novels illustrate many forms of tacit knowledge, such as how Captain Jack Aubrey[10] stays ahead of his adversaries. Sometimes Aubrey has to judge the fighting capability of another ship:

. . . as she came nearer, tacking and tacking again, it was clear that she had had a rough time of it not long ago—her mainsail was double-reefed, presumably from some recent damage; there were strangely-patched holes all over it and more in her foresail and ragged jib; her upper works had a chewed appearance; and one of her seven little gun ports on the starboard side had been hastily repaired. There was not much danger to be feared from her. . . .[11]

He studied them with the most concentrated attention, with a perfectly cold, impartial, expert judgment; and more and more it became evident to him that the heavy frigate, though an elegant ship and a fine sailor, was handled in no more than a conscientious, journeyman fashion—a captain and crew that had spent more time in port than at sea in all weathers. They were not at home in their ship; there was a lack of coordination in her maneuvers, a slowness, a certain hesitancy, that showed they were not used to working together. It seemed to him that they had no great sense of the sea.[12]

If we want to predict where an adversary is heading, we watch it change course and consciously extrapolate its trajectory. That takes too long. Aubrey usually doesn't have the time to wait until the new course becomes clear. He is busy with his telescope, watching the adversary's deck:

[Jack] turned his glass to the French Squadron . . . it was the detail of their trim that would tell him what was going on in Linois's mind. What he saw gave him to comfort. The French ships were crowding sail as though they had not a care in the world.[13]

Both the Frenchmen were filling: did they mean to edge down at last? He clapped his glass to his eye, saw them come right before the wind, and shut his telescope with a smile: from the busy way they were passing their sheets it was obvious that they were merely wearing once again, as they had done five times since dawn.[14]

Example 3.2 contrasts what a typical physician would notice upon seeing a patient, versus what a trained gerontologist sees.

Example 3.2: The fall guy   Imagine that you are a physician encountering a new patient. She is 85 years old and small but sturdy. She walks steadily into the examining room, not needing any support from her daughter who walks in behind her. She has several complaints: She has had a lower-back pain for months, shooting down her leg, sometimes making it hard for her to get out of bed. She has bad arthritis; her fingers are swollen at the knuckles. Her blood pressure is high. She has glaucoma. She is just beginning to experience urinary incontinence and has begun wearing a pad. She has had some bouts of cancer, a previous surgery for colon cancer, and a lung nodule that was diagnosed by a radiologist as a possible metastasis. She manages to live alone in a small house. She struggles to climb onto the examining table. Her balance is a little precarious, and she needs assistance. As a physician, what are your concerns? What are you noticing?[15]

Many physicians might prioritize the long list of problems. They would emphasize possible metastasis as the most serious one threatening her life or the back pain the one creating the most discomfort.

A skilled gerontologist might see things differently. Her greatest risk is falling down and breaking a hip. If that were to happen to her at age 85, the odds were 40 percent that she would wind up in a nursing home and 20 percent that she would never walk again. Elderly people fall because they have poor balance, or because they take more than four prescription medications, or because they suffer from muscular weakness. An elderly person with none of these precursors has only a 12 percent chance of falling in the coming year. The odds go up to 100 percent for an elderly person who has all the precursors. Therefore, an experienced gerontologist would study the patient's balance, her feet (somewhat swollen), and the five medications she took (their cumulative side effects often include dizziness).

An experienced gerontologist would watch as she got out of her chair. (She just stood up and didn't have to push with her arms—a good sign.) A skilled gerontologist would inquire about her eating habits. (She is careful to eat healthy foods. She doesn't seem to drink many liquids during the day, perhaps because of the incontinence, plus one of her medications is a diuretic, so she is somewhat dehydrated, which worsens the dizziness.) An experienced gerontologist would likely conclude that she wasn't eating enough calories to keep her strength up. (When questioned, she admitted that she has lost about 7 pounds in the last half-year.)

A skilled gerontologist would refer the woman to a podiatrist, would try to eliminate some of her medications, would look for a blood pressure medication that wouldn't cause dehydration, and would tell her to throw out her low-calorie and low-cholesterol food and eat more snacks.

The red flags, the risk factors and symptoms that a gerontologist spots are very different from the ones that a traditional physician might attend to. Skilled performance depends on the way we look and listen. It depends on what we can notice and on what kinds of discriminations we can make.

Adapting procedures

Procedures are typically just a series of "if-then" rules. In following procedures, we perform each step until we reach the criterion that tells us that we have finished that step and should start the next one. When we see these steps and the cues and criteria for starting and completing each step, the process looks straightforward. The challenge lies in judging whether the criteria have been met. Is it time to start the next step, or not?

In chapter 2, I presented a range of examples illustrating the importance of tacit knowledge. In the interview with Lia DiBello, the transit mechanic stated that he was just following the inspection checklist, but he wasn't. He was skipping around and using his judgment about what to do next. Scotty and Mad Dog, the F-106 pilots, couldn't squeeze their expertise into a sequence of procedures. They carried out all the actions in the procedural guide they wrote, but they used their experience to tell them which action to perform next and when to initiate it. The example of the metro station at Charles de Gaulle airport illustrated how a template, a procedural guide, was insensitive to the needs of airplane travelers.

In well-ordered and stable domains, we can derive checklists and procedures for people to follow. If it is necessary, we can add branches to the list of procedures. But as the situation gets increasingly complicated, the list of branches and exceptions gets out of hand. Knowing how to violate the procedures is a type of tacit knowledge. The "flying brick" example in chapter 2 described how Al Haynes and the members of his flight crew landed an airplane that had lost all its hydraulics. The Gimli Glider example in chapter 1 described how Bob Pearson and Maurice Quintal landed a commercial airliner that had run out of fuel. Here is another example that shows experts using their tacit knowledge to adapt procedures and to improvise.

Example 3.3: Catching criminals while they are sleeping My colleagues Danyele Harris-Thompson and Sterling Wiggins traveled to Canada to work with a police department that wanted to strengthen its Emergency Response Teams (the Canadian term for SWAT teams).[16] The senior ERT leaders explained that they had worked out clear procedures for just about everything they did—how they approached a house or building, how they entered it, how they systematically cleared it. Everything was proceduralized, everyone knew the procedures, and everyone depended on everyone else to follow the procedures. The ERTs want to make sure that they don't leave suspects behind them, and that they don't create confusion that could result in fratricide. That's why it was so important for them to follow the procedures. But of course it wasn't so straightforward. Once the ERTs started to relax around Sterling and Danyele, they began to describe all the exceptions—all the times they bent the rules.

ERT training and procedure dictate that team members enter a building in formation and clear every room, starting with the ground floor and working up. However, if the operation takes place at 3:00 a.m., the chances are high that the suspect will be sleeping in the master bedroom. One ERT commander put it this way: "If we clear all the rooms, by the time we get to the second floor and the bedroom, we've been in the house for two minutes...the target is awake. Now we're putting ourselves in harm's way and compromising the mission. Therefore, we'll go directly to the master bedroom after breaching instead of procedurally clearing every room first."

Perhaps the ERT procedure should be amended to say "If the assault comes early in the morning, go directly to the bedrooms." But what if there is a light coming from the kitchen? Or what if they hear a door closing to a downstairs bathroom as they are getting ready to rush up the stairs? Each house, each entry, presents its own variations.

In one early-morning incident at a farm, the leader of an ERT noticed a chimney that came from below the first floor, inferred that the basement was heated, and speculated that the suspects were sleeping there. After entering, the team made a cursory inspection of the first floor, then headed straight to the basement and apprehended the people they were looking for. He didn't waste time doing the thorough sweep of the first floor that is called for in the procedure manual.

The members of an ERT obviously don't work in a well-ordered domain. They can't anticipate the kinds of threats they face, or the ways they have to adapt as their mission unfolds. They want to believe that they have broken their job down into procedures, but they adapt these procedures when the procedures don't make sense.

Skilled performance depends on the kinds of perceptual discriminations we can make and on how we interpret, modify, and replace the standard procedures when they don't work. But there is more to expertise than that.

Pattern matching

Every type of expert we have studied has built up a repertoire of patterns to quickly make sense of what is happening. These patterns aren't facts, or rules, or procedures. They are based on all the experiences and events the experts have lived through and heard about. They are the basis of intuitions.[17] The patterns let us judge what category of situation we are facing.

Example 3.4: Tracking the customers   The next time you go into a large retail store, as you walk past the cashiers and the service desk, down the aisles of merchandise, you may find yourself alone—particularly if it is early in the afternoon, a time when the store is pretty empty of shoppers. The store's clerks, usually a scarce commodity, will likely be congregating at the front. You have the entire aisle to yourself. No one seems to be paying attention to you. No one except the store detective, who is probably tracking your every movement, particularly if there aren't many other shoppers.

You don't see store detectives—you aren't supposed to. They work up top, behind windows, with binoculars, using mirrors they have positioned so they can see down every aisle. They are judging whether you might be a shoplifter. They are watching the kinds of items you inspect, the sequence of inspections, your reactions to people walking by, and any other kinds of indications. They are trying to see if your movements fit into a sensible story of a person trying to figure out which product to buy, or if they are the disconnected actions of a shoplifter attempting to create confusion and an opportunity to hide an item, cut off its tag, and smuggle it out. If your actions fit this second pattern—the person who has come to shoplift instead of shop—you will get a lot more attention.

Store detectives attempt to put people into two categories: shoppers and shoplifters. They are studying the pattern of activity, and asking themselves whether this is something a legitimate shopper would be doing or whether it seems like the ruse of the shoplifter.

Firefighters also rely on patterns to size up situations and anticipate what is going to happen next.[18] Firefighters quickly gauge whether they are facing a risk to lives—calling for search and rescue—or a fire that can be extinguished, or a fire that is out of control, calling for containment to prevent its spread.

Sometimes it takes special talent to describe tacit knowledge because people have difficulty articulating it. My friend Jim Staszewski, a psychology professor at Carnegie Mellon University, used cognitive task analysis and other methods to do some detective work involving land mines.[19]

Example 3.5: Detection work   Land mines are a major hazard in many parts of the world that have suffered from violent conflict, such as Cambodia and Afghanistan. The US Army spent almost $40 million over 9 years to develop a new generation of hand-held devices for finding land mines—particularly the low-metal mines that the previous mine-detection devices couldn't find. But tests showed that this new mine detector was still missing 70–96 percent of the low-metal mines. It appeared that the system was a failure.

Enter the researchers. Staszewski and a colleague identified a few experts—people who had lifted thousands of mines and still had their hands and legs. Staszewski spent much of his time with Floyd "Rocky" Rockwell, an Army veteran with more than 30 years of experience who was working with a humanitarian de-mining organization. He was able to use the new equipment to locate low-metal mines. Unfortunately, he couldn't explain how he did it, because he was relying on tacit knowledge. Staszewski interviewed him and watched him in action, prompting him to think aloud as much as possible, trying to figure out what Rocky was noticing and what strategy he was using. Rocky wasn't reacting to sounds—he was picking up patterns. He was using a mental model of how the mine looked and how it might be planted. He was also going much slower than the mine sweeper's official manual advised, using a sweep rate of one foot per second rather than the recommended one meter per second and keeping the head of the detector much closer to the ground than the manual prescribed.

Staszewski then developed a training program to teach Rocky's secrets to other Army engineers. (These secrets had been a secret even to Rocky.) Staszewski designed training drills to impart expertise to others. The results were dramatic. The detection rate improved to greater than 90 percent, whereas without the training it had been only 10–20 percent. The Army adopted the training, and the Department of Defense has called on Staszewski to help train indigenous people in various parts of the world.

Expertise depends on perceptual discriminations, the ability to go beyond standard procedures, and pattern matching. What else?

Typicality and anomaly

We draw on dozens and hundreds of experiences to sense when something seems familiar, or to pick up anomalies. When television commentators explain that the splash a diver makes is very big, they see it as atypical of the splashes they have seen most skilled divers make. When the oil rig manager mentioned in chapter 2 was reluctant to carry out the standard procedure for handling a bubble of natural gas in the pipeline, it was because he had noticed an anomaly: the size and depth of the bubble.

Here is an example I heard from a friend about a time, decades earlier, when he had been a young intern struggling to come up with a diagnosis for a recently admitted patient who complained of shortness of breath. My friend had lots of ideas to check out to make sure he had gotten the diagnosis right. He had arranged for a full battery of tests. Having spent hours pondering their results, he came up with a set of hypotheses. Then the attending (senior) physician came by. Even before reaching the patient's bed, while still at the door, he looked at the patient and announced "Oh, he's got heart failure; but I could be wrong." He made the correct diagnosis just by a quick look at the patient. His experience let him recognize a typical case.

The interplay between noticing typical cases and anomalous ones is a type of tacit knowledge found in many fields. For example, nurses in intensive-care units build up a sense of typicality that lets them notice when a patient looks atypical. The nurses become early warning systems to catch weak signals that a patient is starting to deteriorate. Similarly, weather forecasters build up a strong sense of typical patterns that lets them spot anomalies—unsettled regions that they call "problems of the day." These are the regions to watch carefully because they will govern how the weather fronts play out.

Mental models

Mental models[20] are the stories we construct to understand how things work. They mirror the events or system they are modeling, but they capture only a limited aspect of those events or that system.[21] We form our mental models from the way we understand causes.

In the de-mining example 3.5, Jim Staszewski found that his expert, Rocky, was relying on a mental model of the mines he was looking for and a mental model of how they were set. It wasn't Rocky's skill at using the detector and listening to its audible signals that enabled him to find mines (his hearing wasn't very good); it was his ability to visualize what lay beneath the surface of the ground.

Mental models are even essential for manual work. Shalin and Verdile (2003) described the cognitive challenges of a "simple" manual task: digging ditches. Before the workers are taken to the work site, they must decide which tools to bring with them into the field. They can't bring all their tools—that would be too much to cart around. They must have a mental model of the work they will be doing—for example, digging ditches, laying pipe in the ditches, or filling in ditches. If they leave a necessary tool behind, they may not be able to perform the job. If they are going to be filling in a ditch, for example, they may need some bolt cutters to keep connecting bolts from sticking out if heavy rain erodes the ground.

Mental models are even more critical for other types of work, such as weather forecasting, intelligence analysis, and military command and control, in which success depends entirely on cognitive functions and not on manual strength or dexterity.

It is hard to give people feedback about tacit knowledge. As a result, when settings or tasks are complex we give feedback about departures from procedures instead of helping people to notice subtle cues and patterns.

Except when having a conversation about procedures, we don't know how to learn from one another about tacit knowledge. One human resources director confessed that in her organization, a Fortune 50 company, she never saw executives talk with their predecessors or their successors after personnel transitions. They didn't know how to have such conversations, so they didn't even try. No one she asked could recall ever initiating such a discussion or being invited to have one.

Because tacit knowledge is tacit, we struggle to describe it. If asked about your perceptual skills, your mental models, or your ability to recognize typicality, what would you say? Experts can't articulate what they are seeing—it seems obvious to them. I have had several expert decision makers explain to me that they felt they had made specific life-and-death decisions on the basis of extrasensory perception. It had felt like ESP to them because their decisions weren't based on conscious reasoning. Eventually I got to the bottom of their strategies and showed them that they hadn't in fact used ESP, but getting there took a lot of work.

Example 3.6 presents one of my toughest interviews. I was trying to get at knowledge that a person had and couldn't describe. I have done 15-minute interviews with tank platoon leaders after a grueling day on the training range. I have interviewed the commander of the USS *Vincennes* about how he shot down an airliner. I have interviewed skilled computer scientists about why they were about to leave their jobs—before they had told their boss or anyone else in their company. But this interview took all my skill. It was with my wife, Helen.

Example 3.6: The hidden hotel   Helen and I had arranged a vacation in Bergen, Norway. We came from different locations, met in the Oslo airport, and flew together to Bergen. During the flight, Helen rummaged through her purse and then announced that, as she had feared, she had left at home the information with the name and location of our hotel in Bergen.

When we arrived in Bergen it was raining very hard. We took a bus to the Tourist Information Center in the middle of the city. The kind people there showed us a list of all the hotels and told us that Bergen was overflowing with visitors so every hotel was fully booked. Helen looked over the list and sadly admitted that none of the hotels was familiar. She had booked the hotel through a travel agent, but the agency was closed. The situation had become less amusing.

I wasn't enthusiastic about spending the day at the tourist center waiting for our travel agency in the United States to open. Besides, the telephone at the center (this was in the days before cell phones) had a long line of tourists waiting to use it. I estimated that if I got on that line it would take at least an hour before I got to make a call.

I told Helen I was going to take her through the list again. She explained that this was a waste of time, but as the person who forgot to bring the information sheet she accepted that she didn't have a vote anymore.

I covered up the bottom of the list so I could show her one hotel at the time. "Is it this?" I asked. She shook her head no. "This?" I continued, exposing the next hotel. Again no. And no and no. But midway through the list when I got to a certain hotel (I can't remember the name) her eyebrows wriggled for a fraction of a second before she said "No, I don't think so." But she had paused, and she seemed less than 100 percent confident. None of the other hotel names evoked any response at all.

"OK," I said. "We'll take a taxi over to the hotel from the middle of the list" (the one at which Helen had wriggled her eyebrows). Helen was not enthusiastic about this plan. She didn't think it was the one the travel agent had selected. "Yes," I replied, "but it's the only hotel that got any reaction from you at all."

When we arrived, I strode up to the desk with a surprising amount of confidence. Helen lingered near the front door, where she wouldn't have to be exposed to the embarrassment that awaited me. I announced "Reservation for Gary Klein. K-L-E-I-N." The clerk paged through the reservation slips, stopped at one, looked at me, and shook his head. "Sorry, sir," he said. "Nothing here under that name."

Seeing the disappointment on my face, he added "We do have a reservation for a Helen Klein."

Because we know more than we can tell, trainers gravitate toward describing the explicit parts of the work. These are easier to describe. We find it easier to give feedback about errors than about skillful actions or about improvements in mental models. Furthermore, if we want to give feedback about errors, it is tempting to rely on the official procedures for performing a task so we can let people know when they have failed to follow procedures. That, in turn, leads organizations to issue lots of procedural guides.

In short, when we try to improve performance we usually emphasize explicit knowledge more than tacit knowledge. In giving feedback, we tend to focus on specific procedures. These tendencies aren't problematic in well-ordered situations. However, they are inadequate for improving performance in complex situations. There are techniques, such as Cognitive Task Analysis,[22] that are specifically designed to capture tacit knowledge. But these require training and practice. Jim Staszewski used Cognitive Task Analysis and other methods to figure out the strategy used by Rocky Rockwell, his de-mining expert.

Tacit knowledge is critical for the way we design and use procedures in complex situations. But tacit knowledge resists scrutiny and evaluation. Therefore, it is susceptible to biases. How concerned should we be about judgment and decision biases?

4 How Biased Is Our Thinking?

For more than 35 years, decision researchers have been demonstrating the biases that corrupt our judgments and decisions. They have been showing that our thinking processes are flawed, inaccurate, and unreliable.

Claim 2: Decision biases distort our thinking.

Let's examine three types of heuristics—strategies we commonly use in thinking—that can bias us: anchoring-and-adjustment, framing, and representativeness.

The anchoring-and-adjustment heuristic

When we have to make an estimate and we don't know the answer, one strategy we use is to find a plausible answer and then adjust it up or down. This mental strategy is called *anchoring and adjustment*. It is a type of heuristic, or mental shortcut.[1] The initial estimate is the anchor. People usually don't adjust the anchor very much. Therefore, by suggesting a high or a low anchor we can influence people's judgments.

Strack and Massweiler (1997) used questions to study anchoring effects. One group of subjects was asked this anchoring question:

Was Mahatma Gandhi greater or less than 9 years old when he was assassinated? Pick one:

— Greater than 9 years old.
— Less than 9 years old.

A second group of subjects got a different anchoring question:

Was Mahatma Gandhi greater or less than 140 years old when he was assassinated? Pick one:

— Greater than 140 years old.
— Less than 140 years old.

All subjects then received the same test question:

How old was he when he was assassinated?

The question as to whether Gandhi was greater or less than 9 years old when assassinated was a "no-brainer," and all the subjects picked "greater." The point of this question was to set a low anchor. On average, the subjects given the "9 years old" anchor estimated Gandhi's age at the time of his assassination as 50. The second group of subjects was asked if Gandhi was greater or less than 140 years old when he was assassinated, a high anchor. All these subjects knew that Gandhi was less than 140 years old, but their average estimate of his age at assassination was 67 years. (Gandhi actually was 70 when assassinated. Perhaps some of the subjects were influenced by Ben Kingsley, who played him in the movie. I guess that's another anchor.) Therefore, we can swing the estimate of Gandhi's age at assassination from 50 to 67 depending on the anchor we suggest, even when that anchor is ridiculous. That's what is meant by biasing people's judgments.

Tversky and Kahneman (1974) asked one group of subjects this anchoring question:

In the United Nations, is the proportion of African countries above or below 10 percent? Pick one:

— Above 10 percent.
— Below 10 percent.

A second group got a different anchoring question:

In the United Nations, is the proportion of African countries above or below 65 percent? Pick one:

— Above 65 percent.
— Below 65 percent.

All subjects then received this test question:

What is the proportion of UN members made up of African countries?

The group given the 10 percent anchor judged it to be too low. On the test question, the average guess by these subjects was 25 percent. The second group was asked if the percentage of African nations in the UN was above or below 65. The percentage given in the anchor question seemed too high; the average guess on the test question for this group was 45 percent. The anchor dramatically altered the subjects' guesses. To make matters worse, these anchors (10 percent and 65 percent) were generated randomly by spinning a roulette wheel—while the subjects watched! And the anchor still affected their judgments. (The answer to the test question was about 33 percent.)

The anchoring-and-adjustment heuristic affects real-world judgments, not just toy problems like these. When fund raisers try to get me to contribute to their cause, they use a variant of anchoring and adjustment. They ask for an amount far in excess of what I feel comfortable giving, expecting me to work downward from there. I have never come across a fund raiser who said "How about a dollar? Surely you can give a dollar. You can probably give more than a dollar—what do you estimate you can afford?"

Real estate agents also use anchoring and adjustment to manipulate us into bidding more than we should. And real estate agents are themselves vulnerable to being manipulated. Northcraft and Neale (1987) took dozens of agents through two houses in Tucson, letting them spend 20 minutes in each house, and gave them ten-page packets with all the relevant information, with one twist: some agents got a packet showing that the houses were appraised below the true appraised value, whereas others got a figure greater than the true appraised value. That was the only difference between the groups, but it had a large effect. For the house appraised at $135,000, the agents who were misinformed that the appraisal was $119,900 judged that a reasonable selling price was $117,745. Other agents who were misinformed that the same house was appraised at $149,900 judged that the selling price ought to be $130,981. Thus, merely shifting the anchor resulted in a difference of more than $13,000.

The framing heuristic

The way a question is presented can determine the answer. Eldar Shafir (1993) presented subjects with this scenario:

Imagine that you serve on the jury of an only child custody case following a relatively messy divorce. The facts of the case are complicated by ambiguous economic, social, and emotional considerations, and you decide to base your decision entirely on the following few observations.

The two parents were presented as having the attributes listed here in table 4.1. Shafir then asked half the subjects "To which parent would

Table 4.1
Attributes of parents in decisions on child custody.

Parent A	Parent B
Average income	Above-average income
Average health	Very close relationship with the child
Average working hours	Extremely active social life
Reasonable rapport with the child	Lots of work-related travel
Relatively stable social life	Minor health problems

you award sole custody of the child?" and the other half "To which parent would you deny sole custody of the child?" The only difference was the single word 'award' or 'deny'.

The subjects who were asked about *awarding* custody chose parent B, 64 percent versus 36 percent for parent A. The subjects who were asked about *denying* custody also chose parent B, 55 percent versus 45 percent for parent A.

Parent B had stronger traits for both awarding and denying. When given the 'award' frame, subjects looked for reasons to award custody. Parent B had better reasons: above-average income and a close relationship with the child. When given the 'deny' frame, subjects looked for reasons to deny custody, and parent B had stronger reasons here too: the active social life, the travel, and the health problems.

As in the preceding example, the frame we use will affect which types of data we notice. We can influence people's judgments just by the way we frame the problem.

I remember a workshop in which I used framing to my advantage. I had been invited as an observer, but midway through the workshop I realized that I had recently conducted a research project that would help the participants with their program. Therefore, I wanted to get on the schedule. As I approached the organizer, who knew nothing about me, I thought about asking him "Would you like to have me give a short talk about some of my findings?" But I was pretty sure he would have said no, because he wouldn't have heard any reasons to grant my request. Instead, I asked "Do you have any objection if I take a few minutes to describe some findings that bear directly on the issues we've been discussing?" He thought about it, he couldn't come up with any strong reasons to turn me down (we were slightly ahead of schedule), and he carved out a slot for me. It's all in the framing.

Lawyers try to influence juries by framing incidents in one way or another. Labor negotiators and diplomats do the same. McNeil,

Pauker, Sox, and Tversky (1982) demonstrated framing in physicians, radiologists, and patients. The subjects were asked to choose between surgery and radiation therapy to treat lung cancer. The risk of surgery is that patients have a greater chance of dying during the surgery. The researchers expected that using a positive frame (stating the odds of surviving the lung cancer for each of the two treatments) would increase the selection of surgery relative to a negative frame (stating the odds of dying—the mortality probabilities for the two treatments). The survival data were the converse of the mortality data, so each group got identical data except for the way these data were framed. And that was enough to make a difference. The participants selected surgery 75 percent of the time when given the survival frame, but only 58 percent of the time when given the mortality frame. Even the highly trained physicians showed the framing effect.

The representativeness heuristic

Tversky and Kahneman (1982) provided the classical demonstration of this heuristic:

Linda is 31 years old, single, outspoken and very bright. She majored in philosophy. As a student, she was deeply concerned with issues of discrimination and social justice, and also participated in antinuclear demonstrations. Please check off the most likely alternative:

— Linda is a bank teller.
— Linda is a bank teller and is active in the feminist movement.

In the original experiment, about 85 percent of the subjects picked the second alternative. But the first alternative is statistically more likely, because it includes the possibility that Linda is active in the feminist movement as well as the possibility that Linda is a bank teller but is not active in the feminist movement. Most subjects pick the second alternative because it seems like a fuller and more accurate description of Linda. It seems like a better representation of the kind of person Linda is. The pull of the second alternative shows the representativeness heuristic at work. Here it prevented subjects from judging which alternative is more likely.

The representativeness heuristic also leads to other types of errors. Gigerenzer, Hoffrage, and Ebert (1998) showed that AIDS counselors often get confused by probability data and sometimes misinterpret the results of screening tests. The tests are very good at detecting HIV (the virus that causes AIDS), but because they are so sensitive they also give a positive result to some healthy patients. In this study, the researchers sent a low-risk male client to have an HIV test at each of 20 German public health centers. Part of the protocol for these tests is for counselors to have a pre-test session with the patient, before the results come back. The researchers collected their data during this pre-test session, to witness the way the counselors answered the question of what it would mean if the test came back positive. The counselors knew that people with AIDS almost always test positive, so they used the representativeness heuristic. Fifteen of the 20 counselors claimed that a positive test result meant that the patient would almost certainly have HIV. Actually, low-risk men who test positive have only a 50 percent chance of being infected. This kind of mistaken interpretation can have tragic consequences. Before the development of AIDS medications, some healthy men who were misinformed that they had HIV went home and committed suicide.

The heuristics-and-biases research framework
The decision bias research started in the early 1970s. Danny Kahneman (who would later win a Nobel Prize in economics for these and other studies) and Amos Tversky ran experiments that showed systematic flaws in the reasoning processes of their subjects. Kahneman and Tversky demonstrated that people use heuristics—mental shortcuts or rules of thumb—to make quick judgments, and that these heuristics lead to predictable errors. If people know the answer, they don't need any shortcuts. But if they have to guess at an answer (e.g., Gandhi's age when he was assassinated), they might begin with some sort of estimate and revise it in the right direction. By taking advantage of this strategy, Kahneman and Tversky could lead their subjects to make errors that were wrong in predictable ways.

The heuristics-and-biases paradigm that Kahneman and Tversky pioneered caught on quickly. Other researchers added more and more kinds of biases. As many as 60 biases have been identified in the research literature, including illusory correlation (seeing connections that are just coincidences) and the gambler's fallacy (expecting that the longer a losing streak lasts, the higher is the probability of winning the next wager).

The concept of decision biases is now firmly embedded in the fields of psychology, economics, and business.[2] Many researchers have interpreted these heuristics-and-biases studies to mean that people are defective decision makers. A whole cottage industry has emerged around decision biases.[3,4] The concept of decision biases has been described in a number of books for a general audience, such as *Sway: The Irresistible Pull of Irrational Behavior* by Brafman and Brafman (2008), *Blind Spots: Why Smart People Do Dumb Things* by Van Hecke (2007), *Predictably Irrational: The Hidden Forces That Shape Our Decisions* by Ariely (2008), Russo and Schoemaker's *Decision Traps: The Ten Barriers to Brilliant Decision Making* (1989), and Dawes's *Everyday Irrationality: How Pseudo-Scientists, Lunatics, and the Rest of Us Systematically Fail to Think Rationally* (2001).

The message seems clear: people cannot be trusted to think clearly or to make good judgments and decisions. Inevitably, we will distort the evidence or the logic or our preferences. Even experts are vulnerable to biases.

The people I sampled certainly bought into this message. Their average agreement with claim 2, that decision biases distort our thinking, was 5.35, somewhere between "tend to agree for most situations" and "strongly agree for almost all situations." Only eight of the 159 respondents disagreed.

Disclaimer

Fortunately, the fears of decision biases are overblown. The research doesn't really demonstrate that we are irrational. Rather, we use effective strategies in our thinking but these have some limitations that researchers can exploit. The limitations in our strategies are easier to demonstrate in the laboratory than in the real world. In what follows, I will go into more detail about each of these counter-claims.

The concept of "decision biases" doesn't imply irrationality.

Let us look more carefully at the original heuristics-and-biases research. What really happened is that Kahneman and Tversky designed their studies to demonstrate the limits of classical decision theory, not the limits of their subjects. When Kahneman was teaching a class on applied psychology at Hebrew University, in Jerusalem, he invited Tversky (who also held a position in the psychology department at Hebrew University) to give a guest lecture on Bayesian statistics. Bayesian statistics uses complicated probability calculations to estimate the degree of belief in a hypothesis before and after new evidence has been observed. After the lecture, Kahneman told Tversky "I don't believe it." That is, he didn't believe that people made judgments in the way that Bayesian statistics described. It was at that point that Kahneman and Tversky began their collaboration.

Kahneman and Tversky showed that, when making decisions, people use heuristics instead of formal statistics. They described heuristics as natural reasoning strategies that usually work but aren't perfect.[5] By devising clever examples in which subjects would get the wrong answers if they used heuristics, they were able to demonstrate that their subjects did use the heuristics in making their judgments. These findings, coupled with many other similar studies, showed that the classical decision models and economics models didn't accurately describe how people made judgments. As Tversky and Kahneman (1974, p. 1124) stated, "In general these heuristics are quite useful, but sometimes they lead to severe and systematic errors."

I find heuristics-and-biases research interesting and important. I particularly enjoy the experiments that explore how the reasoning strategies work.[6] This line of research helps us understand how people think.

However, I don't like the term *decision biases*. The word 'bias' has a pejorative connotation of being prejudiced and unfair rather than impartial. It implies a faulty way of thinking and a reason to disregard a person's judgments. Heuristics-and-biases researchers assure me that they aren't demeaning their subjects. After all, we talk about visual illusions where we can fool the eye because of the way the visual system is wired up, so why not decision biases? All the heuristics-and-biases researchers mean by the term is that our heuristics lead to systematic errors.

Unfortunately, heuristics-and-biases research has been "sexed up" in the popular literature. Look for the common theme in these titles: *Predictably Irrational: The Hidden Forces That Shape Our Decisions*; *Everyday Irrationality: How Pseudo-Scientists, Lunatics, and the Rest of Us Systematically Fail to Think Rationally*; *Sway: The Irresistible Pull of Irrational Behavior*. All of them emphasize "irrationality."

Some heuristics-and-biases researchers have confided in me that the word 'irrational' makes them uncomfortable, but that they can't do much about it. The term 'biases', which started out as a synonym for "systematic errors," has now taken on a more dramatic and ominous tone.

We're talking about limitations, not irrationality.

People use heuristics when making judgments. The anchoring-and-adjustment heuristic and the representativeness heuristic are strategies that generally give correct answers when we have to make estimates and we don't know the exact answers. These reasoning strategies aren't perfect. When they break down, we see systematic errors. Most of the time, however, the reasoning strategies work just fine.

Any mechanism will have limitations. Our eyes emphasize contrasts at boundaries in a visual scene. These contrasts help us see the gist of the scene. In situations that require a high degree of accuracy, we have to adjust for this distortion; however, the rest of the time it is quite helpful. In working with any mechanism, we can expect limitations. If necessary, we find ways to adjust to them.

Example 4.1: How to lie to your toaster[7]   One morning, while visiting her family, the communications specialist Susann LuperFoy put some bread in the toaster, set the toaster's dial for the level of toasting she wanted, then found that the toast was under-done. Her mother explained that her brother had just finished using the toaster and it was already warmed up. Susann imagined that the dial was connected to a thermostat. Because her brother had just made toast, the coils and the whole toaster were hotter than usual. Therefore, the toaster reached its thermostat threshold faster than it otherwise would have. That was Susan's mental model. She put the bread back in, turned the dial up to a higher level than she really wanted in order to correct for the pre-heating, and got the slice of toast she wanted. And then she realized she had just lied to her toaster.

We wouldn't say that Susann's toaster was irrational. It had some limitations because of the mechanism for setting the level of toasting. Any toaster strategy would have limitations. If the toaster used photo-cells (a darkness strategy) to gauge doneness, then it couldn't handle pumpernickel and it might be affected by the kitchen lighting. If it used time (a duration strategy), it might give different results on a cold winter morning than a hot summer afternoon. Susann's toaster used a temperature strategy. As long as she understood it, she could communicate with it. By lying.

What about our memories? We may be tempted to say that our memories are flawed. We all know the frustration of failing to remember someone's name. We know the name, but we can't dredge it up. Though we wouldn't call such lapses biases, they certainly seem like flaws in the mental machinery. And it is tempting to say that memory limitations restrict our ability to think rationally. But how damaging are these memory limitations?

Daniel Schacter (2001) has argued that the limitations of memory are actually very useful. Here are a few of the seven "sins of memory" that Schacter has examined:

Transience   In transience, we lose a memory we once had, such as a name or telephone number. Memories degrade over time. The less a person uses a memory, the more quickly it fades. But do we really want to remember all the hotel room numbers we have ever been assigned, all the places we've parked a car, all the seat numbers we're been assigned on airplanes, all the names we've been told at parties? Thank goodness for adaptive forgetting, which gets rid of most of the debris! Sometimes we lose a fact we later need, but we would do much worse if we held onto everything.[8] Our memory systems bet that we probably won't need a piece of information if we haven't used it recently. We get very frustrated when we lose that bet and we do need the information, but we don't notice all the useless items that get thrown out.

Absent-mindedness   Sometimes we forget to do something or to record a fact (such as where we put our car keys), most likely because our attention is directed elsewhere. The cellist Yo-Yo Ma once forgot to get his $2.5 million cello out of the trunk of a New York City taxi. Absent-mindedness may result from the way we focus our attention on some cues and not others; we best remember the cues to which we have attended, and we don't effectively store in memory the cues we have ignored. If we didn't have this mechanism for selectively recalling the cues to which we have attended, we would be inundated with irrelevant details. That's exactly what happens to the rare individuals who seem to have photographic memories: the accumulated details seem to interfere with their abstract thinking.

Blocking   In blocking (sometimes called the "tip-of-the-tongue phenomenon"), we can't recall information we want to remember. Blocking affects our ability to remember facts and incidents. But do we really want every fact we have ever learned and every memory we've ever had to come flooding into our consciousness all the time? Blocking seems to result from memory inhibitions that keep the irrelevant memories bottled up. When the inhibition misfires, we get blocked. It's a small price to pay.

Persistence   We may continue to remember distressing incidents that we would prefer to forget. Although these traumatic memories can cause us unwanted pain, they also make sure we stay alert to danger, and thus they help to ensure our survival.

Schacter's conclusion is clear. We would be foolish to rid ourselves of any of these memory features. They are frustrating when they don't get us what we want, but each one reflects a valuable aspect of memory. A limitation in one setting can be a strength in another. That seems also to be true of the heuristics we use. Even though our reasoning strategies can lead to errors, they generally do an effective job in complex natural settings.

The systematic errors aren't so serious outside the laboratory.
I don't believe that biases are as problematic in real-world settings as the popular books contend. Most of the studies showing decision biases rely on laboratory tasks and on the use of college students as subjects.[9] When heuristics-and-biases researchers study experts such as physicians, auditors,[10] and livestock judges,[11] the decision biases diminish or disappear. Smith and Kida (1991) examined 25 studies of auditor judgments and didn't find the kinds of biases obtained in artificial tasks used with college students. Stewart, Roebber, and Bosart (1997) found that meteorologists were extremely accurate in making short-term weather forecasts and didn't show any evidence of bias.[12]

Reasoning strategies let us do many kinds of tasks without consciously or subconsciously performing calculations to produce an estimate.

Example 4.2: The gaze heuristic   Consider how baseball outfielders catch fly balls. If you are playing in the outfield and the ball is hit in the air right toward you, how do you decide whether to run in or to run back? It's not an easy judgment. Any number of people can still recall schoolyard humiliations when they ran in, yelling "I got it, I got it," only to watch the ball go over their head, to the jeers of the other team.

So how does one catch a fly ball? The rules seem clear: judge where you think the ball will land, estimate how long it will take to get there, and alter your direction and speed accordingly. That should suffice, but it doesn't. We aren't very good at judging the location or the time of arrival.[13, 14] If that was how professional outfielders made their decisions, they would commit many more errors.

Instead, we learn to use something called the *gaze heuristic*. If you are running in at just the right speed, the angle of your gaze—directed at the ball—will stay constant.[15] That's a good feeling. If the angle of your gaze shifts upward, then you are running too fast, and you should slow down or back up. If the angle changes so that your gaze shifts downward, you had better speed up. You just need to find a speed that lets the angle of gaze remain constant.[16]

The gaze heuristic works very well. It takes into account wind, air resistance, and the spin of the ball. Outfielders don't have to know where to go to catch the ball. They just have to maintain a constant angle of gaze in order to get to the right spot. And they don't have to calculate anything—the heuristic does that for them. The gaze heuristic will lead the player to the point where the ball is going to land.

Even major-league outfielders are inaccurate at estimating trajectories. But it doesn't matter. The outfielders use a tactic, a heuristic, that gets the job done better than if they tried to make estimates and calculations.

Unintended consequences

Suppose that we take claim 2 very seriously and worry about biases. Continuing with this thought experiment, suppose we find out a way to eliminate biases. Perhaps laser surgery would let us make brain lesions to burn out the heuristics that produce decision biases but leave the rest of the brain tissue unaffected. Should we have this surgery performed on ourselves? Obviously this elective surgery wouldn't be a big seller, even among heuristics-and-biases researchers. Nevertheless, let us explore the likely effects.

We wouldn't use anchoring to make estimates. But where would our estimates come from, if not from previous cases that we remember?

We wouldn't frame situations when we tried to size them up. But framing just means we use a mindset to judge what is relevant. Without mindsets, we would have to look at every cue, every data element in a scene, and consciously decide whether it was relevant. That sounds like a lot of work. It sounds as if it would paralyze us, especially in complex situations.

We wouldn't size up situations on the basis of representativeness—how well they fit our patterns or our mental model of how things work. Instead, we would have to calculate the likelihood of different possible states of the world every time we needed to figure out what to expect.

I don't think it's necessary to go down the list of heuristics and repeat this exercise.

No one has ever demonstrated that our judgments would be improved if we could be de-biased. No one has ever compared what we would lose versus how much we would gain by giving up any of the reasoning strategies.

Even though the story in the popular press is about irrationality, most members of the heuristics-and-biases community that I know acknowledge the value of the reasoning strategies we use, just as I acknowledge the kinds of errors these strategies sometimes create. The heuristics-and-biases research simply shows the systematic errors that can arise from the limitations of our reasoning strategies. But what is the nature of these limitations?

Some of the so-called biases have nothing to do with flawed reasoning. Look again at the anchor-and-adjust demonstration at the beginning of this chapter. The flaw wasn't in the heuristic; it was that we were suggestible and that we began our reasoning with a misleading anchor (e.g., Gandhi dying at either age 9 or age 140). Look at the framing problem. The flaw wasn't in the framing heuristic. It was in how suggestible we are when given frames, such as whether to accept or deny custody in the divorce example.

No matter how good the reasoning strategy, if it starts with poor data it isn't going to produce accurate results. Garbage in, garbage out. There are cases where the limitations in the heuristics themselves result in systematic errors. However, if the judgment errors are caused by inaccurate data, we shouldn't blame the heuristics.

The original heuristics-and-biases research simply showed that people used heuristics even when the heuristics didn't work well. Few of the so-called biases seem to affect decision making in natural settings.

Some studies have been conducted in real-world settings; I described a few at the beginning of this chapter. Some studies have showed that even experts are susceptible to several of the biases. But most of the research showing how reasoning strategies can lead to errors has been done using novices (college students) performing tasks that are unfamiliar, artificial, and relatively independent of context.

Replacement

Claim 2 states that decision biases distort our thinking—which assumes that there is a "right" way to think. It assumes that we are capable of thinking in the "right" way except when we use mental strategies—heuristics—that are susceptible to errors. I'm not aware of any right way to think.

The way we think, the way we use our experiences to make judgments, is to rely on a set of mental strategies that can sometimes lead to errors, the decision biases. If we were to give up our reasoning strategies, we would be helpless to make judgments in most situations. The biases aren't distorting our thinking. Rather, decision biases *reflect* our thinking. They illustrate the kinds of strategies we depend on.[17] Just as perceptual illusions reveal the ways our eyes work, decision biases reveal the ways our minds work.

Although I still recoil at the term "decision biases," I respect the heuristics-and-biases community greatly for identifying systematic errors and for showing that these errors can be produced or diminished with the right manipulations. The heuristics-and-biases community isn't simply referring to limits in our short-term memory for phone numbers and things like that. It is identifying systematic errors.

The mental strategies we use certainly have their vulnerabilities. Some of the researchers studying biases may have overstated their case, but that's their problem. If we ignore all their warnings, that's going to be our problem. Heuristics-and-biases researchers have demonstrated some systematic errors outside the laboratory.

What can we do to protect ourselves from the limitations without sacrificing the strengths of our mental strategies? A few ways to cope with cognitive limitations are to build expertise, to design more naturalistic judgment strategies that can mitigate the errors, to employ better data formats, and to use choice architects.

Build expertise.
We can help people build expertise so they can use their reasoning strategies more effectively.

If we want to improve decision making, and if we are vulnerable to suggestions about misleading anchors and frames, then we should help people build expertise—particularly by forming richer mental models. Helping people learn more accurate anchors and frames is more likely to succeed than trying to change the way they think in order to de-bias them. For instance, people are often overconfident in their judgments, but overconfidence diminishes as people become more accurate in their assessments of their own capabilities. Greater expertise will help people identify good anchors, which will make them less vulnerable to manipulation by anchoring and adjustment.

Put judgments into perspective.

We can design methods that will reduce problems that stem from the limitations of heuristics. Take overconfidence. As Lovallo and Kahneman (2003) argue, if we ever stamped out overconfidence we would diminish vitality and enthusiasm. Nevertheless, we can benefit from safeguards, particularly if they prepare us to adapt once we encounter trouble.

Lovallo and Kahneman suggest a strategy of taking an "outside view"—that is, using previous projects to suggest how long tasks will take and how many resources they will consume. Instead of basing our estimates on what we hope will happen, we can base them on reality. For example, have projects similar to the one we are proposing taken as much time to complete as we are estimating? If not, then perhaps we are fooling ourselves.

I have come up with another method for tempering overconfidence. I call it the *PreMortem technique*. A postmortem is a procedure done in a hospital to find out why a patient died. The physician benefits, the medical community benefits, and even the friends and relatives benefit from what is learned. However, a postmortem doesn't help the patient. Similarly, after a project has failed, its managers may conduct a postmortem session to figure out what went wrong. But it is too late. The project has already failed. Why wait till the end to find out what went wrong? We can move the postmortem to the beginning to help us anticipate problems and to become more realistic about the challenges. In a PreMortem, you ask your team to pretend that a crystal ball shows that in a few weeks or months your new venture has failed. The team members then write down all the reasons why it failed.[18,19] We can't expect to fix all the flaws, but we can prepare ourselves and our teams by anticipating some of the problems.

Represent data in ways that support intuition.

Many people have difficulty thinking about probabilities. That doesn't mean that their reasoning is faulty, just that they aren't skilled at calculating and combining probabilities. Percentages are tough because they involve ratios and are hard to visualize. If people could see the same data in a different format, they might come up with more accurate judgments. When Tversky and Kahneman (1983) used frequency data (e.g., "How many of 100 participants...") instead of probability data ("What percentage of participants..."), the conjunction fallacy dropped dramatically. Similarly, Gerd Gigerenzer (1991) showed that he can make some systematic errors disappear by presenting data as frequencies instead of probabilities.

For instance, Gigerenzer and colleagues used frequencies to present the "Linda problem" (described above). When Tversky and Kahneman asked subjects which was more probable, that "Linda is a bank teller" or "Linda is a bank teller and is active in the feminist movement," 85 percent chose the latter. But when Hertwig and Gigerenzer (1999) used a frequency representation, the bias disappeared. They stated the problem this way: There are 100 people who fit the description (for Linda). "How many of them are bank tellers? How many are bank tellers and active in the feminist movement?" This time, every participant responded that there were more bank tellers.

Gigerenzer applied the frequency format to help people make better use of base rates. Heuristics-and-biases researchers have shown that people usually ignore base rates when they make estimates. Recall the example of the AIDS counselors who just looked at the results of the HIV test and didn't take into account whether the patients had a low-risk lifestyle.[20] The low-risk lifestyle affects their likelihood of being infected with HIV—that's the base rate that the counselors ignored. Hoffrage, Lindsey, Hertwig, and Gigerenzer (2000) showed that if base-rate data were provided as frequencies, the counselors would take the base rates into account and would make more accurate judgments. Zhu and Gigerenzer (2006) demonstrated that even children use base rates if the numbers are presented as natural frequencies instead of probabilities.[21]

Sloman et al. (2003) and Neace et al. (2008) found that what counts is whether the representation makes it easy for us to see and compare different sub-categories, not the use of frequency data. In the Linda example, people need to compare the number of women who are feminist bank tellers with the total number of women who are bank tellers. Frequency formats usually make it easy to make these comparisons but when probability data portray the relation between sets and subsets they can be just as effective as frequency data. Yamagishi (2003) showed that diagrams also enabled people to make accurate judgments.

Use choice architects.
Richard Thaler and Cass Sunstein are behavioral economists who have used the findings of the heuristics-and-biases research community to

design programs that encourage people to make better decisions about things such as retirement savings. By focusing on a few issues (such as our aversion to losses, our reluctance to change the status quo, and framing), Thaler and Sunstein (2008) have designed programs to help people make good choices about their finances, their health, and their children's education. Thaler and Sunstein describe themselves as *choice architects*.

For example, most workers resist the idea of withholding more money for retirement plans—that feels like a loss of income. The heuristics-and-biases community has shown that we generally are more sensitive to losses than to gains, especially if the losses are going to be incurred immediately through payroll deductions and the gains aren't going to be felt for decades. However, if the withholding comes from future earnings, such as salary increases, then it never feels like a loss, and workers don't resist it as strongly.

I had more difficulty writing this chapter on decision biases than any of the others. I showed an earlier draft to two friends. One of them, a leading heuristics-and-biases researcher, was outraged—he saw it as a polemic that unfairly attacked the heuristics-and-biases community. The other, a leading researcher in my own field of naturalistic decision making, was also outraged, and accused me of being a turncoat because I gave so much credence to cognitive limitations. I suppose I should be comforted to get equal doses of outrage from the two opposite poles.

My position is simply that I dislike the notion of biases because it is tainted by the connotation of irrationality and it encourages contempt for experts in all kinds of fields. It encourages researchers to try to reform the way we think without first appreciating how the heuristics let us think effectively.

At the same time, we have to recognize that, like any mechanism, our minds have limitations that can lead to systematic errors. In some cases we may be able to reduce the problems by helping people gain more experience. In other cases we may turn to different strategies, such as taking an outside view or calling on choice architects.

Whatever our views about decision biases, tacit knowledge and intuitive judgments aren't perfect. Chapter 5 examines whether we would be better off relying on logic and analysis than on our intuitions.

Why claim 2 matters

Claim 2 (that decision biases distort our thinking) matters because the concept of bias encourages organizations to overreact to failures by enacting excessive procedures and counter-productive restrictions. Biases often get invoked whenever a decision turns out wrong. But preventing these "biases" would likely do more harm than good. It could eradicate the beneficial effects of the heuristics underlying the biases.

It matters because it affects the way supervisors diagnose performance problems. Instead of taking a stance of "appreciative inquiry," in which they look for ways that their workers were trying to succeed, claim 2 fosters a "depreciative inquiry" stance which assumes that workers are irrational.

5   Intuition versus Analysis

All responsible people appreciate the value of systematic analysis, logic, and statistics. Claim 2a goes further. It proclaims that we should trust analytic reasoning more than intuition, and that in cases where the two conflict we should suppress our intuitions.

Claim 2a: Successful decision makers rely on logic and statistics instead of intuition.

In chapter 4, I examined decision biases. Regardless of whether our intuitions are biased, this claim discourages us from using intuition.

In 1954, Paul Meehl published *Clinical vs. Statistical Prediction*, a very influential book describing 18 studies that showed the limitations of human judgment. These studies compared the judgments of professionals against statistical rule-based predictions about parole violations, success in pilot training, and academic success. In each study, the professionals had access to the data used by the statistical procedures and to additional data that might not have been included in the algorithm. Despite all their experience, the professionals outperformed the algorithms in only one of the 18 cases. In a few other cases the professionals and the formulas gave similar results, but in most of the cases the statistical rules were superior to the expert judgments. In one example, academic counselors had access to all the data on a school's incoming freshmen plus a 45-minute interview of each one, and still were less accurate in predicting their first-year grades than a statistical analysis based only on the students' high school grades and their scores on a standardized test.

Meehl's work has been repeated in a number of different areas with the same outcome. The statistical methods are more accurate than the expert judgments. In 2000, Grove et al. published a review of 136 studies comparing clinical judgments using experience with mechanical judgments using statistics. Most of these studies involved clinical psychology and medicine. The mechanical methods were superior in 63 of the studies. For instance, the analytic techniques got an accuracy score of 56 in predicting college academic performance, versus 39 for human judges. The analytical method got an accuracy score of 99 in identifying the presence of a throat infection, versus 69 for physicians. The analytical method got an accuracy score of 70 in predicting length of psychiatric hospitalization, versus 34 for clinical staff members. The other 65 studies showed no difference. Only eight studies showed better clinical performance for the experts.

These studies shake our confidence in the judgment of experts. Example 5.1 will shake that confidence even more.

Example 5.1: Panning the pundits   Phil Tetlock (2005) has demonstrated that experts in history and political science are not particularly accurate about predicting world events. One example is the unanimous prediction by the quantitative modelers of presidential elections at the American Political Science Association meeting in August 2000 that Al Gore would defeat George W. Bush by a decisive and possibly a landslide margin. The actual election result was somewhat closer.

Tetlock studied a set of 284 experts, most with PhDs and postgraduate training in fields such as political science, economics, international law and diplomacy, public policy, and journalism. Averaging 12 years of relevant work experience, they came from universities, think tanks, government service, and international institutions. Tetlock's criterion for experts was that they be professionals earning their living by commenting or offering advice on political and economic trends. Their average age was 43. Approximately 61 percent had been interviewed by a major media outlet; 21 percent had been interviewed more than ten times.

Tetlock collected most of his data between 1988 and 1992. He presented these experts with sets of questions and asked them to rate the probabilities. The questions dealt with (among other things) the likelihood of various countries acquiring the ability to produce weapons of mass destruction; the possibility of states or terrorist groups using such weapons; predictions over 3, 6, or 12 years about economic reforms in the former Soviet Bloc countries; adoption of the Euro; the prospects of former Soviet Bloc countries and Turkey joining the European Union; the winners of the American presidential elections in 1992 and 2000 and the margins of victory; the performance of the NASDAQ; the revenues, earnings, and share prices of Internet and information-technology companies such as CISCO, Oracle, Microsoft, Enron, and IBM; and whether Quebec would secede from the rest of Canada.

Tetlock waited a few years to see whether the world events actually occurred within the time frame in the questions. Then he compiled the actual results, to see how well the experts performed in comparison with a control—the performance of a hypothetical chimpanzee who simply assigned equal probabilities to the different events.

The experts barely beat the hypothetical chimp. They were slightly more accurate than chance.

It got worse. Tetlock had tested the experts with some questions from their fields of study and some from unfamiliar fields. The experts didn't do any better on questions from their fields of study than questions on unfamiliar topics. (They did outperform Berkeley undergraduates who received short descriptions of each topic of interest.)

When Tetlock confronted the experts with evidence for their inaccurate predictions, they were unfazed. They explained away the prediction failures rather than trying to improve their mental models. They showed the typical symptoms of fixation. Experts attributed their successes to their own skilled judgment, whereas they blamed their failures on bad luck or task difficulty. The political scientists who predicted a resounding victory for Al Gore in 2000, with confidence estimates that ranged from 85 percent to 97 percent, found no reason to doubt their quantitative equations. The problem, they claimed, was that their models had been fed some misleading economic data. Other modelers blamed the Bill Clinton–Monica Lewinsky scandal and pointed out that their models didn't include variables for promiscuous presidents.

Other experts argued that they were almost right. Thus, experts who doubted that the Communist Party in Russia would be driven from power by 1993 or 1998 responded that the attempted coup in 1991 to overthrow Mikhail Gorbachev almost succeeded. The experts complained that the coup leaders were too drunk and vacillated too much. The experts argued that if some of the military officers had followed the orders to kill civilians who challenged martial law, or if Boris Yeltsin hadn't been so courageous, the coup would have succeeded and the Soviet Union would have survived.

The experts who predicted that the European Monetary Union would collapse complained afterward that it almost happened during the currency crises of 1992 and was only averted by some central bankers. Experts who predicted that Quebec would secede from Canada by 2000 argued that it almost happened in 1995, when 49.4 percent of Quebecois voters voted for sovereignty.

Experts who predicted that a white minority would continue to rule South Africa pointed out the low probability of having leaders like F. W. deKlerk and Nelson Mandela in place to allow for a peaceful transition. And those who predicted that George H. W. Bush would be re-elected in 1992 complained that the Federal Reserve should have started cutting interest rates earlier in 1991 because the United States was obviously entering a recession.

Other experts argued that they were just off on the timing. They continue to predict that Quebec will eventually secede from Canada, that the European Monetary Fund will eventually disintegrate, and so on.

In short, the experts not only failed to demonstrate forecasting accuracy but adamantly retained their views in the face of contrary evidence.

Tetlock and others have shown that we can't trust the so-called experts. And we certainly can't trust our own judgments and intuitions. In his 2001 book *Everyday Irrationality: How Pseudo-Scientists, Lunatics, and the Rest of Us Systematically Fail to Think Rationally*, Robyn Dawes, a professor at Carnegie Mellon University, admonishes us never to rely on our intuitions. Eric Bonabeau, author of a 2003 article in the *Harvard Business Review* titled "Don't Trust Your Gut," makes the same point about the risks of using intuition versus the advantages of relying on mechanical, actuarial methods. This all adds up to a grim picture.

We know that people are getting seriously worried about decision biases and the weakness of experts because those subjects have hit the sports pages. In *Moneyball* (2003), Michael Lewis documents that the seasoned coaches and managers don't have a clue who their best players are. In *The Wages of Wins* (2006), David Berri, Martin Schmidt, and Stacey Brook make the same argument for basketball and football. The message of both books is that we should ignore the advice of the scouts and coaches and turn to statisticians and analysts.

The rallying cry of the decision-research community is "Give us statistics, not stories." Anecdotes may spice up a lecture, but the only way to protect ourselves from decision biases and from pseudo-experts is to have trained analysts pore over the data to tell us what is really going on.

I originally expected the people I surveyed to accept claim 2a, but their average rating was 4.05, almost directly on the centerline of "hard to tell" and in accord with "it depends." Nevertheless, I kept claim 2a in the book because this claim is often made by textbook writers, decision researchers, and college professors teaching graduate and undergraduate courses. Their message is clear: For any important judgment we should call in the decision analysts and operations researchers, not the experts.

Disclaimer

We need both intuition and analysis. Either one alone can get us in trouble. Experts certainly aren't perfect, but analyses can also fail.

Intuition isn't a magical property. I am defining intuition as ways we use our experience without consciously thinking things out. Intuition includes tacit knowledge that we can't describe. It includes our ability to recognize patterns stored in memory.[1] We have been building these patterns up for decades, and we can rapidly match a situation to a pattern or notice that something is off—that some sort of anomaly is warning us to be careful.

Skilled firefighters rely on their intuition to tell them when a fire is weakening, or when one is growing in intensity and becoming a threat. When playing "blitz chess," grandmasters use their intuition, selecting strong moves in seconds. Surgeons, athletes, and other professionals draw on their experience to recognize what to do without having to calculate statistics.

In this section I am going to describe some of the limits of relying too heavily on logic and statistics, and I am going to try to put the anti-intuition research into perspective. In the Replacement section, I will return to the middle ground—that is, that we depend on both intuition and analysis.

Even the research that debunks expertise depends on expert judgment. Studies that contrast the accuracy of judgments made by experts versus statistical formulae conjure up an image of the experts in one room and the decision analysts in another, competing to see who can make the most accurate judgments. That isn't what happened. If we look carefully at the methods used in the studies reported by Meehl and also by Grove et al., we find that the starting point of the research usually was the judgments made by the experts themselves.[2] The decision analysts studied these expert judgments to figure out what factors the experts took into account. Once they got that down, the analysts searched for an effective way to combine the evidence. They took advantage of the fact that experts don't always combine the evidence the best way, and sometimes are inconsistent. In contrast, the analysts' formulas are always consistent and should always come up with a better answer. Sometimes experts give too much emphasis to a factor, whereas the objective data can provide a more accurate weighting.

Therefore, the decision analysts could outperform the experts only after they identified the basic factors the experts were using.

To make predictions we have to do two things: *collect* the data and then *combine* the data. Some of the confusion about logic and statistics and intuition arises from blurring this distinction. Meehl and his followers haven't shown that expert intuitions are useless. They have just shown that statistical formulas for combining the data can be more accurate than the estimates made by experts.

Collecting the data often requires skill, tacit knowledge, intuition, and expertise. A clinical psychologist trying to predict whether a patient will commit a violent crime upon release from jail might make look for evidence that the prisoner expresses hostility, or blames others for his/her own shortcomings, or shows little empathy for the suffering of others. Clinicians make these judgments from interviews and observations with prisoners, judging typicality in reference to hundreds of other interviews they have done, many with similar prisoners. Clinicians use their judgment to identify variables that might be important, something that mechanical systems aren't particularly good at. Meehl never doubted the importance of intuition and expertise in making these judgments.[3]

Next comes the activity of combining all the data to make a prediction. The debate triggered by Meehl's 1954 book centers on this stage. As I noted earlier, about half of the studies reviewed by Grove et al. found no difference between the predictions made by experts versus statistical methods for integrating the data. The other half of the studies found that the statistical methods led to more accurate predictions.

Keep in mind that the predictions made by the statistical methods weren't all that good. The tasks reviewed by Grove et al. involve very complex situations; the statistical forecasts were often wrong, but were less inaccurate than the expert judgments. The research projects reviewed by Grove et al. show that the statistical methods outperformed the experts in half of the studies. The research doesn't show that the statistical methods nailed the predictions and the experts messed up. There isn't any smoking gun here.

Yet some decision researchers treat the findings as if they disprove the existence of expertise. They overgeneralize from such studies to adopt an attitude that demeans experts.

In many of my conversations with decision researchers, I am surprised by how deep-seated this attitude is. The conversation may start off pleasantly, with avowed admiration for experts, but when I describe any example of expertise they usually question whether it is supported by data, or how reliable it is, or make other speculations about why the expertise probably isn't genuine. If I mention the skill of chess grandmasters, they often counter that Deep Blue beat Garry Kasparov. If I talk about the skill of firefighters, they ask if I had any way of objectively measuring the quality of their decisions. If I extol the genius of Napoleon, they point out his defeat at Waterloo. Then we banter about the glass being half-full (my own admiration for all kinds of experts even though I recognize that they are fallible) versus half-empty (the decision researchers' interest in the experts' fallibility).

And although experts aren't infallible, they are able to amaze us with their performance. Consider grandmasters playing blindfold chess, or playing simultaneously against 15 or 20 opponents. Campitelli and Gobet (2004) showed that a grandmaster could solve nearly 50 percent of a set of chess problems within 10 seconds, versus less than 5 percent for a club player.

Skilled chess players rely more on their intuition than on deliberation. Bruce Burns (2004) studied the skill of chess players under blitz conditions—5 minutes for an entire game. In regulation games, chess players have 90 minutes to make the first 40 moves and then 30 minutes for the rest of the game. Under blitz conditions, chess players have to rely more on recognitional processes than on deliberate search strategies. Burns found that if he knew a player's performance in blitz tournaments he could make a very accurate prediction of that player's overall chess rating.[4]

Most of what differentiates skilled from unskilled chess players is their tacit knowledge, not their ability to calculate move quality. Systematic analysis is important in chess, but intuitive skills and tacit knowledge seem to be more critical. As players get stronger, their ability to do deliberate search and analysis doesn't seem to get any better.[5,6] It is hard to reconcile such findings with the claim that successful decision makers rely on logic and statistics rather than on intuition.

The claim that we should trust logic and statistics over intuition is wrong because we need both logic and intuition. Either one, by itself, can get us in trouble. The idea of emphasizing logic and suppressing intuition has led to its share of blunders. It gets repeated so often that we might as well examine its shortcomings.

Here is a simple example in which a manager relied on the analytical formula instead of his intuition and paid the price.

Example 5.2: Location, location, and... dislocation A manager in a large city searched for promising locations for gasoline filling stations. Fortunately, his company had developed an algorithm for locating the best spots. He applied the algorithm and it identified a prime location. The site was available, and he purchased the land. But just before he authorized the construction of the service station, he looked carefully at the plans, then visited the site again. Something was bothering him. He had some familiarity with the algorithm, and he wasn't completely confident in it. He knew many of the shortcuts and assumptions it used. His staff members were all eager to get the project going. He was the only holdout. He explained his uneasiness, but they didn't understand what was bothering him. They were all feeling pressure from the company to get more service stations built in order to meet their quotas and make their bonuses. So he yielded. With misgivings, he gave the go-ahead for the station. The construction proceeded smoothly, and the station soon opened for business. But there wasn't much business. The site wasn't as good as the algorithm had predicted, and the company soon closed the station.

Afterward, the manager was able to articulate what was bothering him. Even though the site was in the right place, on a well-traveled road connecting a residential district with a shopping district, the specific layout was a problem. The road was a divided highway, making it harder for drivers to pull in. And the exit point had poor sight lines for drivers pulling out into heavy traffic. The whole traffic flow intimidated the potential customers. The algorithm didn't capture these kinds of dynamics, but they had bothered the manager from the start. He regretted overruling his intuitions.

Many of us have had experiences like this, in which the analysis didn't quite feel right and in fact was flawed. We've also had other experiences in which our intuitions were wrong. I'm not arguing that we should favor intuition whenever it conflicts with the analysis. My point is simply that analytical rigor doesn't guarantee success. Sophisticated analyses can get it wrong. When we try to make decisions purely on the basis of statistics drawn from previous events, it's like driving while looking only through the rear-view mirror.[7]

One of the most famous blunders that resulted from a reliance on statistics and analysis is the collapse of the investment company Long-Term Capital Management (LTCM).

Example 5.3: The unsinkable hedge fund   Two Nobel Prize winners and several Harvard professors took an active role in establishing and governing Long-Term Capital Management. The founders had developed complex mathematical models for certain types of bond trading, enabling them to make profits based on very small differences in time-related trends. LTCM produced annual returns of up to 40 percent. Like the *Titanic*, it seemed unsinkable. But somehow, to the amazement of the financial community, LTCM sank. Or rather, it was in the process of sinking in 1998, losing $4.6 billion in just four months. At that point, the federal government arranged a bailout to prevent a financial crisis that stemmed from loss of investor confidence. What happened?

LTCM collapsed for several reasons. The strategy itself had a flaw. It relied on mathematical calculations that occasionally uncovered a very small discrepancy that could be exploited. Taking advantage of the discrepancies required a lot of transactions. To make profits, LTCM had to take highly leveraged positions. As it grew, the company faced increasing pressures to maintain its profit levels. This pushed it into riskier and riskier deals. The downturn started when LTCM hit a patch of negative net returns. In 1998, when LTCM was struggling with a loss of capital of almost $500 million, Russia defaulted on its government bonds. Suddenly, investors began pulling their money out of the bond market and out of LTCM. LTCM, heavily leveraged (to try to squeeze profits out of tiny rate differences), faced collapse. Their mathematical model was correct—the values of the government bonds did eventually converge, but by that time LTCM was defunct.

In this case, rigorous use of systematic analysis still resulted in a collapse. We are not talking about a clever scheme that didn't work very well. We're talking about a monumental failure that threatened to destabilize the US economy.

We saw a repeat of the LTCM episode during the Wall Street collapse in 2008. Once again sophisticated investors relied on statistical analyses to assure themselves and others that they were in good shape, and once again they almost succeeded in destroying the US economy.

These examples illustrate why a reliance on analysis and statistics won't prevent blunders. It may even lead to a dysfunctional condition of overthinking.

The failures of systematic analysis—overthinking
Logic and statistics are useful, but they aren't sufficient for making good decisions, and they sometimes result in worse decisions. Let us now look at the results of a study in which some people were asked to systematically think through their decisions and others were prevented from deliberating.

Example 5.4: Deliberation without attention   Are you better off relying on conscious thought to make choices, or on unconscious thought? The answer seems obvious—we should rely on conscious thought. That's what a team of Dutch researchers led by Ap Dijksterhuis found when they asked subjects to make simple choices, such as selecting towels or oven mitts (Dijksterhuis et al. 2006). But when the researchers turned to complex[8] choices, such as selecting an automobile or an apartment, the subjects did better with *unconscious* thought. In one study, participants read about four apartments that differed in desirability, then either chose immediately, chose after thinking hard about the alternatives, or chose after being distracted for the same period of time. This last group, the unconscious thinkers, made the best choices, picking the apartments that got the highest ratings from judges.

In another study, participants tried to select a car from among four different models.[9] The option that was considered the best was the one with the highest proportion of positive features. In the simple condition the participants had to consider only four attributes of the cars; in the complex condition they had to consider twelve attributes. Some of the participants had a chance to think deliberately about the options for four minutes; others were distracted by another task for four minutes. Then they made their choice.

The conscious thinkers made the right choice in the simple condition (only four attributes to think about) but not in the complex conditions. The people who were distracted—the unconscious thinkers—made the best choice in both the simple and the complex conditions.

To verify these results in real-world conditions, Dijksterhuis and colleagues asked shoppers how they made decisions about actual purchases, and then contacted the shoppers again a few weeks later. The shoppers who reported that they relied on deliberate thinking were more satisfied than the unconscious thinkers, but only for the simple items. For the complex items, the shoppers who hadn't consciously deliberated said they were much happier than the deliberate and systematic thinkers.[10]

We can't easily explain these findings away, because other researchers, including Timothy Wilson, Jonathan Schooler, and John Bargh, have all reported the same results—that conscious deliberation seems to make people less satisfied with their decisions.[11] Conscious thought doesn't necessarily help us make better choices. Any systematic strategy exposes us to the risks of overthinking.[12]

Radiologists worry about overthinking. If they look at a film too long, they start seeing things that aren't there. After about 38 seconds, they begin to overreact to slight irregularities in normal structures and identify non-existent malformations.[13]

What causes overthinking? One possibility is that we can think of only a few things at a time, so our cognitive bandwidth prevents us from considering all the variables when making choices. Unconscious thought lets us integrate lots of information. Another possibility is that when we consciously deliberate we may over-emphasize some of the features—the features that are easier to verbalize. We may ignore or downplay important features that don't have convenient verbal tags. Conscious deliberation seems to impose serious penalties on us.

Conscious deliberation presses us to view the world through a keyhole—the limitation of attention. And what gets missed by this keyhole view? Often we fail to notice the context. We happily flag three or four variables and think systematically about these, ignoring the background of what is going on. But when we tell stories, we tend to capture much of the context—that's the whole idea of a story, to embed facts within contexts. If we try to think about facts without the story (the context), we risk overthinking. It is very easy to miss what is really going on by attending just to the facts.

Example 5.5 shows that the objective data may give us a distorted picture of what is really going on.

Example 5.5: Who is leading the race? My youngest daughter Rebecca was the captain of her college rowing team. During the winter, when it is too cold to race outdoors, teams compete in indoor meets using rowing machines. In one contest, Rebecca sat next to a rower who was her toughest competition in that race. This young woman was much taller than Rebecca (height matters a lot in rowing) and looked pretty fit.

A typical strategy is to sprint for the first 400 meters (these indoor races are 2,000 meters long), do the next 1,400 meters at a good, strong pace, then finish with a powerful kick in the last 200 meters. Rebecca had decided a few weeks earlier that she needed a different race plan. She wasn't comfortable sprinting as fast or as long as most people at the beginning, and she thought that if she shortened that sprint she wouldn't have to ease up as much as most rowers did. She also believed that if she started her final kick a little earlier, at the 1,500-meter point, the excitement and adrenaline would get her through the end, even after her lungs and her legs wanted to stop. When the race started, the other woman opened up a large lead as Rebecca did her weak initial sprint and quickly settled into a nice pace. Rebecca was tempted to try to close the gap but decided that if her opponent could keep that pace up for the whole race she was unbeatable so it wasn't worth trying to challenge her. Rebecca was way behind after 500 meters. However, as she expected, her opponent slowed down in the next 500 meters, and Rebecca had closed the gap considerably when they reached 1,000 meters. At that point, Rebecca knew how the race would proceed. She knew that she was now rowing more strongly than her opponent and would be within distance to challenge her within the next 500 meters. And she had enough energy left to begin her kick early. She was pretty sure she was going to win the race.

No one else in the gymnasium realized this. Looking at the results, looking at the fact that Rebecca was still behind, her teammates tried to encourage her. "Hang with her, Rebecca," they urged. "You've still got a great shot at second place. Don't give up."

Even though she was rowing hard, Rebecca couldn't keep from reflecting on what they were telling her. No one else in that gym understood that she was almost certain to win. They saw the current results, saw the data, calculated the trends, and wanted to keep Rebecca from giving up.

Of course, the rest of the race unfolded as Rebecca imagined. (Why else would I include this story?) Rebecca had almost caught up by the 1,500-meter point, then started her kick. By the time her opponent started her own kick, the race was over.

Without context, we can't reliably make sense of data, particularly in complex settings. Without knowing Rebecca's strategy or how much energy she had saved, the objective data meant little. The notion of favoring logic and statistics over intuition leads to overthinking. It pretends that we can make sense of facts without taking context into account.

Research on people with brain damage shows the effect of overthinking. Damasio and colleagues[14] studied patients who suffered damage to brain areas (due to strokes, accidents, or tumors) that connect emotions with decisions. Such patients make decisions without any emotional/intuitive inputs. The results aren't pretty. In extreme cases, patients may deliberate for very long times about trivial choices, such as which restaurant to select, because they just don't have a good basis for making decisions. Patients who had previously led successful lives suddenly deteriorated. They could still speak well, handle logic problems, learn new material, retrieve material from memory, and score well on intelligence tests. They appeared fine, but they weren't. They lost their jobs and their families. The research suggests that normal people depend on emotion to trigger intuitions and guide their preferences.

Unintended consequences

It's time for some more imaginary surgery. After listening to a leading decision researcher give a lecture on decision biases and the perils of intuition, I asked him if he would be willing to have an operation that destroyed the part of the brain that translated emotions into the decision process. We know where this pathway is because of the findings of Damasio and others who have studied brain-damaged patients. After this surgery his judgments wouldn't be clouded by impulses anymore. He looked at me in disbelief. There was no way he would even consider such an operation. So we shouldn't be swayed by the rhetoric. Intuition and emotions are an important part of good decision making. Nevertheless, let us explore the likely effects. Or, if these surgical procedures are making you squeamish, imagine that we did convince people to rely on logic and statistics instead of intuition.

We would eliminate about 80 percent of the skill of chess grandmasters. They depend on their intuition to see what is going on in a game; we would force them to count everything out, the same as computers.

We would put managers under the thumb of operations-research specialists, replicating the helpless feeling of the manager in the earlier example who knew that the gasoline station was going to be put at the wrong location but couldn't articulate why.

We would make overthinking the ideal, even in complex, shadowy situations that aren't readily analyzed.

We would never use any hunches. But where would our new ideas come from, if not from our previous experience?

We would have trouble with data overload, because we would have to pay attention to everything to see what is important rather than relying on our intuition about where to focus our attention and what to ignore.

We would turn everyone into facsimiles of the brain-damaged patients Damasio studied, who had to calculate everything.

Replacement

The replacement for the claim that we should rely on logic and statistics over intuition is straightforward: *We need to blend systematic analysis and intuition.* Neither gives us a direct path to the truth. Each has its own limitations.

Analytical and statistical methods can pick up subtle trends in the data that our intuitions would miss. They can show us when the regularities we think we see are really just chance connections. They can help us appraise the size of different effects so we can take the effects into account more accurately. On the other hand, analytical methods often miss the context of a situation, and they can result in misleading recommendations.

Intuitive judgments reflect the experiences we've had and can help us respond quickly to situations. They are sensitive to context and nuance, letting us read situations and also read other people. We can make successful decisions without using analytical methods, but we cannot make good decisions without drawing on our intuitions. Yet our intuitions aren't foolproof, and we always have to worry that they are going to mislead us.

Research showing that a statistical formula can outperform an expert doesn't mean that the expert is flawed. It just means that the statistics do better in certain types of circumstances. Analytical methods can sometimes outperform experts, particularly if these methods improve on the judgments made by experts, but the methods may not be as valuable as their developers argue.

We can make good use of analytical tools and statistical methods that let us gain a clearer picture of trends. But that isn't the same as handing decision authority over to statisticians and analysts.

When I first decided to include claim 2a—that we should depend on logic and statistics instead of intuition—I worried that readers would dismiss a suggestion that logic, statistics and analysis might have any limitations, but I think that the failures of analytical methods during the financial crisis of 2008 have made such arguments more palatable. Wall Street firms had come to rely on analytical methods such as Value at Risk (VaR) to calculate how much to hold in reserve. The VaR analyses were insensitive to the pending collapse of the housing market, and the loss of liquidity that followed. Many now blame the VaR method for the failure of the investment firms to anticipate the financial collapse.

Long Term Capital Management had relied on VaR as one of its risk models. In the aftermath of the LTCM debacle, the Merrill Lynch annual report stated that mathematical risk models "may provide a greater sense of security than warranted, therefore, reliance on these models should be limited."[15]

Defenders of VaR explain that it is very useful, but that it has limitations. They argue that the decision makers failed to put it in perspective. "The problem on Wall Street at the end of the housing bubble," one commentator concluded, "is that all judgment was cast aside. The math alone was never going to be enough."[16]

Here we have a restatement of my replacement for claim 2a. We need both systematic analysis and intuition. The defenders of systematic analysis argue that of course methods such as VaR have their limitations but they also have their benefits—mirroring the defense of intuition I have made in the last two chapters. We'll get back to this topic in chapter 15 when we examine the process of risk management.

The examples in the Disclaimer section showed that we can't rely on the claim that successful decision makers rely on logic and statistics instead of intuition. However, the examples don't mean we trust intuition over logic and statistics. For instance, we should be careful in interpreting the findings of Dijksterhuis et al., because Newell et al. (2009) didn't find much difference between participants who used conscious deliberation versus participants who were prevented from engaging in conscious deliberation through distraction. Conscious deliberation doesn't always interfere with complex decision making, but that's still a long distance from claim 2a.

What should we do when logic and analysis suggest one answer and intuition suggests another? Which answer should we favor? As I said in chapter 1, it depends. The next chapter considers what it depends on, and how we combine intuition and analysis.

Why claim 2a matters

The claim that successful decision makers rely on logic and statistics instead of intuition matters because systematic analysis may work for well-ordered tasks. But it runs into difficulty in complex settings, and it leads to overthinking. We can make very poor decisions when we rely solely on systematic analysis. Recall the study in which Dijkster-huis et al. asked shoppers to deliberate without using intuition. Recall Damasio's brain-damaged subjects, who were crippled when their decisions were disconnected from their emotions.

It matters because it encourages organizations to set up procedures and analytical practices that make it harder to develop good intuitions —that is, to develop expertise.

It matters because we have to stop sending MBA students out into the world armed only with analytical and statistical methods. We should also help them appreciate the limits of these concepts. We should teach them to recognize experts in the workplace and to take advantage of the tacit knowledge these experts possess.

6   Blending Intuition and Analysis to Make Rapid Decisions

In chapter 5, I explained why we rely on both intuition and analysis. Here, I examine how to use both in making decisions.

Claim 3: To make a decision, generate several options and compare them to pick the best one.

Claim 3 is taught in business schools, in schools of engineering, and in military academies. It has shaped generations of leaders. These leaders believe that all they need is more good options and stronger methods to select the best.

Often we do have to compare options—for example, when picking a selection from a menu, choosing a detergent or a breakfast cereal from those never-ending supermarket aisles, or settling on which job candidate to hire. These decisions take attention and deliberation.

Claim 3 makes a stronger statement: that when faced with a decision we should go through the drill of listing a set of alternatives and then contrasting them.

In addition to claim 3, here are five more claims that I will dissect in this chapter:

- When people get better at making decisions, they consider more options and evaluate them more deliberately.

- Only novices rush ahead with the first option that pops into their minds.

- We make decisions by comparing options, using the same criteria to find the best one.

- Decision analysis will improve the quality of our choices.

- The closer the alternative options are matched, the harder we must work to pick the best one.

Table 6.1
The Rational Choice model of decision making.

Evaluation dimensions	Option		
	A	B	C
1 Price	✓		
2 Reliability		✓	✓
3 Safety	✓		
4 Gas mileage	✓	✓	✓
Total	3	2	2

These beliefs encourage us to think carefully when making decisions. Thinking carefully means identifying a range of different options so that we don't miss anything by being too impulsive, then setting up a common set of criteria so we evaluate each of the options using the same standards.[1] Sometimes we want to give more weight to the most important evaluation criteria rather than counting every dimension equally. I'll refer to this type of analysis as a Rational Choice method.

Imagine that you have to buy a car, that you have narrowed the decision down to three options, and that the features you want to take into account in comparing the three cars are price, reliability, safety, and gas mileage. Table 6.1 shows how the spreadsheet might look. Option A comes out on top with three check marks. It satisfied three of the four evaluation criteria. The other options satisfied only two criteria.

Analytical methods like this are general—once we learn them, we can use them for all sorts of decisions. They are reliable, and they tend to give the same result over and over. They are comprehensive, and they can easily expand to include all the criteria and options we want to add. And they are quantitative. They give precise answers that can be audited to trace where the numbers came from.

Another technique is to use a decision tree. Decision-tree diagrams represent different options, the probability of success with each, and the anticipated benefit if that option is successful. The result of each branch is an expected value for that option, letting the decision maker see which option to select. The option with the highest expected value will have the greatest chance for success.

Decision researchers have developed elaborate strategies for carrying out these kinds of methods. One strategy, described by Edwards and Fasolo (2001), consisted of a 19-step process for making decisions.

Most professional communities treat analytical methods such as rational choice diagrams and decision trees as the gold standard for rational decision making. When I criticize these methods to Army and Marine generals, many of them bristle. They were taught this strategy at the beginning of their careers and have become increasingly committed to it. Decision researchers are just as adamant. This is the only rational way to make decisions. If people don't follow these strategies— well, it's not clear how else you could make decisions.[2]

The survey showed that claim 3 was strongly accepted. Respondents averaged 5.51 on the seven-point scale. Only nine of the 163 respondents showed any disagreement.

Disclaimer

People and organizations rarely use formal methods of decision making, such as the Rational Choice method (table 6.1). Many decision analysts have come to recognize that decision makers hardly ever set up formal evaluation methods or rate different options on the same dimensions.

Think about the decisions you have made in your life. I doubt that you set up a matrix to compare your choices very often, if ever. Why not?

One reason why people and organizations rarely use formal methods of decision making is that they require too much time and effort. You can't use them if you have less than half an hour to make the decision.[3]

A second reason is that the formal methods require a lot of data to fill in all the cells of the decision matrix, or to estimate all the probabilities. If you want to use the methods, you have to make up ratings and probabilities that you don't have any way to confirm. You can't put much faith in the results if you don't believe the estimates that go into those results.

Third, it is much harder to estimate complex variables than well-ordered ones. In buying a car, we can pin down reliability records and fuel economy and crash protection ratings. On the other hand, we have trouble estimating how comfortable a car will be on long trips. How enjoyable is it to drive? How easy will it be to strap a child into an infant seat? As a result, we either ignore those features or we rate all the alternatives as average, which washes out this variable from the decision.[4]

Recall Dijksterhuis's study of shoppers in chapter 5, which showed that when subjects had to consider twelve variables instead of four they made better decisions when they were *prevented* from deliberating consciously. Johnson, Driskell, and Salas (1997) found that subjects in an experiment who were directed to use a decision matrix performed worse than the controls who were allowed to make the judgments any way they wanted. Additionally, Nygren and White (2002) reported that college subjects who relied on an analytical style of decision making performed worse on a complex decision-making task in a flight simulator. Those who relied on an intuitive approach didn't have any trouble with this decision-making task, and also did better as their workload increased, which is consistent with the Dijksterhuis study. These findings mesh with the discussion in chapter 5 that logic, statistics, and analysis don't take precedence over intuition.

Fourth, I am not aware of any evidence that these analytical methods help people make better decisions, or that training in formal decision making results in better performance.[5] Decision analysts now argue that their goal is to help people make more consistent decisions with clearer justifications, not necessarily decisions that are better.

And we all know what happens if we do these kinds of analyses and get an answer we don't like. For example, if we don't like Option A in table 6.1, we go back and fiddle with the evaluation criteria or the ratings until the results come out the way we want. We game the method.

The more skilled one is, the fewer options one thinks about. The only population I studied that compared multiple options for most decisions was the least experienced—tank platoon leaders in their initial training. Novices have to compare options because they don't have the experience base to recognize what to do. However, comparing options doesn't substitute for experience.

A final weakness in these analytical methods is the Zone of Indifference.[6] When one option is clearly better than the others, we need not do any analysis. We immediately know what to choose. The closer the options become, the more the strengths and weaknesses are balanced, the harder the choice. The hardest decisions are those that must be made when the options are just about perfectly balanced. Paradoxically, if the options are perfectly balanced it doesn't much matter which one we choose. We agonize the most, spend the most time and effort, making choices that are inside this Zone of Indifference, when we might as well flip a coin. The analytical methods are designed to help us make the toughest choices, but once we realize we are inside the Zone of Indifference we should stop right there, make an arbitrary choice, and move on.

What if we don't move on? Herbert Simon argued that any company that attempted to optimize its returns and make the best decisions would fall into a never-ending quest to find the best decision. Simon (1957) coined the term *satisficing* to describe what we all do just about all the time—pick the first option that seems to get the job done and not worry about whether it is the best.

In a well-ordered world we might have a chance at finding a best option, but in a complex world with goals that are unclear and changing, the concept of a best option doesn't make much sense. Statisticians may enjoy speculating about optimal strategies, but the rest of us have to get things done.

The more choices we are given, the harder the decision. For example, Tversky and Shafir (1992) offered subjects the opportunity to buy an attractive appliance whose price was dramatically marked down. The subjects recognized this opportunity as a bargain. But when a second item, also at a reduced price, was offered alongside the first, the subjects vacillated, and the sales were lower than when the subjects had only one good option. The extra item put the subjects inside the Zone of Indifference and turned an easy decision into a difficult one, with the paradoxical result that a number of subjects no longer took advantage of the bargain.[7]

The field of decision making searches for ways to help people make better choices. Yet in study after study we find that people don't compare any options, let alone systematically review those options' strengths and weaknesses. Even for difficult decisions, we go with the first workable course of action in 90–95 percent of cases. We contrast options in perhaps 5–10 percent of cases.[8] If we usually don't compare options, how do we make decisions?

Replacement

How do we make decisions, especially under some time pressure and uncertainty? That was the question my colleagues and I set out to answer in 1985. We had received funds from the Army Research Institute to conduct a small research project, and we decided to study firefighters because making decisions is what they do for a living. I expected that the firefighters would compare only two options, because they didn't have time to go through a comprehensive review. As you can see, at that time I was still accepting claim 3; I was simply adapting it for time-pressured situations.

We interviewed 26 highly experienced firefighters—commanders who averaged 23 years of experience.[9] That's more than 500 years of cumulative wisdom. To our surprise, the commanders insisted that they didn't compare any options. They looked at a situation and just knew what to do. That created two mysteries: How could they be so confident in their initial impulses? How could they evaluate an option except by comparing it to others?

The answer to the first mystery is that with 23 years of experience you recognize situations as familiar, or typical. The patterns you recognize include typical ways to react. Therefore, the first option the commanders thought of was usually going to get the job done. They were satisficing (looking for a good workable option, not necessarily the best), and their first impulses were very effective.

Example 6.1: Pushing the fire out   An interview with a commander was going badly. I asked him for challenging incidents. He couldn't remember any. I asked about difficult decisions. Again, a blank. I asked for incidents showing the importance of experience. Nothing. So I changed my interviewing strategy and asked him about the last fire he had handled. He explained that it had occurred about a week ago but had been trivial, requiring no decision making at all. I reasoned that at least we had an incident to talk about. And it is rare to probe an incident without learning something, so I asked him to tell me what had happened. A simple house fire, he said. He and his crew had pulled up to a single-family house. They could see smoke coming out of the back, so the commander immediately figured it to be a kitchen fire. As he began to walk around the house to do his inspection, he told his crew to get ready to go in through the front door with a $1\frac{3}{4}$-inch line (hose). When he completed his circuit, he gave the go-ahead. They charged the line (filled it with water from a nearby hydrant), hit the fire, and extinguished it. He gave me a triumphant look—see, there wasn't any decision making at all.

Something didn't feel right to me. I told him that I was always taught to go out of a building if it was on fire. He sent his crew into the building. Why didn't he just take the hose around the back and hit the fire from the outside?

He looked at me with contempt. That's what a volunteer fire department might do. The problem is that by hitting it from outside you're going to push it into the house where it can spread in all kinds of ways. No, it's much better to go into the house and push it outside. Of course, if there is another exposure outside, say another building right next to it, then you might have to do an external attack, but that's really a last choice.

The commander had made a decision in this incident, but it was so natural that he hadn't realized it. That's what his 20+ years of experience bought him: the ability to recognize just what to do.

The last example was mundane. It showed how firefighters make routine decisions. The next example involved higher stakes.

Example 6.2: Good to the last drop The volunteer fire department was called out to a three-story apartment complex. When they arrived, they saw heavy smoke and some flames coming out of one of the basement units.

The commander, who had a lot of firefighting experience, sent some of his crew into the building in order to locate the seat of the fire. He sent another crew to ventilate the roof—cut a hole in it to allow the smoke and heat to escape. He also ordered one of his engine crews to attach their hoses to a nearby fire hydrant.

Then he got the word—the hydrant was dry. There must have been a problem with the water supply pipes in the village. However, he had no time or need to speculate. He had to extinguish the fire, which was growing in intensity, even though he hadn't determined where the seat of the fire was and the only water he had was the little that he brought with him on the fire trucks. The apartments had been constructed with a common attic, making it likely that the fire would destroy the entire unit if he didn't quickly get it under control.

Without hesitation he ordered his crew to aim all of their water at the point that he judged to be the seat of the fire. All of the water. If he guessed wrong he would just have to watch the fire destroy the entire building.

His guess was right. The water he had was enough to extinguish the blaze, barely.

Afterward, he explained to my research team that fires grow exponentially. By the time he was certain of the location of the seat of the fire, the fire would have been too large to contain. He had to rely on a blitz attack to catch it while it was small. He had to rely on his judgment.

My colleagues have used this scenario to test commanders in other fire departments. Experienced ones make the same decision—hit the fire with everything they've got. The newly promoted commanders hesitate. They aren't confident in their judgment and they fear the consequences of using up all the water. They tend to keep some water in reserve even though that decision will make it less likely that they'll put the fire out, and the amount in reserve won't be useful. Experienced commanders have learned to rely on their first judgment because they usually don't get a second chance.

The answer to the second mystery, how to evaluate an option if you don't compare it to others, is that the commanders evaluated an option by imagining it. They played it through in their mind, conducting a mental simulation. If it worked, they carried it out. If it almost worked, they altered it to make it better. If they couldn't make it work, they discarded it and looked at the next most typical action, continuing on until they found an adequate course of action.

Klein, Calderwood, and Clinton-Cirocco (1986) called this strategy a Recognition-Primed Decision (RPD) model. (See figure 6.1.) The pattern recognition suggested an effective course of action and then the firefighters used a mental simulation to make sure it would work. This

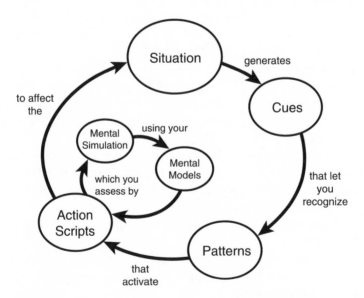

Figure 6.1
The Recognition-Primed Decision (RPD) model. Source: Klein 2004.

RPD strategy combines intuition with analysis. The pattern matching is the intuitive part, and the mental simulation is the deliberate analysis.

Therefore, I would replace claim 3 (To make a decision, generate several options and compare them to pick the best one) with the RPD model: *Good decision makers use their experience to recognize an effective option and evaluate it through mental simulation.* Our research shows that the more experience people have, the more likely they are to make decisions without deliberately contrasting options. The action scripts are hunches for how to decide. The scripts get developed further during the mental simulation of how they might play out. Novices, lacking the experience base to recognize patterns, must generate a range of options in the hope that one of them might work.

The first study of firefighters showed that about 80 percent of the difficult decisions followed the RPD model. Later research with a wider range of settings has upped the estimate to around 90 percent. Other researchers, using offshore oil installation crisis managers and Navy technicians,[10] have replicated our findings.[11] The incident in which a US Airways pilot safely landed in the Hudson River illustrates recognition-primed decision making.

Example 6.3: Miracle on the Hudson On January 15, 2009, at 3:25 p.m., US Airways Flight 1529, an Airbus 320, took off from LaGuardia Airport in New York on its way to Charlotte, North Carolina. Two minutes after the takeoff the airplane hit a flock of Canada geese and lost thrust in both of its engines. The captain, Chesley B. "Sully" Sullenberger III, and the first officer, Jeffrey Skiles, safely landed the airplane in the Hudson River at 3:31 p.m. All 150 passengers plus the five crew members were rescued.

Media reports and interviews with Sullenberger allow us to describe his decision strategy after he lost thrust in both engines.

Option 1 was to return to LaGuardia Airport. Sullenberger's initial message to the air traffic controllers was "Hit birds. We lost thrust in both engines. We're turning back toward LaGuardia." But he quickly realized that the airplane was too low and slow to make it back, so he abandoned that plan.

Option 2 was to find another airport. Sullenberger was headed west and thought he might be able to reach Teterboro Airport in New Jersey. The air traffic controllers quickly gained permission for him to land at Teterboro, but Sullenberger judged he wouldn't get that far. "We can't do it," he stated. "We're gonna be in the Hudson."

Option 3 was to land in the Hudson River.

Sullenberger's decision strategy fits the RPD model. He considered three courses of action, one at a time, starting with the most typical and ending with the most desperate. It is instructive to think about what he didn't do. He didn't set up the kind of decision matrix shown in table 6.1, listing these three options and contrasting them on common evaluation dimensions such as shortest distance, best runways, least inconvenience to passengers who might need to re-book their flights. Sullenberger was satisficing, looking for the first option that would work.

Before the firefighter studies that we conducted, researchers didn't know how people actually made decisions. The formal decision models described a set of ideal strategies. While many decision researchers understood that people didn't use those strategies, it wasn't obvious what people did instead. They may have carried out a simplified and corrupted form of the strategies, or they may have made arbitrary choices. Most of the experiments used college students performing artificial tasks, and didn't involve any experience. Researchers hadn't considered the possibility that when people used their experience the first option they considered could be a good one.

How good are these first options? Maybe the first options satisfied the decision makers' needs but were pretty mediocre. To examine this question we designed a study using skilled chess players. We showed them challenging game positions and asked them to think aloud as they studied the boards. We really just wanted to identify the first move option they thought of. We evaluated these first impulses using grandmaster ratings. The grandmasters assessed that only one-sixth of the legal moves were worth considering. Therefore, if the players were just randomly coming up with possible moves, only one-sixth of their first moves would have gotten acceptable ratings from the grandmasters.

We found that the players were much, much better than chance. Two-thirds of their moves received acceptable ratings from the grandmasters, versus the one-sixth we would expect by chance. The chess players in our study, even the mediocre ones, weren't randomly spinning out options. Most of their first choices met the standards of grandmasters.[12]

The RPD model shows how we can make good decisions—using our experience—without comparing options and without even generating more than one option. The decision-analysis model, as stated in claim 3, shouldn't be our gold standard for good decision making, because we rarely use this strategy and because it doesn't seem to result in better decisions.

Now that we have covered what is wrong with claim 3, and how people actually make decisions, let's re-examine the connection between analysis and intuition.

Two systems of thinking

Many researchers are now advocating for a dual-system mode of thinking.[13,14] The automatic system is fast, automatic, effortless, and emotional, and uses tacit knowledge. The reflective system[15] is slower, conscious, effortful, deliberate, logical, and serial, and uses explicit knowledge. These two systems, which work in different ways, complement each other, just as the rod cells and cone cells in our eyes complement each other. The two systems are different mental gears that we can use.

The connection between the two systems isn't always perfect. Consider this problem: A bat and a ball cost $1.10 in total. The bat costs a dollar more than the ball. How much does the ball cost? For most of us, the immediate reaction is 10 cents. Yet the correct response is 5 cents. Think about it. If the ball is worth 10 cents, then the bat has to cost $1.10, which totals $1.20. Why do most of us jump to the wrong conclusion—that the ball costs 10 cents? Shane Frederick (2005) has studied this and similar problems as examples of a failure of the reflective system to do its job. The initial impulse seems so obvious that we don't think twice—and therefore we don't engage the gear for our reflective system. Frederick composed a cognitive reflection test to distinguish people with strong and weak reflection tendencies, and found that the test scores identify people who are more generally impulsive or reflective in their choices. It also works in the other direction. We need the automatic system to check up on the reflective system. Even when we calculate mathematics problems, we depend on our intuitions. Halberda, Feigenson, and Mazzocco (2008) studied our "approximate number sense"—our "ballpark" intuition. They tested the approximate number sense of 14-year-olds by showing them very short images (one-fifth of a second—about as long as it takes to blink an eye) of slides with yellow and blue dots. The subjects had to press a button to indicate whether there were more yellow or blue dots. Some of the teenagers could tell the difference between nine blue dots and ten yellow dots. Others had trouble distinguishing five yellows from three blues, which is about the level of the average 9-month-old. The teenagers who did the best, who had the strongest approximate number sense, also had the best performance on standardized math tests, starting in kindergarten and continuing to their current grade. Their number intuition seemed to help them do better when deliberating and calculating the answers to math problems.

This two-system Automatic/Reflective framework fits the RPD model. The intuitive pattern-recognition part of decision making uses the automatic system to size up situations and form initial impulses about what to do. The deliberate mental simulation uses the reflective system to assess the options suggested by the patterns.

Claim 3 (to make a decision, generate several options and compare them to pick the best one) is part of the rational mind set that says the more we deliberate, the better off we'll be. It ignores System 1, the automatic system, and the contributions of our experience and tacit knowledge. As we saw in chapter 5, we need both intuition and analysis—both the automatic system and the reflective system. If we were just using intuition, we would be making lots of blunders. And if we just tried to use analysis, we would never get very far, as shown by the brain-damaged patients Damasio studied. Those patients lost the connection between their emotions and their decisions and had enormous difficulties making even the simplest kinds of decisions. They were forced to use the reflective system to reason about everything.

Additional claims about decision making
Now that we have replaced claim 3, let us clean up all the other claims I listed at the beginning of the chapter.

When people get better at making decisions they consider more options and evaluate them more deliberately.
Not true. As people gain experience, they consider fewer options and evaluate them using mental review rather than by comparing them using the same evaluation criteria. A study by Monique Cesna and Kathy Mosier (2005) is typical of the research here—they found that highly experienced nurses generated many fewer options than nurses with less experience.

Only novices would rush ahead with the first option that popped into their minds.
Not true. Novices don't feel comfortable going with the first option—they don't have the experience to trust the first option, or to gauge its quality except by contrasting it to others. Research by Raanan Lipshitz and Orit Ben Shaul (1997) is consistent with what numerous other studies have found: novices tend to deliberate about which option to select, whereas experts deliberate about what is going on in the situation.

We make decisions by comparing options using the same criteria to find the best one.
Not true. When we try to use the same criteria for all the options, we wind up discarding some important considerations and distorting others. That's when we try to force the outcome to mirror our intuition, fiddling with the criteria until we get what we want.

Decision analysis will improve the quality of our choices.
Not true. I am not aware of any evidence that decision analysis improves the quality of judgments and decisions.

The closer the alternative options are matched, the more we must work to pick the best one.
Not true. When the options match up too closely, we are in the Zone of Indifference. Sometimes we would be better off just flipping a coin instead of continuing to struggle. For higher-stakes decisions, such as whether to attack a country suspected of developing nuclear weapons or just continue to apply political and economic pressure, decision makers aren't going to flip a coin. They are likely to look for more options, or to shift from decision making to problem solving, trying to find ways to make some options work better.[16] Regardless of the tactic, when we reach a point where further analysis is unlikely to break an impasse, we should recognize the futility of endless debate.

Comparing options
Sometimes we do face situations in which we do have to contrast different courses of action. We may have a choice between a few different job applicants, or between a few different jobs, or different colleges that have accepted us, or we may have to figure out which computer to

buy. We may have to decide whether to move to another state to be with a spouse. What do we do then?

We can learn from skilled chess players.[17] They don't settle for the first satisfactory option. They really do want to play the best move possible. Their strategy is to conduct mental simulations of each one of the promising moves, imagining how the option would play out deeper and deeper into the future. Then they take stock of their mental and emotional reactions to what they see in this mental review. If they feel that a line of play is going to get them into trouble, they reject that move. Other moves may have potential and are worth thinking about, and some just feel right—they just seem to be more promising than the others. Thus, the players are considering several moves, but their choice is based on how each move stands up to the mental simulation, not on a comparison of moves using standard criteria.

Skilled chess players don't compare options using the Rational Choice method (table 6.1), because there is little benefit to rating options on the same evaluation dimensions, such as controlling the center of the board, increasing the defense around the king, and making a good shape with the pawns. These kinds of ratings don't capture the dynamics of the game position. Instead, the mental-simulation strategy lets chess players appreciate how a move works for that game. The mental simulations capture the context rather than filtering it out through a Rational Choice method.

The Rational Choice method might be useful when we do have to make choices and don't have very much experience. The process of setting up a matrix such as that shown in table 6.1 can help us clarify what matters to us. Howard Raiffa, who originated this method, wanted to help people notice when their intuitions didn't match their analyses. When that happened, Raiffa didn't recommend that we should automatically go with the analytical choice. Instead, he suggested that we should re-examine the analysis to see what it left out, and review the intuition to see if it still felt compelling.[18]

According to Raiffa we shouldn't trust either analysis or intuition. When they give us different answers, we should use this as a signal to re-examine each one.

In most situations in which we do have to compare options, we may not gain much from the formal Rational Choice strategy. It may be enough just to list the different options in order to keep track of our thoughts, and help us discuss the issues with others. Then we can list the strengths and weaknesses of each option to make sure we have captured everything.[19]

In some situations we would benefit from the Rational Choice method. A company trying to decide in which city to open its next branch office might find it useful, for example, to compare the candidate cities on common dimensions. Most of the time, however, we borrow from the firefighters and chess grandmasters and do a mental simulation of each option to imagine how it might play out.

Example 6.4: ApartMental simulation   Several years ago, my daughter Rebecca went apartment-hunting in Washington. She knew what neighborhood she wanted to live in, and she found a few good options. One of her friends had recommended one of the buildings in that neighborhood as "the best deal in DC," so Rebecca was happy to see that it had a vacancy. She was pleased that her search was going so well.

Rebecca went to visit the apartment the next day and loved it—huge windows, beautiful hardwood floors, a great kitchen. The rent was a little more than she hoped but still within her budget. The apartment would be available just about when she was ready to move in. Electricity wasn't included in the rent, but Rebecca decided that paying for utilities would be a good way to encourage her to be more environmentally conscious.

The layout of the apartment was a little awkward; the only way people could get to the bathroom was to walk through her bedroom. Rebecca convinced herself that this was really a virtue because it would force her to keep her bedroom tidy. The building's elevator was small and rickety, and Rebecca found it a bit frightening, but she figured it would be better for her to get a little exercise by walking the five flights up to the apartment anyway. The apartment didn't have central air conditioning, which could be a disadvantage in the hot and muggy Washington summers. Rebecca saw this as another plus; she could use window air conditioners whenever she got too warm rather than being at the mercy of the building superintendent. In her current apartment, the superintendent went by the calendar, and Rebecca suffered a little during the warm days of early spring. Rebecca was concerned about the cost of buying the window units but figured it was a fixed cost that would balance out in the long run.

It was, surprisingly, the lack of a garbage disposal that prompted Rebecca to change her mind. When she took stock of all the negative features she had been explaining away, she realized it was time to continue her apartment search rather than sign the lease.

Rebecca wasn't really relying on intuition. She was relying on emotion—she wanted to like this apartment. She turned weaknesses into strengths until she reached a point at which she couldn't tolerate the cognitive strain of explaining away so many problems. She realized the mismatch between her emotions and a deliberate analysis.

Making decisions in organizations

We make many decisions in teams and organizations, rather than alone. The Rational Choice approach lets us direct the behavior of team members. We can use teammates to gather data on each of the options in parallel. Sub-teams can compare the options on each of the evaluation dimensions in parallel. Then we just combine their estimates to get scores for the options.

Because of misplaced faith in claim 3, and because of its advantages for coordinating planning teams, some organizations mandate these methods. For example, the US Army has a Military Decision Making Process that centers around generating three courses of action and evaluating each option on a common set of dimensions, as illustrated in table 6.1. The Marine Corps has its own version of this process.

The trouble is that very few military headquarters ever follow this doctrine. My friend John Schmitt, a former Marine, developed a Recognitional Planning Model to expand on the Recognition-Primed Decision model. Building on the RPD research, Schmitt's model jettisons all the busy work of three courses of action and instead encourages the leader to use intuition to identify a favored course of action. (The leader is free to consider several courses of action if there is no favorite.) The planning staff reviews and details this course of action, along the lines of a reflective system evaluation. We tested this approach to planning at Fort Leavenworth. Participants (retired Army colonels) judged that the Recognitional Planning Model was faster than the traditional Military Decision Making Process.[20]

Does the Recognitional Planning Model increase speed at the cost of plan quality? Peter Thunholm (2005) investigated this possibility in a study with the Swedish Army and got the same quality of plans in 20 percent less time. As a result, the Swedish Army has adopted Thunholm's version of the Recognitional Planning Model for tactical operations.

Unintended consequences

Imagine that we have taken the pledge to adopt claim 3 and make all important decisions by generating several options and comparing them to pick the best one. Does that commitment fill us with pride, or with dread? We certainly won't be making rapid decisions anymore. In fact, every decision from here on is going to be a chore.

But we'll still have to make decisions. For any important decision we'll have to decide which options to study and which to dismiss. Which evaluation dimensions should we use and how many? How are we going to make those decisions—more analyses? That sounds like an infinite regress of analyses before we even get to make the decisions.

Of course, we won't be making decisions. We'll just be judging which boxes to check in a Rational Choice table. Why do we think we can make that judgment better than judging which option looks better?

And what are we going to do in complex situations? Even the situations Dijksterhuis et al. studied, comparing cars using twelve uncomplicated features instead of four, showed that conscious deliberation resulted in worse decisions. And the more choices we include, the more decision paralysis we are going to suffer.

Furthermore, there is no place in this rational strategy to use intuition to monitor the analysis.

Years ago a prominent decision researcher took the pledge to adopt claim 3.[21] He was about to move to another university, and he needed to find a new house. He had been teaching decision-analysis methods to his students and now it was time for him to walk the walk and use the techniques of decision analysis to make the decision about which house to buy. It didn't take him long to give up his pledge. He usually knew within ten minutes of walking into a house if he wanted to buy it, but the analyses took much longer to work out. In each case, another bidder had already made a successful offer by the time he finished his calculations. Worse, he had trouble comparing different houses on the same evaluation dimensions because each house was different. The context of the houses and the relationship between features got in the way of making clean comparisons or even isolating comparable features.

In this chapter, I have distinguished between an automatic and a reflective system of thinking. Claim 3 puts too much emphasis on the reflective system—that's the one we can control better. Because we rely on both systems, we have to resolve conflicts between them.

We have to gauge how much we trust our intuitions and our analyses. And that depends on how skilled we are. The next chapter takes up the topic of expertise, its strengths and its limitations.

Why claim 3 matters

It matters because claim 3 (to make a decision, generate several options and compare them to pick the best one) doesn't help anyone make better decisions. It ignores the way experienced people actually make decisions. It just gets in the way of their effective strategy, and yet it doesn't really help novices.

It matters because of the advice we give to people. Currently, we are advising people to make decisions in ways that are unrealistic and ineffective.

It matters because we have to stop treating decisions as gambles. It is certainly convenient to boil the decision making down to probabilities and costs/benefits. However, this view assumes that the decision maker is passively awaiting the outcome of the gamble rather than actively managing the situation and shaping options.

7   Experts and Errors

According to legend, a famous composer was asked how long it took to write one of his operas and replied "One week, and all my life before that."

Many of the claims discussed in this book relate to the nature of expertise. These claims rest on assumptions about our ability to gain experience, about the reliability of the intuitions that emerge from that experience, and about the kinds of errors our experience might allow. Experts sometimes make errors, and aren't infallible but that shouldn't lead us to dismiss their abilities.

The mental models of experts

Experts are not just accumulating experiences. People become experts by the lessons they draw from their experiences, and by the sophistication of their mental models about how things work. Stephen Ceci and Jeffrey Liker (1986) studied the way people handicap horse races. They visited race tracks on the East Coast and talked to the regulars to find out which bettors were the most experienced. Ceci and Liker excluded bettors who relied on their dreams, or their license plate numbers, or the color of the horse's warm-up blanket. They picked a small sample of 30 bettors who seemed highly knowledgeable (they had a good track record of winning money) and studied them intensely. Fourteen of them could correctly pick the winners 93 percent of the time, and picked the top three finishers in the correct order 53 percent of the time. These were the true experts. You could see it in the way they interpreted the racing program. A racing program usually contains 20–30 categories of information. A program might give a horse's speed, with upwards of 30 different computations. The program also describes each of the tracks the horse had raced on, and this information affects the way one interprets the horses' speeds. A mile race on a half-mile track means that the horse had to negotiate four curves, each of which slows the horse down. Thus, a time of 1 minute and 59 seconds on a half-mile track is more impressive than a time of 1 minute and 58 seconds on a mile track. One of the experts, MM, was a 62-year-old crane operator who only went to school through the eighth grade. The question put to him was "Which horse do you think will win the next race?"

Example 7.1: Horse sense

Q: Which horse do you think will win the next race?

A: The 4-horse should win easy; he should go off 3-to-5 or shorter or there's something wrong.

Q: What exactly is it about the 4-horse that makes him your odds-on favorite?

A: He's the fastest, plain and simple!

Q: But it looks to me like other horses in this race are even faster. For instance, both the 2-horse and the 6-horse have recorded faster times than the 4-horse, haven't they?

A: Yeah, but you can't go by that. The 2-horse didn't win that outing, he just sucked up.

Q: Sucked-up?

A: You gotta read between the lines if you want to be good at this. The 2-horse just sat on the rail and didn't fight a lick. He just kept on the rail and sucked-up lengths when horses in front of him came off the rail to fight with front runners (i.e., attempt to pass them on the outside).

Q: Why does that make his speed any slower? I don't get it.

A: Now listen. If he came out and fought with other horses, do you think for one minute he'd have run that fast? Let me explain something to you that will help you understand. See the race the 4-horse ran on June 6 (pointing to the relevant line of the racing program)?

Q: Yes.

A: Well, if the 2-horse had to do all this fighting (pointing to indications of attempts to pass other horses) he'd run three seconds slower. It's that simple. There ain't no comparison between the 2-horse and the 4-horse. The 4 is tons better!

Q: I think I see what you're saying. But how about the 6-horse, didn't he do some fighting and still run faster than the 4-horse (pointing to indications of attempts to pass front runners)?

A: Yeah. I like the 6-horse a little, but you can't bet him against this field because he's untried.... He's been running in cheap company (pointing to the 6-horse's purse sizes).

Q: Why is purse size that crucial? He's still running faster than the 4-horse and fighting front runners while he's doing it. What difference does the purse make?

A: It only makes all the difference in the world, that's all. Do you think for one minute that he can pull those stunts with good horses (pointing to an indication of the 6-horse going around a "wall" of three horses)? Hell, if he tries to go three-wide in $15,000 company, they'll eat him up.

Q: What do you mean?

A: You can't do these cheap tricks with horses of this caliber. They'll sit back and wait for him to get even with them on the outside, then they'll speed up and make him stay on the outside. You see, horses of this caliber ($15,000 claimers) can generate the speed to keep you parked outside the whole race. $10,000 claimers don't have the stamina, as a rule, to do that.

Q: And the longer you're on the outside the longer the race you have to run, right? In other words, the shortest route around the track is along the rail and the farther off it you are, the longer the perimeter you have to run.

A: Exactly. Now with $10,000 claimers, the 6-horse is a different story. He can have it all his way. But there's another horse in this race that you have to watch. Do you know who I mean?

Q: The 5-horse?

A: No! He'll still be running this time tomorrow. No, I'm talking about the 8-horse. He don't mind the outside post because he lays back early. Christ, he ran a monster of a race on June 20. He worries me because if he repeats here, he's unbeatable.

Q: Do you like him better than the 4-horse?

A: Not for the price. He'll go off even money. He isn't that steady to be even money. If he's geared up, there's no stopping him but you can't bet on him being geared up. If he were 3 to 1 I'd bet him because he'll return a profit over the long run. But not at even money [i.e., 1 to 1].

MM used data in the racing form to imagine the different races and then judge the real potential of each of the horses. He used his mental model to take many kinds of variables into account. Mental models are developed through experience—individual experience, organizational experience, and cultural experience. The richer mental models of experts like MM include more knowledge and also enable the experts to see more connections.[1] These are two defining features of complexity. The mental models of experts are more complex than those of other people.

We need not conduct research projects to appreciate the mental models of experts. We can see it all around us. As I am writing this chapter, my doorbell rings. It is an appliance repairman. I called him because my dishwasher has stopped working. He questions me: How did I notice that it stopped? I answer that it just stopped—I pressed the buttons and got no response. I checked the fuse, but it was fine. It just stopped. "That sounds terrible, doesn't it? I'll probably need a new dishwasher." He explains to me that it sounds promising. When it just stops like that, it means some sort of electrical problem rather than a mechanical problem. If it had failed more slowly and noisily, then I should worry. He gets down on the floor, removes the dishwasher's bottom panel, tinkers with it for about 10 minutes, and solves the problem. It was a weak connection between the thick wire from the house and the braided wire from the machine. Whoever had installed the dishwasher had failed to make that connection as strong as it should have been. The repairman reconnects it, and I go back to my writing, thinking about his rich mental model of how appliances fail and my impoverished one.

Expertise and errors

Ideally, experts wouldn't make any mistakes. But we know that's not true. In fact, expertise gives rise to errors. With experience we learn more and more patterns. These patterns let us size up situations quickly and accurately. The experience and the patterns enable us to judge what to pay attention to and what to ignore. That way, we usually reserve our attention for the most important cues and aspects of a situation. However, if the situation is deceptive or is different from what we expect, we may focus our attention on the wrong things and ignore important cues. That's why the concept of "mindsets" creates so much controversy. Our mindsets frame the cues in front of us and the events that are unfolding so we can make sense of everything. Experience and patterns produce mindsets. The more experience we have, the more patterns we have learned, the larger and more varied our mindsets and the more accurate they are. We depend heavily on our mindsets. Yet our mindsets aren't perfect and can mislead us. With more expertise, we may become more confident in our mindsets, and therefore more easily misled.[2]

As we saw in the previous chapters, every mechanism has limitations. The mindsets that reflect our experience and power our expertise can, on occasion, cause our downfall. Mindsets aren't good or bad. Their value depends on how well they fit the situation in which we find ourselves. Mindsets help us frame situations and provide anchors for making estimates. With more experience, our frames will be effective and our anchors will permit accurate estimates. When we are in unfamiliar situations, this same use of mindsets won't work as well. Our frames may distort what is going on, and we may be susceptible to irrelevant anchors.

Jim Reason, now a professor emeritus at the University of Manchester, spent most of his career investigating the basis for human error.[3] He worked in fields as diverse as aviation and health care. His "Swiss Cheese" model of errors has had a major influence in deflecting blame for errors from the person working at the "sharp end," the pilot or nurse, to a broader perspective that includes the training these people received and the kinds of organizational pressures placed on them.

Reason has contrasted two aspects of human performance that come up again and again in treatment of errors: the human as a hazard and the human as a hero.

If we want to cite the human as a hazard, it isn't hard to spot slips, lapses, mistakes, and violations of procedures. People forget things, stop paying attention, get distracted, suffer from carelessness, and so forth.

If we want to cite the human as a hero, we can make note of adjustments, compensations, recoveries, improvisations. In this view, errors result from organizational failures. The people at the sharp end aren't the instigators—they merely inherited the failures of the organization and system. The Gimli Glider incident (which I first heard about from Reason) exemplifies both. Captain Pearson created a crisis because he was badly mistaken in taking off in an airplane that lacked fuel gauges. After he ran out of fuel, he was a hero for landing that airplane without any loss of life.

According to Reason, if we over-emphasize the human-as-hazard model, we wind up blaming and shaming people at the sharp end, and ignoring the organizational forces acting on them. If we over-emphasize the human-as-hero model, we may fail to address early signs of organizational dysfunction and the erosion of standards. The hard part is to balance these two views, each of which captures part of the error picture.

This account of error meshes with the debate that has been running through the last few chapters on whether to rely on analysis and procedures versus intuition when the two conflict. Those who urge us to curb intuitions line up with the human-as-hazard model. They worry about overconfidence in biased judgments. They point to examples such as amateur pilots who suffer from vertigo or confusion in cloudy, low-visibility situations, and follow their erroneous intuitions into a plane crash.

Those who urge us to listen to intuitions follow a human-as-hero model. They worry about the consequences of making people distrust their intuitions. They point to examples such as firefighters and military leaders who notice subtle cues that others have missed and give the right orders. They are said to have "the right stuff." As Jim Reason pointed out, the human-as-hazard model and the human-as-hero model are both justified, and we must find ways to balance them.

The Central Intelligence Agency may be leaning too strongly toward the human-as-hazard model in the wake of its incorrect assertion that Saddam Hussein possessed weapons of mass destruction. After Operation Iraqi Freedom in 2003, when the American troops didn't find any WMDs, the CIA commissioned a group to examine what had gone wrong, and what lessons could be applied to improve its work. The CIA subsequently provided training for its entire analytic workforce to advance its tradecraft standards, e.g., tracking critical assumptions, being sensitive to the effects of mindsets and the tendency to fixate on the first hypothesis.[4]

Some of the tradecraft guidance I have seen creates the impression that if intelligence analysts carefully follow the steps, they can avoid biases and also put out insightful forecasts. I am worried that the analysts will see their job as a process of gathering, verifying and combining evidence streams. I am worried that the insights will dry up and the expertise will diminish.

Several leaders in the CIA are resisting the tendency for the agency to over-emphasize the human-as-hazard model. One of them, a person who favors the efforts to strengthen standards, wrote to tell me this: "The hard part is to balance what we teach so we don't give analysts the impression that their job is to just turn the crank of some analytic methodology machine. We need to worry that the structuring process may get in the way of insights."

I want the CIA analysts to use their mindsets and hunches and intuitions. I wish they had done more of that before September 11, 2001, and that leaders had listened more carefully to their concerns about a terrorist attack. Overreacting to the errors of judgment that led to the failed prediction of Iraqi WMDs could reduce the chances of spotting another 9/11-style attack.

The fear of human error also influences health care. Hospitals and insurance companies are increasingly turning to evidence-based medicine, the process of relying on statistical analyses of which treatments work most effectively. Hospitals and health insurance companies expect physicians to comply with the best practices.

Some physicians are resisting this trend. They feel uncomfortable subordinating their judgment to statisticians. They are unwilling to make judgments that conflict with the guidelines, for fear of being sued or even prosecuted if the patient shows adverse effects. They don't want to subordinate their judgments to "best practices" that may not apply in specific instances. They echo the reactions of the expert forecasters at Accuweather (discussed in chapter 2) who disliked the procedural guidelines that restricted them to making "adequate" forecasts.

Expanding expertise

Balancing the human-as-hazard and the human-as-hero models isn't simply giving each of them equal time or equal weight. We should find ways to blend them, expanding the role of expertise when procedures and analyses aren't sufficient.

Example 7.2: Outsmarting diabetes   Diabetics can't rely on their bodies to automatically adjust the level of glucose in their bloodstreams. For a variety of reasons, diabetics have lost this protective homeostatic ability. As a result, they are vulnerable to swings in which their blood glucose gets too low or too high.

High blood glucose is much harder to detect than low blood glucose. Over time, the toxic levels of blood glucose can result in blindness, kidney failure, amputations, strokes, heart disease, and early death. The World Health Organization estimates that 171 million people around the world suffer from diabetes. As of 2005, there were nearly 21 million diabetics in the United States.

We would expect people who face these risks to work hard to keep their blood glucose under control. However, 88 percent of diabetics don't follow the guidelines put out by the medical community; 63 percent of diabetics have dangerously high blood glucose levels.[5] As a result, in the United States alone, hundreds of thousands of diabetes patients either die or suffer serious diabetes-related complications every year.[6]

Helen Altman Klein, a psychology professor at Wright State University (and my wife), has been studying the way people manage Type 2 diabetes.[7] She has tried to understand why they have trouble adhering to the rules.

Most diabetics can successfully control their blood glucose levels by just following a few simple rules, as long as they lead stable and predictable lives. But if they have to travel, eat at unfamiliar restaurants at unpredictable times, vary their exercise schedule, or manage unexpected stresses, they can't rely on the rules. Instead, they have to form a mental model of how these different conditions are affecting their blood glucose and how to adjust.

Think of the task of controlling a nuclear power plant. If you insert the graphite rods too far into the core, you slow the reaction and the plant doesn't produce much energy. If you withdraw the graphite rods too far, the reaction will speed up too much and the uranium in the core may overheat and melt. The technicians in the control room have an array of sensors and computer aids with which to determine what is going on inside the reactor.

Now let's complicate this picture to more closely resemble the condition of diabetes. We strip away most of the alarm systems and all of the automated fail-safe mechanisms. We vary the purity of the uranium rods and graphite rods so the controllers don't know what they are working with. They'll have to figure it out on the fly. We unpredictably create a water leak in the system to mimic the effects of stress. We make some valves stick open a bit and others lock closed. And we scramble the feedback cycles so that the operators' control actions can take minutes or hours to take effect, just to make it harder to figure out what is causing the odd reactions.

That's the challenge facing Type 2 diabetics. Even when they test their blood glucose every day, or several times a day, they still have to struggle to figure out why they are getting a high reading. Was it something they ate this morning, or yesterday? Different foods, even different kinds of carbohydrates, metabolize at different rates. Maybe the problem was that they exercised for only 15 minutes that morning, or perhaps they are worrying about what to say to a rude cousin at a family gathering this coming weekend.

One diabetic, a physician, described her dilemma when she wanted to go out drinking with her friends in medical school. She knew that alcohol reduced blood glucose levels but the sugar in the drinks would increase it. Did they offset each other? Did they operate at the same rate of speed? What would be the effect of each drink? And, more worrisome, how could she keep track of this after two to three drinks?[8]

Diabetics often don't understand the rules they are given. One patient explained that once he was diagnosed with diabetes, he avoided all foods with sugar. However, he ate lots of bread and potatoes because he hadn't learned that carbohydrates also metabolize into blood glucose. Some communities encourage their members to drink more lemonade, on the belief that they need sour foods to balance their increased blood sugar, which is viewed as excessive sweetness.

My friend Herb Bell falls on the other end of the spectrum. He is outsmarting diabetes. When Herb (a PhD in visual perception) was diagnosed with diabetes, he began logging his activities and his blood glucose readings in order to find relationships and to figure out time lags. Herb is trying to turn himself into an expert on the blood-glucose variations in his own body. As a result, Herb has little trouble controlling his blood glucose despite his heavy travel schedule. As Herb exemplifies, many of the diabetes-related deaths and disabilities are unnecessary.

Helen found that patients who are successful, such as Herb, can build mental models of how their own blood glucose works. Everyone has a different metabolism and physiology, so you can't rely on standard rules. You can't boil diabetes management into one-size-fits-all procedures. The successful patients learned offsetting strategies, such as going for a walk, to get the levels down.

One Air Force pilot explained that controlling his diabetes was like flying an airplane when you couldn't use autopilot anymore and had to take over manual control. That illustrates his attitude as well as the strategy of learning the handling characteristics of his condition. The successful diabetics had learned what caused their blood glucose to go up and down, and what the time lags were. Diabetics need procedures when they first get diagnosed. They have to start with some simple guidelines about what to eat, but then they have to build good mental models in order to figure out their own routines and adaptations.

Unfortunately, very few diabetics are shown how to build good mental models for controlling their blood glucose, or even encouraged to do so. They are asked to test themselves in order to provide data for their physicians, not to help them make sense of what might have caused high or low readings. They are admonished to follow rules, even when the rules are inadequate.

Many diabetics are contributing to their condition because of their poor eating habits, obesity, and lack of exercise. Other diabetics are victims; their condition is so unpredictable and brittle that they cannot manage it no matter how hard they try. And some diabetics are heroes—they have learned to take responsibility for a very complicated biological function, blood glucose regulation. One diabetic told me that when he was diagnosed with Type I diabetes as a boy, his physician explained that he could let the disease control him or he could control it. He chose the latter path. Instead of encouraging diabetics to curb their intuitions, we can help them build better mental models for taking control of their disease.

Under what conditions can people develop expertise? This was a question that Danny Kahneman and I explored over several years. We were trying to de-mystify intuition by investigating the conditions under which reliable intuitions can develop. We reviewed a range of situations in which people had developed reliable intuitions (including firefighting, health care, weather forecasting, aviation, and driving) and a range of situations in which efforts to develop reliable intuitions had failed (including selecting stocks, predicting the recidivism of criminals, and predicting the course of world events).[9]

Kahneman and I concluded that two conditions are necessary for reliable intuitions to develop: the situation must be reasonably predictable and people must have opportunities to learn. Low-predictability situations make it unlikely that people can develop expertise because it is so hard to identify reliable cues.

By these criteria, diabetics should be able to develop good mental models that would enable them to control their disease. The existence of experts suggests that this is possible. It may not be possible for all diabetics—those with highly variable metabolisms. Nevertheless, it seems that many diabetics could do a better job than they are now doing. They don't have to settle for rules and procedures that are too simplistic.

Positive psychology

Think back to the talented television sports commentators reporting on swim meets who can describe what went right or wrong with a platform dive. We appreciate the way they notice things that are not visible to the rest of us.

In contrast, when we watch people who work in well-ordered and stable domains, who carry out rules, and who remember facts, we don't find much to admire. We evaluate their performance by counting how often they make mistakes.

Look at the difference between appreciating talents and catching mistakes. One is positive, the other is negative.

Most tools for improving performance are aimed at reducing mistakes. The survey claims listed in chapter 1 are aimed at reducing mistakes. The claims advise us to adhere to procedures, to worry about decision biases if we use our intuition, and to rely on statistics and analysis.

Contrast this emphasis on avoiding mistakes with the field of positive psychology, which was started by Martin Seligman, a clinical psychologist and a former president of the American Psychological Association. Late in his career, Seligman concluded that the field of clinical psychology had fallen into a rut. For a century, ever since the time of Freud, clinical psychology had been devoted to healing people by reducing their misery, their neuroses, and their depressions. The field had almost nothing to say about making people happy.

According to Seligman, even if therapists are successful in eliminating a condition such as depression, they just move their patients up to zero. They haven't helped the patients become happy. Patients who at least had an identity ("I'm just a sad case") now have none. Seligman

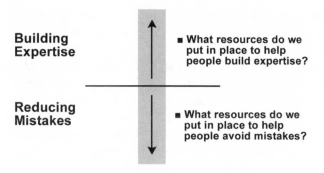

Figure 7.1
Developing tacit knowledge.

initiated a new field—Positive Psychology—to help people move above the line and have satisfying lives.

Seligman's views apply to cognitive psychology—to the way people think and reason and make decisions and diagnose events. They apply to executives, housewives, students, and soldiers. The guidance we tend to hear is about reducing mistakes. Procedures, checklists, and decision aids are all designed to catch and correct possible mistakes.

But eliminating mistakes isn't the same thing as gaining expertise. (See figure 7.1.) One of the themes of this book is that a fear of mistakes should be balanced with a pursuit of expertise. I think most organizations overdo the human-as-hazard model and put too much effort into reducing or eliminating mistakes. I don't think organizations do enough to help their workers become skilled. In pointing out the limitations in the ten survey claims, I am trying to restore a balance.

In many cases, our aversion to mistakes may be counter-productive. We must make mistakes in order to learn.[10] R. Buckminster Fuller once said "If I ran a school, I'd give the average grade to the ones who gave me all the right answers, for being good parrots. I'd give the top grades to those who made a lot of mistakes and told me about them, and then told me what they learned from them."[11]

When organizations crack down on mistakes, they may unwittingly slow the rate of learning. Employee evaluations usually highlight mistakes and failures because these are easier to spot and document. In the health care industry and in the aviation industry, prosecutors sometimes press criminal charges against people who make mistakes. Some people may get satisfaction from seeing nurses or pilots hit with fines or jail sentences. However, as Sidney Dekker (2003) has complained, in his article "When does human error become a crime," these sanctions reduce safety rather than increasing it. We learn from mistakes by diagnosing why they happened, but if an organization is overzealous about reducing mistakes then workers may spend more time covering up their mistakes than they spend trying to figure out what caused those mistakes and how to do a better job in the future.

8 Automating Decisions

One reason the claims in part I on decision making matter so much is that they affect the designs of devices that are created to help us make better decisions.

Claim 2 (that decision biases distort our thinking) invites developers to build systems that will take over control for decisions and prevent human biases from getting in the way.

Claim 2a (that successful decision makers rely on logic and statistics instead of intuition) inspires developers to construct information technologies that interfere with skilled judgments and that make it harder for people to gain expertise (Klein 2004). Too often, the result is a lower quality of decisions. Smart technology can make us stupid.[1]

Claim 3 (to make a decision, generate several options and compare them to pick the best one) guides developers to design systems that help us visualize the different options and the evaluation dimensions. These decision aids make it easier for us to enter our check marks in the right boxes.

And yet many decision-support systems are rejected or fail. The developers think that people will welcome decision aids that make it easier to conduct decision analyses. The developers often can't believe that decision makers are too stupid to appreciate all the benefits of such decision aids. But decision makers are not just rejecting the aids—they are rejecting the mindset that keeps churning out this kind of system. Decision makers are rejecting the mentality that idealizes reflective, analytical thinking and marginalizes automatic, intuitive thinking, instead of blending the two kinds of thinking.

Developers of decision-support systems wrestle with the dilemma of whether to cede control to the human or the algorithm. As statistical methods get more sophisticated, advocates brush off criticisms of previous failures by explaining that the new decision-support systems are more powerful, more comprehensive, more everything. Those who advocate for a balance between the automatic (intuitive) system and the reflective (analytical) system are continually challenged to ensure that their organizations value their employees' tacit knowledge. Once the balance shifts, expertise may begin to wither away.

Instead of getting ground down by pointless arguments about whether the human is better or the computer-based system is better, let's recognize that they both have their strengths.

Four types of decision-support systems

In my conversations with Danny Kahneman we identified four approaches to decision-support systems:

a. The decision is made by the decision maker alone.

b. The decision maker is helped by a support system or an algorithm.

c. The decision-support system has the final say, with inputs from the operators.

d. The decision-support system makes the entire decision on its own.

What are the boundary conditions for these four categories?

The decision maker alone.
Kahneman and I think that most judgments and decisions fall into the first category. We don't see much to be gained by incorporating information technology when people can attain a reasonable level of expertise. Information technology makes even less sense in the face of unstable, shadowy conditions that are heavily dependent on context. We are most comfortable relying on decision makers when they can develop tacit knowledge as a basis for their intuitions. For that to happen, the environment must have some predictability and decision makers must be able to get feedback on their choices and to gain some level of proficiency.

The decision maker is helped by a support system or an algorithm.
How hard should I exercise? Many gyms have diagrams showing heart-rate guidelines. By looking at the column for my age, I can see the level I need to get a good workout and the suggested maximum heart rate. What price should I set for my car when I list it for sale? By entering the year, model, and condition of the car and the geographical

area, I can find out what price the car is likely to fetch. Should we drill for oil in a certain region? Geologists have powerful analytical tools that can provide useful advice, even though the tools aren't good enough to replace the seasoned veterans.

The decision-support system has the final say, with inputs from the operators.
Should a bank lend me money? Intelligent systems now can do a more reliable and unbiased job than most of the people who have this authority. Drivers can tell their GPS systems if they want the fastest or the shortest route, and get a recommendation. Let the humans feed data into the program, but let the program make the final decision or recommendation. This approach means giving up authority to the decision-support system. However, in cases where our judgment is not particularly accurate (for example, selecting job applicants or finding our way in unfamiliar cities, or guessing future revenues), we'll probably get better decisions by relying on a formula than by using our judgment.

When I served as the marketing director for my company, our survival depended on my ability to accurately forecast how much revenue we were likely to have. I was aware that my intuitive judgments about future revenues were too unreliable. My level of optimism depended on how many unsolicited queries we had gotten in the past week, our level of anxiety about covering the salaries of the staff members, and other considerations. Therefore, I replaced my intuitive guess with a more structured method. For each potential new contract, I entered when the contract was likely to start, how large it was likely to be, and a guess of our probability of winning the contract. From these data I could calculate our probable revenue: estimating the likely size of a contract, discounting that number by the probability of winning it, and summing the results. This procedure had room for intuition—our guesses about the likely size, start date, and chance of winning each proposal we wrote. The final estimate, however, came from my calculations and not from my intuition.

The result of my simple algorithm was a surprisingly high level of forecasting accuracy. Using it, my estimates for the revenue for the coming year were generally ±10 percent of the actual revenues. It took me a few years to reach this level of accuracy. I had to diagnose the reasons why some forecasts were inaccurate, such as delays in the actual award for contracts we won. This method is fairly standard for most companies. It was a discipline that my own company hadn't previously imposed on itself.

The decision-support system makes the entire decision on its own. There is no point in letting experts do a job that a machine can do better. If I'm driving on an icy road, my car's anti-lock braking system can figure out when to kick in and how to pump the brakes better than I can. My car's traction-control system can figure out better than I can how to transfer power from wheels that are starting to slip to those that are solidly contacting the road.

Some risks in using decision-support systems under complex conditions

The last two of these four approaches cede decision control to the equations. They are best suited to well-ordered domains that have enough structure to get the systems organized, enough stability to make the programming economical, not too much complexity or interdependencies, little need for tacit knowledge, and clear criteria for good decisions.

What about using these last two approaches in complex domains? At first glance, any time an algorithm can outperform the people doing the job, we should rely on the algorithm for making decisions. It is usually cost-effective to rely on decision-support systems. People are expensive to train and are prone to getting sick, getting careless, and leaving their jobs. But, of course, we have to take practical considerations into account.

Algorithms are brittle and often don't work well in the shadows, whereas skilled decision makers are more resilient and sensitive to context and nuance. Therefore, we may not want to rely on statistical methods if there is a reasonable chance that conditions may change. We need to be confident that the algorithm takes into account all the relevant variables. We also depend on having a relatively large body of similar cases from which to extract the rules. Algorithms aren't used where flexibility is demanded, because they are carefully tailored to narrow conditions.

In addition, algorithms can get in the way when we need people to develop and sustain skill and expertise. When the algorithms are making the decisions, people often stop working to get better. The algorithms can make it harder to diagnose reasons for failures. As people become more dependent on algorithms, their judgment may erode, making them depend even more on the algorithms. That process sets up a vicious cycle. People get passive and less vigilant when algorithms make the decisions.[2]

We can safeguard the use of algorithms by ensuring that people are watching over the recommendations and ready to overrule the decision-support systems when necessary. Unfortunately, this safeguard goes away if people become complacent and simply rely on the decision-support systems.

Another disadvantage of using decision-support systems is that we shouldn't replace human judgments with algorithms if we want to make discoveries. Even in fairly chaotic environments, human intuition may provide clues about the way different factors relate to one another. Replacing human judgment with algorithms reduces opportunities for discovery.

Aside from these practical objections, decision-support systems run into a further problem: people tend to reject them.

The rejection of decision-support systems

If decision biases are pervasive and crippling, then various decision-support tools should improve performance. Decision researchers often formulate various kinds of decision-support systems and tools to help people make better judgments and avoid biases. Decision Analysis uses decision trees or influence diagrams to structure the process. De-biasing methods should help us assess uncertainty. Techniques such as Multi-Attribute Utility Analysis should help us combine information about our preferences.

Yet people don't use these systems. Again and again, researchers sadly report that people in the field rejected their systems. Decision researchers develop de-biasing workshops and programs, but target audiences don't adopt the methods. Why should this happen? Some researchers blame the subjects for being so wedded to their ways and to their biases that they can't be helped. I think that a more likely reason is that the de-biasing methods and the decision-support systems aren't helpful under complex real-life conditions. By now, the decision-research community isn't asking *whether* the tools and systems are used; it is asking why they *aren't* used.

What must a decision-support system do in order for us to judge that it helped us make good decisions? Frank Yates, co-editor of the

Journal of Behavioral Decision Making, has shown that the answer to that question depends on what we mean by "a hard decision." What ordinary people mean by "an easy decision" or "a hard decision" is different from what the system designers mean. Yates et al. (2003) investigated this issue by asking 99 students in an introductory psychology course at the University of Michigan to describe easy and hard decisions. The students described a few things that made decisions hard. One was the seriousness of the outcome, particularly if the decision maker might suffer a significant loss. Another was having too many or too few options. Another was how much the students had to struggle with the process—the amount of effort, emotional strain, time pressure, uncertainty, and lack of expertise. Clarity was a fourth factor, involving the difficulty the students had in gauging whether an option was in fact superior to the competitors. Finally, the students said that decisions were hard when they weren't sure how they would feel about their choice later.

Next, Yates et al. asked another group of students to reflect on whether difficult decisions they had actually made were good or bad. The students reported that they were pretty pleased with their decisions, even the bad ones. Among the things that made a decision bad were having a bad outcome, missing out on good outcomes, limiting future options, using a poor process to make the decision, and feeling bad while making the decision or afterward.

Researchers who design decision aids don't worry about most of these issues. Their goal is usually to help people eliminate inconsistencies—to give the same ratings the same preferences throughout the choice process. Decision analysts worry about inconsistencies because the analysts have been able to demonstrate that people aren't as consistent as statistical formulas, so one way to help people is to make them more consistent.

However, Yates and colleagues found that not many people worried about inconsistency. The decision aids are solving a problem people don't care about.

People like to feel good about the process they use to make decisions. Yates et al. found that decision-support systems make people uncomfortable. These systems marginalize the decision makers themselves. The methods take away control in ways that people may not understand. People may also worry about extenuating circumstances that the decision aids might not capture.

In short, Yates et al. found that decision aids make the decision process unnatural and difficult. The decision aids are trying to change and improve on the way we think, not to support or amplify our thinking. But we aren't comfortable with letting decision analysts or techniques usurp our decision authority. We are responsible for the outcomes, not the analyst or the method.

Raanan Lipshitz, a professor at Haifa University, has seen the same reactions in applied courses he has taught to business leaders: "Low to high ranking executives have consistently stated that they had no use for the formal models to which they had been exposed in a variety of university and executive development courses."[3]

Yates et al. also criticize methods to reduce biases, such as hindsight bias and overconfidence: "We have seen little evidence that debiasing techniques are frequently employed in actual practice." (p. 34) Why not? The students Yates et al. studied weren't worried about biases, so removing judgment biases didn't matter to them. Remember that decision biases may not be a big problem outside the laboratory. (This was discussed in chapter 4.) Because the students' decisions were complex, bad outcomes seemed unpredictable. Even if the students had worried about biases (which they hadn't), the impact of biases didn't seem as great as the influence of chance. And those students who might worry that decision biases were distorting their judgments may not have had confidence that de-biasing would help.

These reasons explain why Baruch Fischhoff (1982) found that the de-biasing strategies he reviewed were not very successful. Bazerman and Moore (2008) report that Fischhoff's pessimism still seems justified 25 years later.

Adding to the factors that Yates et al. identified, my own dissatisfaction with decision-support systems is that they generally ignore expertise. They treat decision makers as sources of ratings and preferences, and they try to pack all the statistical expertise into the tools. Because you can't pack tacit knowledge into computerized aids, the systems may miss important connections. They may miss the context of the situation, as shown in the next example.

Example 8.1: Racking and stacking[4]   Software developers have to decide what features to include in the release of the next system. To help with this challenge, Carlshamre (2002) built a prototype planning aid that balanced the costs of the new features and their value to the client.

His system would "rack and stack" the proposed features, to help the developers decide which ones to select for the next version.

But the simple tradeoffs that Carlshamre built into his planning aid didn't work. Software developers rejected this system. They weren't just trading off costs and benefits. For instance, a given requirement might depend on an employee who was going on maternity leave, so the requirement had to be delayed until a subsequent version.

Carlshamre also discovered that the concept of "value to the client" combined the strategic business value for the customer, long-term and short-term value for a range of consumers with differing importance in different markets, compliance with laws and regulations, compatibility with new computing platforms, and internal cost savings. In estimating the resource demands for a new feature, the developers considered factors such as individual employee's workload and vacation schedules and their company's recruitment plans.

Carlshamre's system required users to assign values to the requirements but to the software developers these values were arbitrary and unconvincing. The criteria couldn't be defined in advance, because many essential parameters are never quantified. The developers were always discovering properties as they planned—some criteria were only realized after solutions were presented. And as they worked the developers were continually gaining new insights about the relationship between features that were treated separately by Carlshamre's program.

Carlshamre concluded that a simple tradeoff—calculating the value of a feature against the resource required to field it—was actually a "wicked" problem (Rittel and Webber 1984) that doesn't permit optimal solutions. People who develop decision support systems find it convenient to simplify the complexities that surround so many difficult decisions. The developers may get the details right, but may miss which way the wind is blowing. And that brings us to the topic of weather.

Project Phoenix

Few decision makers have been studied as carefully as weather forecasters. They make predictions every day. They make short-range predictions about the next few hours, medium-range predictions about the next day or two, long-range predictions about the rest of the week, and seasonal predictions about the severity of the winter, the summer, or hurricanes. And we can check their predictions for accuracy.

Researchers find that weather forecasters are very accurate in making short-range predictions of 1–2 days. Then they fall off a bit.

Good weather forecasters have one big drawback: they cost money. By building decision-support systems, organizations can get away with hiring relatively inexperienced forecasters and still hope for the same level of quality. That's why Canadian forecasters are ordered to use large-scale programs providing Numerical Weather Predictions (NWP)—computer-based systems to generate forecasts. The theory is that these automated systems will help the forecasters do a better job.

The actuality is that system isn't perfect. Project Phoenix, conducted at the Prairie Storm Prediction Center in Winnipeg, is a set of studies that compared the accuracy of automated forecasts to the accuracy of forecasters who didn't have access to NWP (McCarthy, Ball, and Purcell 2007). The skilled forecasters did a better job on their own, without the automated forecasting system. After nine Project Phoenix experiments, administrators finally directed the staff to take the training to upgrade their skills rather than relying on the system.

The NWP system was so awkward to use that forecasters just accepted what the system said unless it really made a blunder. The experts forced to use it found themselves accepting forecasts that were sort of good enough. They knew that they could improve on the system, but they didn't have the time to enter the adjustments. As professionals, they felt dishonored to be doing less than their best. This problem will probably disappear once they retire. The newest forecasters won't know any better, and so expertise will be lost to the community because systems like NWP get in the way of building expertise. Snellman (1977) used the term "meteorological cancer" to warn about the trend for forecasters to cease being professionals and instead rely on computer-generated information.

The Canadian government does not seem particularly worried about meteorological cancer, or about sustaining expertise. It is eager to use information technology and artificial intelligence for making forecasts as a way of cutting costs. After all, NWP is almost as good as the human forecasters in the short range. However, the errors that the system makes usually involve high-impact weather, such as severe storms and extreme temperature events. One proposed strategy was to use forecasters to check the outputs of NWP but panels of experienced forecasters objected. They don't believe the forecasters can adequately monitor the systems if they haven't been actively engaged in collecting and analyzing the data.[5]

In chapter 3, which explored tacit knowledge, we saw that Accuweather, in the United States, pursues the same policy as Project Phoenix. It uses procedures that help the less-experienced forecasters make adequate predictions while forcing the highly experienced forecasters to make only adequate predictions.

Decision aids aren't doing very well in the field of medicine, either. One review of 100 studies of clinical decision-support systems over a six-year period[6] found that if we discount evaluations done by the people who built the systems, fewer than 50 percent showed an improvement in performance. Wears and Berg (2005) argue that we can't blame the problems on bad programming or poor implementation. Rather, these systems are usually designed with the idea that health-care workers make neat and discrete decisions by themselves, whereas health-care settings are highly social and filled with competing demands. The decision-support tools simply don't match the tasks and context of work in health-care environments, and that's a major reason why people reject them.

When decision-support systems are designed by people who are insensitive to tacit knowledge, their devices and strategies are likely to interfere with expertise rather than support it. For example, my former colleague Rebecca Pliske conducted a study of skilled weather forecasters and described the kinds of strategies they used. She explained that skilled forecasters needed to build their own understanding of how a weather system was operating. They would ignore the automated computer forecast, ignore the forecast from the previous shift, and go directly to the data for the previous 6 hours. Once they were comfortable with their understanding, they would consult the automated forecast and the forecast from the previous shift to see if they missed anything. If they had started by consulting the other forecasts (and many mediocre meteorologists did just that), they wouldn't get the same feel for what was happening in the different layers of the atmosphere.

After the project had ended, Pliske gave a presentation on the results at a conference attended by professional weather forecasters as well as researchers. Her talk was well received. Then the next speaker got up and talked about a new system that his company had designed. It would analyze all the data and present meteorologists with a complete set of forecasts, saving them time and effort. Pliske, who is ordinarily very patient and gentle, couldn't believe what she was hearing. She raised her hand during the question-and-answer period and explained that this was exactly what skilled forecasters did not want. The automated system being described was going to interfere with expertise, not support it. The unusual part of this story is what happened next. The professional forecasters in the room began clapping. Then some of them cheered. Few, if any, researchers, are ever cheered at a professional conference. The professionals were excited that they finally had an advocate who understood them.

I am not criticizing the use of computers and information technology to improve performance, though the examples I have given may convey such an impression. What I am criticizing is decision-support systems that rely on shaky claims and misguided beliefs about how people think and what they need.

Fortunately, in the past few decades the discipline of cognitive systems engineering has emerged to help designers develop information technologies that more effectively support decision making. A number of books have described ways to conduct Cognitive Systems Engineering projects. Perhaps the best introduction is *Stories of Modern Technology Failures and Cognitive Engineering Successes*, by Nancy Cooke and Frank Durso (2008). Other Cognitive Systems Engineering books have been published by Kim Vicente (1999), Mica Endsley and her colleagues (2003), Don Norman (1988, 1993), and David Woods and Erik Hollnagel (2006).

I am saddened to see ineffective decision-support systems that are designed in accordance with ideology rather than observation. If we try to balance the human-as-hazard model with the human-as-hero model, and to balance the automatic, intuitive system with the reflective, analytical system, we should have more of a chance to create decision-support systems that will get used.

II   Making Sense of Situations

We often have to make sense of highly uncertain situations, but uncertainty isn't always reduced by gathering more and more information. Sensemaking is not just a matter of connecting the dots. Sensemaking determines what counts as a dot. Jumping to conclusions is sometimes the right thing to do even before all the dots have been collected. Feedback depends on sensemaking. Our minds are not computers—they don't connect dots in the same ways that computers do.

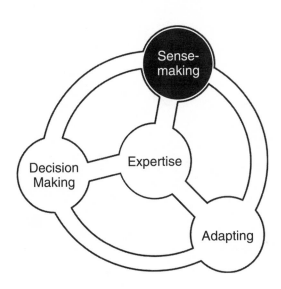

9   More Is Less

Uncertainty is caused by not having the information we need. Therefore, adding more information will reduce uncertainty. That certainly seems simple enough.

Claim 4: We can reduce uncertainty by gathering more information.

The people in our sample agreed with this statement. Their average rating was 5.57. Of the 164 people who responded to this statement, eight indicated some degree of disagreement.

Disclaimer

There are different types of uncertainty. Sometimes we are uncertain because we don't have the information we need. That's the type of uncertainty that claim 4 covers. Sometimes we have the information but we don't know if we can trust it. Sometimes we trust it but it conflicts with other information we also believe. And sometimes we believe it but we can't figure out what it means.[1] Claim 4 covers only the first type of uncertainty, which stems from missing information.

When we are faced with the other types of uncertainty, adding more information may not help at all. If I'm going to doubt the accuracy of any information I receive, adding more information just gives me more to doubt. If I believe in a data point but it conflicts with others, then adding more data may add to the conflicts instead of resolving them. And if the situation is too complex to sort out, adding more data may increase the complexity, not decrease it.

I believed in claim 4 until I studied the kinds of uncertainty faced by the members of a Marine Corps regimental command post.[2] I tried to identify each instance of uncertainty that the Marines faced, and then afterward I sorted these instances into categories. The Marines struggled more with uncertainty caused by ambiguous and conflicting information than with missing information. Helping them gather more data points wouldn't have reduced their uncertainty unless those data points enabled them to resolve ambiguities.

A useful way to think about uncertainty is to distinguish between puzzles and mysteries.[3] A puzzle is easily solved with the addition of a critical data point. For example, as I write this (in 2008) we don't know exactly where Osama bin Laden is hiding. That is knowable. He is somewhere. We just don't know where he is, or even if he is alive.[4] But if an informer were to provide bin Laden's current location, the puzzle would be solved.

A mystery isn't solved by critical data. It requires more analysis, not more data. If we want to know what the future will bring to Iraq, no data point will give us the answer. No amount of data will eliminate our uncertainties about whether China is a potential business partner of the United States or an inevitable military, political, and commercial threat.

Claim 4 aims to solve puzzles, not mysteries. Mysteries emerge from ambiguous and complex situations. Even if we have the data we need, and know what data points to trust, and they aren't inconsistent with each other, we still aren't sure how to explain past events or anticipate future ones. Mysteries require sensemaking. Adding more data doesn't necessarily improve success in resolving mysteries.

Well-ordered situations abound with puzzles. They can also have mysteries. The structure of DNA, for example, was a mystery that yielded a clear answer. However, puzzles primarily appear in well-ordered situations, whereas complex situations are filled with mysteries. Claim 4, like the other claims, holds for well-ordered but not complex situations.

The saturation point
Too much information can make things worse. As we add more and more information, the value of each successive data point gets smaller and smaller while the strain of sorting out all the information keeps increasing. Eventually, we may reach a point where the additional information gets in our way. We would do better to stop gathering more information before this point, but most of us keep seeking more data. We can't stop ourselves. We have become data junkies. As

Friedman, Treadwell, and Beal put it (2007, p. 98), "the pursuit of data, in almost any field, has come to resemble a form of substance abuse."

Obviously, if we start out with no information, the first data points are likely to be very helpful. I'm not arguing that we would be better off with no information at all.[5] That's why this chapter is titled "More Is Less" rather than "None Is Best." The initial data are helpful, but we then reach a saturation point, and after that little is gained by the additional information, which may create more rather than less uncertainty.

In a study that showed this more-is-less effect, Stewart et al. (1993) gave 29 meteorologists the task of forecasting severe weather conditions that are associated with summer thunderstorms in Colorado. Meteorologists do a very good job of forecasting temperature and precipitation, but they have much more trouble with rare events, such as hail, high winds, and tornados.

Stewart et al. found that, after a point, the more information the forecasters had, the worse their reliability and skill in using the information. Some meteorologists did show a small improvement in skills with more information, but this difference was statistically significant in only one of the three experiments that Stewart et al. ran. A number of the meteorologists became less accurate when they got more information. (See figure 9.1.) Why did this happen? In addition to the argument that the marginal value of each additional data point gets

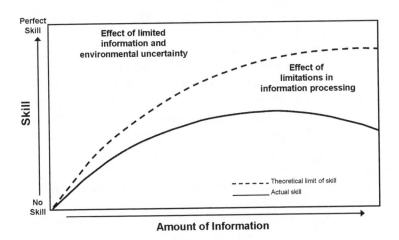

Figure 9.1
The relationship between amount of information and skill. Based on figure 5 of Stewart et al. 1993.

smaller and smaller, as shown in figure 9.1, Stewart et al. suggest that the additional information gets harder to integrate with all the other data. Stewart and colleagues concluded that it makes more sense to help meteorologists improve their use of information than to simply collect more and more information.

Stewart et al. also reviewed a number of studies showing that experts ask for more data than they use. Most experts use fewer than five cues when making judgments. That doesn't mean we should stop gathering data after we get five cues. Experts know which five cues will matter. However, even experts ask for more than they need. Gathering the extra information is the easy part. Thinking about what the extra information means takes real work. We would be better off thinking more about what we have learned instead of continuing our pursuit of data.

Omodei et al. (2005) came to the same conclusion in a study of firefighters. The researchers presented experienced commanders a set of decision scenarios of simulated forest fires. The teams with incomplete information performed better than the teams with detailed information. Omodei et al. speculated that the additional information created its own burdens. The firefighters had to prioritize and inspect all the data, and they felt compelled to look at all the information they received. In contrast, the teams with incomplete information could spend more time integrating the material. Omodei et al. concluded that the commanders had trouble managing the excessive data. They tried to use everything available, working harder to review more data than to integrate the data they had.

Other researchers have reported the same findings. Smallman and Hegarty (2007) found that Navy weather forecasters selected weather maps that had more information than the task needed, rather than maps that were easier to follow and had all the relevant information. In a follow-up study with undergraduate students, Canham, Hegarty, and Smallman (2007) offered the students maps with just the relevant information and other maps that had extra details and irrelevant realism. As in the earlier work, more than one-third of the students preferred displays that were unnecessarily detailed, even though they had more trouble answering questions as the number of irrelevant variables increased. The extra realism slowed the response times by about 10 percent, an effect that got worse the more irrelevant details the students were given. The students preferred displays with unnecessary details that just slowed them down.

Oskamp (1965) gave experienced clinical psychologists more information to use in diagnosing a patient's condition. The additional information didn't improve the accuracy of their judgments, but their confidence ratings got higher as they received more information. Therefore, their confidence was misplaced. It reflected the amount of data the judges had, not their accuracy.

We have to be careful not to overplay these kinds of studies in which the experimenters control which data to feed to their subjects. In practice, we usually decide for ourselves which data we will examine. We decide when we will stop seeking more data. Look at Mauboussin's (2007) study of horse-racing handicappers. The more information the handicappers got, the more confident they were, just as Oskamp found with clinicians. Further, the handicappers' predictions were less accurate when they got 40 pieces of information than when they got five pieces. Once again, the more information, the worse the performance. But Ceci and Liker's racing handicappers (discussed in chapter 7) were able to integrate lots and lots of information. In a natural setting, the handicappers were deciding for themselves what information to use, rather than having the information thrust on them. It makes a difference.

Therefore, even though I like the studies showing that people reach a saturation point and their performance gets worse when we drown them in too much data, in real-world settings experts usually can protect themselves. They self-select which types of data to seek. For example, in a study of professional auditors and accounting students, the experts primarily relied on a single type of information, whereas the novices tried to use all the data (Ettenson et al. 1987). The experts, using their single data source, were more accurate and showed greater reliability and consensus than the students.

The biggest danger of claim 4 (that we can reduce uncertainty by gathering more information) is that it invites a mindless search for more data. It invites a search for anything that might be relevant. It invites abuse, encouraging us to move past our saturation point. Even when we control our own searches for information, we tend to gather more than we need, and the extra information can get in our way.

We do this to ourselves. How many times have we gathered information we didn't use? The real reason for gathering extra information isn't to make a better decision; usually it is to stall for time.

I have anecdotal evidence from observations of exercises at military command posts that the information technologies designed to speed decision making may have the opposite effect. Some commanders seem to put off decisions and wait for additional information. New data points keep arriving every few seconds, so the commanders keep hoping that the next message will clarify their choices.

In well-ordered settings we can do a good job of identifying what critical data point we need and going after it. But in complex settings, the additional information can exponentially increase the number of connections instead of pruning them, resulting in more rather than less uncertainty.

The saturation point, the point at which our attempts to resolve uncertainty by getting more information become counterproductive, is technically referred to as *information overload*. Sutcliffe and Weick (2008) argue that information overload reduces our ability to take a good perspective on events, or to identify which cues are the most relevant, because we get so distracted by all the other irrelevant cues. These are the kinds of problems that Omodei found in her study of wildland firefighters. Sutcliffe and Weick argue that the problem isn't merely the quantity of information but rather our inability to make sense of the data, to see their significance and put them in context.

An illustration is provided by Hurricane Katrina, which hit New Orleans in 2005. The Federal Emergency Management Agency (FEMA) made sure the White House knew exactly what was going on. FEMA briefed the White House on Monday, August 29 (the day Katrina made landfall in Louisiana) that at Camp Beauregard in Louisiana it had 17 trailers of ice, 32 trailers of water (with eight more in transit), 15 trailers of Meals Ready to Eat (MREs), six trailers of tarps, 14 trailers of cots, and three trailers of blankets. On August 31, FEMA briefed the White House that it had staged ten trailers of water at the Superdome (a football stadium in New Orleans) and 22 trailers of water at Camp Beauregard, 23 trailers of ice at Camp Beauregard, 14 trailers of MREs at Camp Beauregard (and another two diverted to the Superdome), and so forth. This is an impressive litany of resources. But nowhere in the briefings did FEMA indicate how many trailers of water, ice, MREs, etc. were needed. In fact, the four hurricanes that hit Florida in 2004 suggested that Louisiana would need hundreds of trailers of ice. The flow of Katrina data to the White House didn't give a useful picture of whether the supplies were sufficient. The top officials at FEMA, lacking disaster-relief experience, didn't think to add this perspective. The White House didn't ask "How does this compare with what was needed in comparable disasters?" The White House staff believed they knew the logistics picture of the flow of supplies, but they really didn't. Adding more details isn't the same as creating meaning.

The White House also didn't understand the timing of when the resources had to be delivered. Not enough resources were delivered in the early phases, when they were most needed; there weren't enough commodities stockpiled, and transportation was difficult. Within a few weeks, however, there was a surplus of ice and other commodities. The flow of detail to the White House didn't portray the degree to which FEMA was out of step with the time cycle of the disaster.

There is no point at which enough data will magically coalesce and produce meaning. People have to make sense of the details.

Information overload isn't just having too much information. After all, we already have more information than we can absorb, but it doesn't bother us as long as we can skillfully redirect our attention. Information overload—the saturation point—becomes problematic when we have trouble focusing our attention on the relevant signals. That's what happens when people interpret claim 4 as an invitation to turn on the information spigot in order to reduce uncertainty. They start by collecting more and more data, then they complain that they have too much.

We can label this the Goldilocks Effect.[6] Goldilocks wanted her porridge not too hot, not too cold, but just right. She wanted her bed not too hard, not too soft, but just right. Decision makers want not too much information, not too little, but just the right amount. They want the peak of the curve in Tom Stewart's diagram (figure 9.1).

The Goldilocks Effect assumes that there is a "right" amount of information, that we can know what it is, and that we can aim for it the way we might set a thermostat. None of these assumptions holds. There is never a right amount of information.

People sometimes try to use filtering strategies to get the right amount of information. Information filters let us design a search that returns mostly relevant material. We want to filter out the chaff and find what we need. The trouble with filtering is that we tend to spend more time tuning the filters rather than looking at the information. The idea of setting filters comes from the Goldilocks Effect—a belief that perhaps we can find just the right amount of information.

We would be better off if we stopped worrying about getting the right amount of information and instead tried to see the meaning in the data that we do have.

Let's examine a few examples of events that caught people by surprise.

Historical examples of "surprises"

Consider some cases in which people were surprised by events. "If only we had more information"—that's the common complaint. But in case after case we find that the information was there but it got ignored or rejected. The additional data obscured the pattern. Pearl Harbor is a famous example.

Example 9.1: The failure to detect the attack on Pearl Harbor[7]   In retrospect, all the data needed to draw a clear conclusion of an imminent attack on Pearl Harbor were available: a gathering momentum of Japanese troop and ship movements (these were public and visual); two changes in the Japanese naval call signs (highly unusual, interpreted as preparation for an offensive); loss of contact with the Japanese aircraft carriers. Decoded messages indicated that the new military cabinet in Tokyo was more aggressive and had set a deadline for success in negotiations with the United States; Japanese Army and Navy messages implied that an attack was planned for the weekend of December 7.

Another signal was that the Japanese were compiling a list of British, American, and Dutch targets. The Japanese were particularly diligent in sectoring Pearl Harbor into zones and identifying which zone each ship was in. The United States knew this from intercepted messages. The US knew that the Japanese were increasing their reporting at several sites around the world, but in the weeks before December 7 the message traffic to Japanese sources in Manila and Pearl Harbor, but nowhere else, had increased. (The Japanese attacked the American forces in the Philippines 10 hours after their strike against Pearl Harbor.)

According to cryptographers who had decoded a message, Japanese embassy officials were instructed to burn most of their code books. There was even a rumor from the Peruvian embassy in Tokyo about a planned strike at Pearl Harbor. The Peruvian ambassador to Japan relayed this rumor to the American ambassador. An hour before the attack, a Japanese submarine was sunk near the entrance to Pearl Harbor. And just before the attack, a radar operator spotted the Japanese airplanes approaching Pearl Harbor.

Yet the Americans could explain away most of these clues. The loss of contact with the Japanese aircraft carriers? They must be near their homeland, and using different wavelengths. The diligence in sectoring Pearl Harbor into zones? That just showed the Japanese passion for thoroughness; it also was a way to shorten messages, so no one told Admiral Kimmel, the head of the Pearl Harbor fleet. Japanese alerts were not unusual, and had occurred on a number of previous occasions. The burning of the code books? This might mean that the Japanese were anticipating an American attack. Code books had been burned before. Besides, the message ordered Japanese embassies to destroy "most of their secret codes." If the Japanese were going to war, they would have ordered the destruction of *all* their secret codes. So the decoded message suggested that war was not imminent. The rumor from the Peruvian ambassador? The American officials didn't take it seriously and never passed it along; they lost some of their respect for an official who would waste his (and their) time on such an absurd tale. The increased message traffic to Manila and Pearl Harbor? No one noticed this pattern because no one was monitoring the worldwide picture. The Japanese submarine that was sunk? How could anyone be sure it was Japanese—better get confirmation before jumping to conclusions. The radar signals of the advancing Japanese airplanes? They were reported to Lieutenant Colonel Kermit Tyler, who told the radar operator not to worry about them. Tyler assumed the radar blips were a group of American B-17s coming in from the mainland; he had a friend who was a bomber pilot who once told him that any time the radio station played a certain type of Hawaiian music all night long, that was a good bet that B-17s were coming in because they used that radio music for homing. When Tyler drove to work that morning and heard the Hawaiian music, which was playing by coincidence, he figured he would be seeing the B-17s. So when he heard from the radar operator, he just assumed it was the returning B-17s. Less than an hour later, when Tyler stepped outside and saw planes coming down to Pearl Harbor, he assumed they were US Navy planes. When he saw that anti-aircraft guns were being fired, he assumed it was a training exercise.

The Americans also struggled with additional signals that created uncertainty. Some pointed to the USSR as the target of attack. Some pointed to a Japanese advance through Southeast Asia.

In addition, there were reasons not to believe that the Japanese could attack Pearl Harbor. The harbor was too shallow to permit torpedoes to be dropped from airplanes (torpedoes would detonate prematurely unless the water was deep enough), so no anti-torpedo netting had been laid in the harbor. The United States didn't know that the Japanese had figured out a way to modify their torpedoes to operate in a shallow harbor.

There were also reasons to resist going to a full alert. A full alert would increase the possibility of shooting down an unknown aircraft, so it might provoke the Japanese. Furthermore, if pilots had to fly additional reconnaissance missions, they would get less training, become more fatigued, and wear out their equipment faster.

On top of all these difficulties, the signals were scattered. Some were received by different agencies, some were decoded but others not, some were sent rapidly, and others were blocked. The intelligence analysts who broke the Japanese "Purple" diplomatic code safeguarded their work by carefully limiting the distribution list for intercepts, not always informing officers higher up in the chain. Decrypted information was provided without any context, which made it hard to interpret. To maintain security, the recipients weren't allowed to retain this information or make notes about it. Some signals never reached a decision center.

The military officers couldn't believe that the Japanese might attack Pearl Harbor. Their mindset got in the way. With so much information, it was easy to explain away data that didn't fit the mindset. Tossing more information into this mix wasn't likely to increase the chances of anticipating the attack. The officers would just have explained these cues away.

The 9/11 attack is another example of how information gets lost within a system or organization, and why additional information is unlikely to help.

Example 9.2: Anticipating 9/11   How could the American agencies have anticipated that terrorists would use commercial airplanes to attack New York and Washington? Who would have expected such a thing?

The notion that Islamic terrorists might use airplanes as weapons emerged in the 1990s. An Algerian group hijacked an Air France jet in 1995 and threatened to crash it into the Eiffel Tower, but commandos killed the hijackers before they could succeed. In 1994 a Philippines Airlines flight to Tokyo was bombed, and in 1995 the intelligence community figured out that this was a practice event for a larger hijacking during which a light airplane would fly into CIA headquarters. The World Trade Center itself was attacked by a truck bomb in 1993. In

1998, on the basis of these and related events, terrorism specialists provided the Federal Aviation Administration with two scenarios that seemed reasonably plausible: terrorists crashing planes into nuclear power plants, and terrorists hijacking Federal Express planes and crashing them into targets such as the World Trade Center, the Pentagon, the White House, and the Capitol.

The FBI had determined that al-Qaeda had been behind the attack on the USS *Cole* in October 2000 and the attacks on American embassies in Africa in August 1998. The CIA knew that al-Qaeda was plotting further attacks on the United States. Yet these hints didn't alert authorities to mobilize their defenses. Today we might be more sensitive and likely to act, but in the days leading up to 9/11 we didn't have a mindset to take the threats seriously.

Some of the clues got ignored because of information overload. The National Security Agency intercepted communications between September 8 and September 10 about the plot but didn't translate them until after September 11.

Some of the warnings got deflected. By the summer of 2001 the intelligence community was receiving more and more warnings of an al-Qaeda plot, but most officials believed that the plot would be overseas. Many of the messages hinted at overseas targets; these obscured the data suggesting that the US itself was the target. The officials believed that a domestic threat was unlikely, and that mindset shaped their review of the data.

Most of the warnings simply got dismissed. The intelligence agencies learned in 1998 about a plot in which a group of Arabs would fly a plane loaded with explosives from a foreign country into the World Trade Center. The FBI and the FAA judged that the plot was far-fetched.

On July 10, 2001, an FBI agent in Phoenix sent a message (the "Phoenix memo") to Washington informing his superiors that he was concerned that terrorists were getting training at flight schools in Arizona. The agent warned that these suspects might be preparing to conduct a terrorist mission. The agent further suggested that the FBI investigate flight schools around the country, engage the intelligence community in a dialog about this danger, and obtain visa information on applicants to flight schools. Unfortunately, the people who reviewed the Phoenix memo decided not to act on it and never notified higher managers. One alternative explanation was that Osama bin Laden needed pilots to move materials within Afghanistan.

In August 2001, the FBI's Minnesota office asked for permission to investigate Zacarias Moussaoui, a member of al-Qaeda (and possibly a potential 9/11 hijacker). But the FBI turned down this request.

Between June 22 and July 31, the FAA issued four information circulars to the aviation industry alerting them about a possible terrorist action, possibly involving hijackings. The FAA did not give these alerts a high priority.

Even when the CIA alerted the White House to impending terrorist attacks within the United States, these warnings got little attention.

Some warnings got embargoed. This happened because federal agencies didn't coordinate effectively.

The CIA knew that two al-Qaeda operatives had entered the United States in 2000 and again in the spring of 2001. The CIA (which is not permitted to operate inside the United States) never told the FBI about this. The FBI only found out for itself on August 22, 2001, too late to track the two down. Both of them were among the 9/11 hijackers. (And, true to form, the FBI decided it couldn't assign any criminal investigators to the hunt for fear that would compromise any legal action. Besides, the FBI only had a single, inexperienced intelligence agent available.) One CIA agent, a liaison at FBI headquarters, did ask CIA officials for permission to tell the FBI that the two al-Qaeda operatives were in the United States, but he never got a response to his request.[8]

Could the events of Pearl Harbor and 9/11 have been thwarted by additional information? Perhaps, but not necessarily. At the time, additional cues would have been ignored, lost in the noise, and suppressed by the disbelief.

Why bother to gather more information if it won't be used? If the United States had been able to double the amount of information it had, the extra information also would have doubled the messages that weren't truly relevant, and the connections between all these messages would have gone up exponentially. Adding more information wasn't going to prevent these events unless there was also a way to analyze the messages better. And if the agencies had that capability, they wouldn't have needed additional data. They already had enough data. They squandered the data in bureaucratic inefficiencies.

When the data collectors don't believe that an attack is plausible, they are likely to explain away any additional data. The mindset that the Japanese weren't going to attack Pearl Harbor, or that al-Qaeda wasn't going to attack the United States directly (despite the CIA's warnings to the contrary), would likely have trumped most new messages the US government might have received.

Had the FBI received some of the information the CIA possessed, it might have prevented 9/11. In that sense, the FBI would have benefited from the additional information. However, this argument misses the point. The US government possessed all the information it needed. The agencies failed to use that information. The country paid the price for organizational barriers and for within-agency blindness. These dysfunctions were more serious than a lack of data.

And then there's the case of Enron.

Example 9.3: Catching on to Enron   It is popularly believed that Enron, an energy trading corporation, misled the investment community, its shareholders, and most of its employees as it rapidly slid into insolvency. Instead of revealing its difficulties, the firm managed to hide its problems until the very end. As a result of the Enron case and similar abuses, Congress now requires large corporations to disseminate much more information about their operations.

However, Jonathan Macey (2003) pointed out that the cues were there. A few people did pick their way through the data, did notice the discrepancies, and did report their observations. But no one listened. Macey (ibid., p. 331) argues that the American system of mandatory reporting worked fairly well: "Enron did make disclosures that should have led reasonable market participants to uncover grave problems within the company . . . the market did an astonishingly poor job of both interpreting Enron's disclosures and 'decoding' the information contained in the trades conducted by Enron insiders."

The people who did recognize early cues to Enron's impending collapse included tax specialists, a group of business school students, and a financial reporter.

Enron wasn't paying any taxes. Some thought that Enron had figured out how to avoid taxes on its massive earning, but the tax accountants saw that Enron simply wasn't generating any income. By clearing debt off its balance sheet, Enron fooled most observers, but that was a non-event from the perspective of the tax system. No financial observer or analyst picked up on the discrepancy between Enron's tax reporting and its reports to the Securities and Exchange Commission. Or if they did, they explained away the tax data.

In 1998, several business school students at Cornell made Enron a case study, using publicly available data. They published an investment report raising red flags about Enron's financial condition and urging investors to sell Enron stock. Troubled by a drop in net income the year before, they even suggested that Enron might be manipulating its earnings. (The sales figures Enron reported seemed implausible.) The Cornell students reached this conclusion several years before Enron unraveled. Enron's stock doubled in value in those years before the rest of the community caught on.

In September 2000, an article by Jonathan Weil in the Texas edition of the *Wall Street Journal* pointed out that Enron's annual and quarterly reports described how the company had removed assets from its books and replaced these with revenues. Enron's large reported profits consisted of large, unrealized non-cash gains. Enron reported that its earnings had increased by 26 percent for the quarter, but if Enron hadn't reported those unrealized gains it would have had a loss for the quarter. The transaction was legal but highly speculative.

James Chanos, an investor, double-checked Weil's analysis and began to short-sell Enron stock. He told Bethany McLean, a reporter for the *Fortune* magazine, about this, and she wrote about it in the March 2001 issue. McLean's article set off a round of scrutiny. Enron's stock fell, and the company filed for bankruptcy in December, 2001, more than a year after the *Wall Street Journal* broke the story.

Because of their inattention, hedge funds and other short-sellers missed a wonderful opportunity to make a fortune betting against Enron. The data were there.

Macey concludes that disclosure is necessary but not sufficient. We also need an infrastructure to receive, analyze, and interpret that information. Otherwise, why spend huge amounts of money on corporate governance systems?[9]

All these examples show how decision makers ignore weak signals or explain them away when the signals didn't fit with the prevailing mindset. The data were there, but the sensemaking broke down.

The US financial meltdown of 2008 provides another example. The data were there. For years, economists had warned about the housing bubble. Economists and politicians alike had worried about the complexity of transactions involving sub-prime mortgages. The collapse was a question of when, not whether. No one fully appreciated how the collapse would play out, or that most of the big investment banks on Wall Street would disappear, either swallowed up by other companies (Bear Stearns, Merrill Lynch) or forced into bankruptcy (Lehman Brothers). But in hindsight, anyone who was paying attention could have known that a day of reckoning was approaching. No additional information was required.

I have personal experience on this point. In March 2007, I participated in an international conference on early detection of major threats. Most of the talks covered threats such as terrorist attacks or outbreaks of viruses. One of the speakers, David Martin, discussed financial threats. He warned us about collateralized debt obligations and what a complex web they had spun through global commerce. His analyses showed a frightening danger of a global meltdown, particularly when the US housing bubble burst.[10] The Dow Jones Industrial Average closed at 12,288 on the day of his talk, on its way up to 14,000 in October 2007. I doubt that anyone at the conference acted on his warning. I remembered his talk in February 2009, with the Dow Jones index around 8,000 and the world economies in recession. Martin had made his predictions more than eighteen months prior to the dramatic crash of the US stock market in the fall of 2008. He had not only made the predictions, he had explained the causal chain reaction that we could expect. We listened to him, and we ignored him. His message was too inconsistent with our worldview.

Woods et al. (2002, p. 27) put it well: "The meaning of a particular piece of data depends on what else is going on, what else could be going on, what has gone on, and what the observer expects to change or happen." Because the same message can mean different things in different contexts, a mindless search for more data can't be successful. Woods et al. gave the example of an alarm in a control room. The operators' responses to the alarm depend on context. It may not be important, or if it has gone off repeatedly it is no longer meaningful, or it may demand immediate attention, or it may be important only if other alarms have started to go off. That's what we see in the cases of Pearl Harbor, 9/11, and Enron. The messages and clues seem ominous today, now that we know what happened. But at the time, without being able to relate these clues to the other clues, the analysts struggled to see their significance. So why collect data if we aren't going to believe them?

Unintended consequences

If we adopt claim 4 as our creed, we will know just what to do when we feel uncertain.

We will gather more data. The more the uncertainty, the more strenuous the data gathering. We won't stop until our uncertainty disappears or we become exhausted, whichever comes first.

Sometimes we will notice that the information we need is already in our "in" boxes. Therefore, we'll decree that every message must be read in its entirety, to make sure we don't miss anything. If we can't personally read every message, we'll have to hire additional staff members, and somehow work out how all those involved will collaborate.

Because of the potential for overload, we will have to invest in information technology to collect and categorize and analyze all the data. And we'll have to store the data in a way that will let us retrieve what we need instantaneously (as long as we remember it and the label we used to store it).

We will also have to develop intelligent filters to figure out what is relevant and what we can ignore.

To make sure this all works efficiently, we'll develop measures and standards for the right amount of data with which to make any type of decision.

Does that fill anyone with confidence?

Replacement

The claim that we can reduce uncertainty by gathering more information is sometimes accurate but sometimes misleading, especially under conditions of complexity. It is accurate for cases in which the uncertainty stems from a lack of data, as opposed to conflicting or ambiguous data. Of course, in the case of a well-ordered task, such as being uncertain about the telephone number for a restaurant, we can reduce the uncertainty by looking in the phone book or checking the website. We know exactly what data point we need, and where to find it. Even in complex situations, more information can help up to a point.

When dealing with a mystery, instead of a puzzle, we enter the realm of complexity. We have to pick our way through the shadows. What is the future of the relationship between Islamic and Western civilizations? No data point will solve this mystery. The more books we read, the more lectures we attend, the more we have to think about, the more complicated it all gets. Information will not cure these kinds of uncertainty. And a non-directed search for more information can just add to the confusion.

Richards Heuer wrote in *Psychology of Intelligence Analysis* (1999) that the intelligence community needs more analysis, not more data. His recommendation applies to many other communities as well. The replacement for that claim is that *in complex environments, what we need isn't the right information but the right way to understand the information we have.*

Further, under complex conditions, we need to manage uncertainty more than we need to reduce it. To manage uncertainty we have to know how to seek and prioritize information. We need to fill gaps with assumptions. We need to know when to wait for the situation to evolve. We need the cleverness to act in a way that structures the situation.[11]

Managing uncertainty also means managing the teams and organizations that exchange messages or suppress them. The examples of Pearl Harbor, 9/11, and Enron show that we need to improve team sensemaking, because teams may ignore the weak signals that individuals notice. The Phoenix Memo, which preceded the 9/11 attack, illustrates how easy it is to suppress suspicions.

In 2006, Dave Snowden and I, working with Chew Lock Pin, Holly Baxter, and Cheryl Ann Teh, performed a study for the Singapore Armed Forces on the dynamics of weak signals (Snowden et al. 2007). We set up "garden-path" scenarios in which the initial, obvious account of events was wrong and the weak signals started to dribble in. We ran seven groups of military and intelligence specialists in teams of four. Not a single team talked about the weak signals when there was time to take early and preventive action.

However, we had asked the participants to keep private diaries, and in every team at least one member noted the weak signals in his or her diary. Sometimes half the members of a team noted the weak signals in their diaries. In other words, each team had the potential to surface the weak signals. But not a single team talked about them. Somehow the climate of teamwork suppressed these cues. We need to find ways to encourage team members to voice suspicions and hunches without inviting ridicule or losing credibility.

Managing uncertainty means that people have to escape from the mindsets that explained away or suppressed critical clues to Pearl Harbor, 9/11, and Enron. People also have to build and use mindsets so they can spot anomalies such as the future terrorists who were taking flying lessons.

Claim 4 emphasizes the quest for more information, whereas in facing mysteries people need to focus on the ways they are interpreting and anticipating events. Managing information puts the emphasis on what we understand, not on how many signals we have collected. It's usually more valuable to figure out how the data connect than to collect more data. The next chapters will examine the process of sensemaking—understanding situations by finding connections between the data.

Why claim 4 matters

It matters because claim 4 (that we can reduce uncertainty by gathering more information) oversimplifies the nature of uncertainty. It misses the uncertainty caused by distrust of data, conflicting data, and complex data.

It matters because our ability to obtain information has overwhelmed our ability to make sense of it.

It matters because an age of information leads to the tyranny of information. If information is good, more information is better, pushing us past the saturation point. We devote more energy, resources, and funding to gathering more information than to sorting it out. Organizations put resources into acquiring and cataloguing more information rather than into improving the way the information gets shared and integrated.

It matters because, in an age of information, people are less comfortable making decisions under uncertainty. Instead, we delay. We wait for more information even when that information will not affect our decisions.

10 When Patience Is a Vice

Whenever you hear about a dramatic news event, track the initial account and watch as it changes over the next few days. Sometimes we don't get the real story for months. Sometimes we never do. But when we find out what really happened, it's likely not to be what we believed from the first story. After the 1995 bombing of the Alfred P. Murrah Federal Building in Oklahoma City, the first story implicated Islamic terrorists.

When Valerie Plame was publicly identified as a CIA employee, the initial story was that senior officials in the White House had punished her because her husband (Joseph Wilson, a former ambassador and diplomat) hadn't cooperated with its scheme to show that Iraq was developing weapons of mass destruction. Many people still believe that Plame was deliberately identified in order to get even with her husband, but the source of the leak was Richard Armitage, a senior official in the Department of State who was actually a critic of the plan to invade Iraq. Armitage "outed" Valerie Plame by carelessness in a discussion with a reporter, not by design. However, once a story takes hold and fits our expectations, it is hard to dislodge.

Claim 5: It's bad to jump to conclusions—wait to see all the evidence.

Not only is the first story likely to be wrong, it clogs our minds. It gets us thinking in the wrong direction, and it makes shifting over to the truth more difficult. When we get contradictory evidence, we fixate on the first story and preserve our mistaken impressions.

Bruner and Potter (1964) demonstrated how fixation works in a simple experiment.[1] They showed 89 college students a set of blurred photographs of common objects. For each photo, Bruner and Potter kept improving the focus until the object was reasonably clear—that is, to the sharpness of focus at which 25 percent of the subjects in a group who had not seen the progression identified it accurately. When the image reached that sharpness, which was the termination point, the researchers asked the subjects to guess the object. Some subjects began when the photo was severely blurred; others began later in the sequence, when the photo was less blurred.

The subjects who started with the severely blurred images had the most trouble identifying the objects. They correctly recognized 23.3 percent of the pictures. The subjects in the medium blurred condition got 44.7 percent correct, and the subjects in the lightly blurred condition identified 59.8 percent of the objects. Remember, all subjects made their guesses at the termination point when the picture was at the same level of blurriness. The subjects starting out with the very blurred image did the worst. Their initial guesses about the very blurred image were way off, and those incorrect guesses interfered with their official attempt to identify the image at the termination point. Perhaps they would have done better had they stifled their initial guesses.

Bruner and Potter tried another strategy. In Group A they had nine subjects view the photographs going from medium blur to the termination point. In Group B, another ten subjects did the reverse—they viewed the photographs starting with the termination point and moving to the point of medium blur. Group A saw the photographs coming into focus and scored 44 percent accuracy, about the same as in the initial experiment. Group B saw the photographs going out of focus and scored 76 percent accuracy. Both groups saw the exact same images, but in two different orders. Because Group A started with a blurry image, their interpretations went off in the wrong direction and they couldn't easily recover.

Feltovich, Coulson, and Spiro (2001) took this research out of the laboratory and studied pediatric cardiologists in a hospital setting. Their experiment used a garden-path scenario in which participants form an incorrect initial explanation, and then get messages that contradict the initial story. The researchers measure how long people stay on the garden path—how much contrary evidence they need before they come to their senses. In this study, the cardiologists read a description of a new case and tried to find a diagnosis while receiving more and more information about the fictitious patient. The initial description made the diagnosis seem fairly obvious. However, that obvious diagnosis was wrong. The subsequent information contradicted the obvious diagnosis. Feltovich et al. found that some cardiologists stayed on the garden path for a very long time. Some never got off. They remained fixated on the initial "obvious" diagnosis.

Political leaders have been known to get trapped by their initial beliefs. This may come as a surprise to some readers, even after the review of Phil Tetlock's study of pundits in chapter 5, so let's look at another example.

During World War II, at a point when Germany and the USSR were still allies, the Americans and the British tried to inform Stalin that Hitler was about to launch Operation Barbarossa and attack the USSR without warning or provocation. Stalin ignored these warnings. Germany's ambassador to the USSR met with Stalin and told him about the impending attack. When the ambassador left the room, Stalin commented to aides that the disinformation campaign was reaching high levels. Two weeks later, Germany attacked the USSR. A few hours before the attack, a German soldier who was a dedicated communist slipped across the border and revealed what was coming. Stalin, who had lost patience with attempts to deceive him, had the man shot.[2] Historians have estimated that Stalin received more than 50 different warnings about Hitler's pending attack; some of them came months in advance. Stalin ignored the warnings because they were so inconsistent with his world view.[3] If he had followed the advice of claim 5, Stalin would have waited to see all the evidence.

At times, our fixation on our initial beliefs becomes comical. The following example comes directly from an interview my colleagues conducted about a US Army unit in Kosovo that used an Unmanned Aerial Vehicle (a drone aircraft that can fly over areas of interest and send back live feed pictures) to track a gang of thugs in a city.

Example 10.1: Chasing their tail   After the disintegration of Yugoslavia, a United Nations force attempted to keep the peace in Kosovo, with uneven success. The Presevo Valley, patrolled by the American forces, had more than its share of arsons, beatings, and multiple murders. Once someone shot at the Army unit's Brigade Commander. At night, small groups of young men roamed the city streets, often going to a specific house to beat someone up.

In the spring of 2000, when the staff in the Army headquarters in the Presevo Valley saw eight men going in a direct path through the town, it matched the pattern they expected. From their experience, groups that big walking around town were usually up to no good.

Fortunately, the Army unit had just gotten their Unmanned Aerial Vehicle to begin sending them visual feeds, which ran live in the update room, where everyone could see them. They oriented the UAV to stay in the area of the suspicious activity. The Brigade Commander came in to watch. The gang of eight men were moving quickly, jumping fences, and appearing to be wreaking havoc.

The Brigade Commander gave soldiers on the ground orders to find the bad guys. Then the men who were being watched on the UAV feed began running around. The HQ staff speculated about why the men had started running; perhaps they heard the UAV, or heard a helicopter, or heard the American soldiers moving toward them. Regardless, the staff still thought the behavior was consistent with being "bad guys," so they weren't really trying to figure out why the men were running. As seen on the UAV feed, the suspicious band of men would start running down an alley, then turn around and run in the other direction. Their movements became pretty erratic, but this didn't send up a red flag. Because it was dark, it was hard to make out how the men were dressed. The Army staff knew the coordinates of the UAV and the general location of the thugs, but wasn't sure. There were no distinguishing landmarks.

The staff believed that the group was moving with a purpose. The cues were that there were eight of them, they were tightly knit, and they were looking into windows. The cohesiveness of the group seemed to be a cue; it didn't seem to be just a group out walking. Everyone seemed to know where the others were going, and they were moving fairly fast. When they would stop running, it seemed that they were trying to re-organize, that they didn't feel that they were in any immediate danger anymore, and that they were trying to figure out what to do next.

Toward the end of this incident, an intelligence analyst from another unit came into the update room to see what was going on. He never said anything or asked for information from anyone. He just said "Hey, those are our guys." The soldiers on the ground were also the "bad guys" they were trying to catch! When asked how he had figured it out, the intelligence analyst said he could hear the commander saying "move right" and then saw the people on the feed move right.

The whole incident took approximately 15 minutes. The intelligence analyst only came into the room for the last 2–3 minutes.

No one on the staff who had been there from the start of the incident realized that the men they observed were responding to the commander's orders. Some people did notice a connection between the orders and the reactions of the "bad guys," and explained it away: "They must be intercepting our radio communications."

This example and many others point to the importance of claim 5. Yet our survey respondents gave this claim an average rating of only 5.06, "Tend to agree for most situations." They weren't entirely convinced of it. Twenty out of 164 disagreed with it.

Disclaimer

Claim 5 (that we shouldn't jump to conclusions but instead wait to see all the evidence) has two weaknesses: we can't follow the advice to keep an open mind, and we shouldn't follow that advice because it will make us passive.

We can't keep an open mind.
Elstein et al. (1978) studied the way physicians made diagnoses. The physicians knew they were supposed to gather all the data before starting to speculate about what was wrong with the patient, just as claim 5 states. But they couldn't stop themselves. As they got more information, they naturally began to imagine what it meant.

And we shouldn't keep an open mind.
An open mind equates to an empty mind. How will we know when we have seen all the evidence? How long are we supposed to wait while we leave our minds on idle? The advice is impractical.

Worries about keeping an open mind echo the theme of chapter 7 about the way experts rely on mindsets. Mindsets are neither good nor bad. They are how we apply our experience to understand events.[4]

The advice is also misguided.
Keeping an open mind can make it harder to figure out what is happening. To understand why, look at a study conducted by Jenny Rudolph (2003).[5] She studied 39 resident anesthesiologists in a lifelike simulation setting to see how they interpreted evidence and diagnosed a problem. All these resident anesthesiologists were taking a course in introductory crisis management.

Example 10.2: The plugged breathing tube   Rudolph used a garden-path scenario to study the anesthesiologists. In the scenario, an anesthesiologist-in-training was called into a simulated but fully outfitted operating room to provide anesthesia for a woman (actually, a very lifelike mannequin) who was being prepared for an appendectomy. After getting the breathing tube into the mannequin's airway and putting "her" to sleep, somehow the ventilation stopped working very well. Why could that be? (The actual reason is that the "woman" exhaled some mucous into the tube and this mucous plug hardened inside the breathing tube.)

The anesthesiologists struggled to diagnose what was going wrong because the timing of the ventilation problem and the patient's history of mild asthma suggested that the cause might be a bronchospasm (an asthma attack). When treating the bronchospasm didn't work, another common reaction to the ventilation problem was to suction the breathing tube to remove any blockages. This treatment, however, also had no effect because the mucous plug had hardened. This is a rare development. Worse, the surgical team was under time pressure to remove the inflamed appendix.

Rudolph divided her subjects into four categories based on their reactions to this scenario: Stalled, Fixated, Diagnostic Vagabonds, and Adaptive Problem Solvers.

Two of the anesthesiologists fit the "stalled" category. Neither of them could find any pattern that showed them how to proceed. They couldn't generate diagnoses, and they didn't try different treatments. Neither figured out the problem.

The eleven physicians categorized as fixated (including one chief resident) usually jumped to the obvious diagnosis of bronchospasm. This diagnosis fits perfectly with the timing of the ventilation problem, which began after the breathing tube was inserted. These physicians tended to repeat one treatment for bronchospasm over and over rather than experimenting with different treatments. They rarely reconsidered whether the ventilation problem was in the tube rather than in the patient. Six of these fixated physicians did wonder about secretions in the breathing tube, and two of them tested for a blocked tube. The test is to see if secretions come out when the tube is suctioned. Because the mucous plug had hardened, no secretions came out, so they mistakenly concluded that the tube itself was clear.

The physicians also erroneously interpreted distant breath sounds as wheezes, a sign of bronchospasm. None of the eleven anesthesiologists in the fixated group diagnosed the problem.

The 17 open-minded anesthesiologists fared no better. Rudolph called their pattern "diagnostic vagabonding," because these anesthesiologists wouldn't commit to any diagnosis but instead treated all possibilities as tentative. Was the problem bronchospasm, too little muscle relaxant, or a wrongly placed tube? These physicians would consider each possibility but quickly jump to the others, and never engaged in a course of treatment that would let them probe more deeply. None of them figured out the problem.

Last, we have the nine physicians who jumped to conclusions but tested those beliefs. Rudolph called them "adaptive problem solvers." Like the fixated problem solvers, most of them immediately identified the bronchospasm as the most likely cause. But when their treatment didn't work, they turned to other diagnoses (e.g., allergic reactions, pulmonary embolisms), testing and rejecting each, eventually speculating about an obstructed breathing tube. Their active exploration style let them use initial diagnoses as springboards for conducting subsequent tests and treatments. Seven of these nine physicians discovered the hardened mucous plug. They tested in different ways—with fiber optic scopes, by the feel of the suction catheter, by the dry sound as they did the suctioning, by comparing how far they could insert the suction catheter versus the length of the breathing tube. Four different strategies that all led to the same diagnosis. No physician in any of the other categories got there.

Rudolph expected that the anesthesiologists who jumped to a conclusion and held on to it would be unsuccessful, and she was right. None of them ever figured out the problem. Rudolph also expected that the anesthesiologists who kept an open mind while receiving the stream of information would be successful at making the right diagnosis, and here she was wrong. The ones who kept an open mind, absorbing data like sponges, also failed. The only ones who succeeded had jumped to conclusions and tested them. They hadn't fixated on their first explanation. Instead, they had used that explanation to guide the tests they had performed and the way they had searched for new information. They exemplified the strategy of "strong ideas, weakly held."

Now we have a conflict. Rudolph found that the physicians who kept an open mind didn't make the diagnosis, but Bruner and Potter found that the subjects who speculated too soon, when the image was too blurry, did the worst. Where does that leave us?

Maybe it depends on whether people are active or passive. Bruner and Potter's subjects, college students, couldn't direct their own search; they just had to sit there, watching a fuzzy image, describing what they thought they saw. In contrast, Rudolph let her subjects—anesthesiologists—actively gather information. Perhaps that's why their early speculations became a basis for testing and inquiring.

Unintended consequences
Claim 5 (that it's bad to jump to conclusions, and one should wait to see all the evidence) fits an orderly situation where we can use past experiences to estimate the flow of information and pick a point where it is safe to begin guessing. It fits the conditions under the streetlights, with everything in the open. But how can we know when to begin guessing in a complex situation? How can we know what we'll be learning as we examine more data? To be on the safe side, we might refuse to speculate at all until all the data are in, but if the situation is complex how will we know that there aren't any surprises left?

Claim 5 just doesn't work under conditions of complexity.

Replacement

The replacement for claim 5 is to speculate actively, but to test those speculations instead of getting committed to them. Rather than advising people to keep an open mind, we can encourage them to engage in a speculate-and-test strategy.[6] Cohen, Freeman, and Thompson (1998) have developed a training approach to support the speculate-and-test strategy, and have demonstrated its effectiveness.

Here is an example of speculate-and-test.

Example 10.3: The triple helix[7]   The discovery of how DNA carries genetic instructions is one of the major scientific accomplishments of the twentieth century. James Watson and Francis Crick, two newcomers, cracked the code, astonishing the rest of the field. How did they figure it out?

Watson and Crick met at Cambridge University in 1951, where Crick was a graduate student and Watson was working on x-ray methods by which to explore the structure of the protein hemoglobin.

Watson was consumed by his intuition that a breakthrough to the discovery of the structure of DNA was near. In 1944, Oswald Avery had shown that DNA carries information. Erwin Schrödinger had argued in 1946 that genes carry information. Perhaps DNA in the genes was what carried the information. DNA was crystalline and had a regular structure. Maybe Watson and Crick could crack what that structure was.

Careful scientists gather precise data, adding their observations to the collection of established relationships for all to build upon. That's not how Watson and Crick worked. They read a paper by Linus Pauling, who had used x-ray diffraction data to demonstrate a helix structure for protein. Watson and Crick liked the helix structure and wondered if it fit DNA. A single strand of a helix couldn't do much to carry genetic information. Watson and Crick speculated that DNA was made up of more than one helix. They speculated that DNA was composed of three strands—a triple helix.

Watson and Crick expected that Pauling would soon apply his work to genetics. That left them only a small window of time to try to determine the structure of DNA. Politically, they shouldn't have pursued the topic of DNA structure. Each of them had other responsibilities. Besides, another British laboratory, run by Rosalind Franklin, was using x-ray diffraction methods to study the structure of DNA. By engaging in their own investigation, Watson and Crick were poaching on Franklin's project. Yet they couldn't stop themselves. They didn't own the idea of DNA-as-helix. The idea of DNA-as-helix owned them.

Instead of collecting new data, Watson and Crick started from the idea of a triple helix and tried to build models using the available data in the published literature and from unpublished sources as well. They quickly assembled a three-dimensional physical version of their triple-helix model. Franklin came up from London with her laboratory's director, Maurice Wilkins. She quickly spotted all the flaws in Watson and Crick's triple-helix model. After this debacle, Cambridge University's research director told Watson and Crick to end their investigations into DNA and to leave that topic to Franklin.

The Watson-Crick story should have ended there, but Linus Pauling's son, who had come to Cambridge to pursue a PhD degree, showed Watson a pre-publication paper in which Pauling speculated about a triple-strand helical version of DNA along the same mistaken lines that Watson and Crick had taken. They knew Pauling's version was wrong, and they expected him to discover his mistake and soon find the actual DNA structure. Rosalind Franklin didn't seem interested in the notion that DNA was a helix. It was up to Watson and Crick to beat Pauling. Having obtained some preliminary x-ray diffraction photographs from Franklin's lab, they were more confident than ever that DNA had a helical structure. They decided to take one last shot at it.

Back in the research laboratory, Watson and Crick divided up their attack. They didn't see any way a single helix would work. They still thought the triple helix was the most likely structure. Crick went to work on revising their triple-helix ideas to accommodate Franklin's criticisms and the data in her newest photographs.

Still, Watson and Crick had never really investigated the idea of a double helix. They didn't think that a double helix would work, because that entailed attaching the four bases (adenine, thymine, guanine and cytosine) on the inside of the helix, which didn't leave much room for variability and for rich information. They had been caught up—fixated, we might say—in the idea that the sugar-phosphates carried the information, not the bases, because there were only the four bases. That's what they liked about a triple helix. The sugar phosphates could go in the inside. Nevertheless, to be systematic they decided to try a double helix. Crick admonished Watson not to waste every afternoon playing tennis but to see what he could come up with.

Obediently, Watson went to work. The next morning, while waiting for some model components from the shop, he began playing with some two-dimensional components, pushing them around to see how they could fit together. "Suddenly," Watson later recalled, "I became aware that an adenine-thymine pair held together by two hydrogen bonds was identical in shape to a guanine-cytosine pair held together by at least two hydrogen bonds."[8] In that instant, the double-helix model (figure 10.1) sprang to life. Watson realized the symmetry. Every A-T pair matched its complement in a G-C pair. Now Watson appreciated the significance of Erwin Chargaff's findings that in DNA the proportion of adenine and thymine matched the proportion of guanine and cytosine. In retrospect, it was so clear. Crick had even

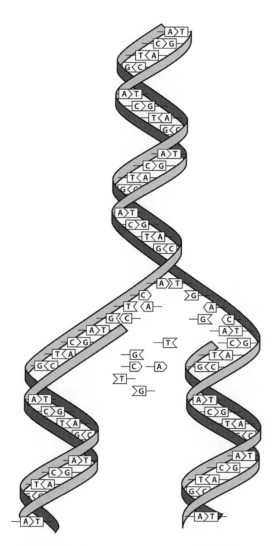

Figure 10.1
The double-helix model of DNA (based on a figure on p. 123 of Watson's book *The Double Helix*).

mentioned Chargaff's work to Watson earlier, but Watson dismissed it because Chargaff wasn't considered a careful researcher.

Watson had solved eight puzzles simultaneously. He and Crick had simply been trying to find a structure for DNA. Now they knew that structure: a helix. They knew how many strands: two. It was a double helix. They knew what carried the information: the nucleic acids in the gene, not the protein. They knew what maintained the attraction: hydrogen bonds. They knew the arrangement: the sugar-phosphate backbone was on the outside and the nucleic acids were on the inside. They knew how the insides matched: through the base pairs. They knew the arrangement: the two identical chains ran in opposite directions, so they were mirror images. And they knew how genes replicated themselves: through a zipper-like process.

The notion of a double helix alone wouldn't have made headlines. What struck everyone was the way all eight puzzles were resolved. As Crick put it, this was too beautiful not to be true.

The story of the triple helix shows two scientists who didn't have an open mind. They started out with a set of beliefs, which guided their investigations. Like Rudolph's Adaptive Problem Solvers, they tried to make their beliefs work but honestly admitted failures, regrouped, and tried again. They showed active exploration and a speculate-and-test mentality.

There are times when it is reasonable and practical to keep an open mind. Skilled weather forecasters report that when they come on shift they look at the data for the previous shift rather than reading the analysis prepared by the forecaster on that shift. They want to form their own mental model of the weather, and they don't want their judgments to be influenced by what someone else believed.

Claim 5 appropriately warns us that we can get fixated. Its recommendation to keep an open mind usually isn't realistic in most complex settings, but there are other ways to protect ourselves. They will be described in chapter 17.

Anticipatory thinking

I think that in complex and ambiguous settings people should actively speculate, instead of passively absorbing data. This advice is just the opposite of claim 5. Experts distinguish themselves by their ability to anticipate what might happen next. Even while doing their work, they are positioning themselves for the next task. Their transitions from one task to the next are smooth instead of abrupt. By forming sharp expectancies, experts can notice surprises more readily. They notice novel events and the absence of expected events.[9] As Weick and Sutcliffe (2007, p. 45) observed, experts "don't necessarily see discrepancies any more quickly, but when they do spot discrepancies, they understand their meaning more fully and can deal with them more confidently."

When we anticipate, we get ourselves ready for what may come next. We redirect our attention. We also can prepare for a few different possibilities. We don't know for sure what the future will bring, but we aren't going to stand idly by. And we can't engage in anticipatory thinking by forcing ourselves to keep an open mind, waiting until we receive enough information before we begin to explore ways to react.

Anticipatory thinking lets us manage our attention so that we are looking in the right places to spot anomalies in case they appear. Pradhan et al. (2005) studied eye movements to see if skilled drivers do more speculative scanning for possible problems than novices, and their findings also demonstrate the importance of anticipatory thinking.

Example 10.4: Looking for trouble[10]   What do you look for when you drive your car? Novices try to keep the car in the lane and not too close to the car ahead. The rest of us can control our cars automatically. We are more likely to look for hazards that might arise. If we see children, we prepare ourselves in case one of them impulsively runs into the street. If a truck blocks our vision of a crosswalk, we watch for signs that a pedestrian is starting to walk in front of us. If a large bush occludes our vision of a side street, we keep glancing over to make sure a car isn't running through a "yield" sign. We aren't predicting these events. We're just readjusting our concerns and focusing our attention on the hot spots. In 2005 Pradhan et al. reported the results of an experiment on the attention of skilled and novice drivers. The experienced drivers were 60–74 years old; the inexperienced drivers were 16–17 years old and had been driving for less than six months. Pradhan et al. put the drivers into vulnerable situations. The researchers monitored the eye movements of the drivers to capture what they were looking at in the scene. As expected, the skilled drivers looked to the places where trouble was most likely to arise. They weren't predicting trouble but were preparing for it. The novices weren't as proactive.

They kept looking at the road ahead. By failing to anticipate problems, they cut into their margin for reacting. The experienced drivers spotted potential risks 66 percent of the time, versus just 36 percent for the novices.

In one scenario, the driver was waiting at a red light, behind two other vehicles. The vehicle directly in front of the driver was signaling for a right turn. A pedestrian was on the corner this vehicle was going to turn past. Eighty-nine percent of the experienced drivers looked at the pedestrian to see if he was going to cross the street when the light changed, because that would cause the turning vehicle to slow down and wait. But only 43 percent of the novices looked at the pedestrian. They didn't appreciate how the pedestrian's actions might interfere with the turning vehicle and might force that driver to brake sharply to avoid a collision. (See figure 10.2.)

Driving a car depends on being able to anticipate dangers, and is a metaphor for many other activities. Good drivers aren't waiting for data. They are using their experience to actively scan for possible threats and hazards.

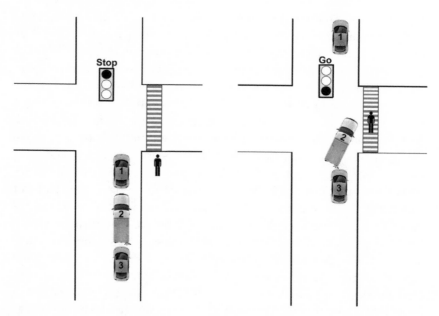

Figure 10.2
The turning-truck scenario.

We can scan while driving because we have lots of experience, as drivers and as passengers, with different types of hazards. In other situations we may have to anticipate novel events. At these times, anticipatory thinking may depend on how skilled we are at seeing connections between innocuous events and grasping their implications. We have to notice an "ominous intersection" of conditions, facts, and events.

Here is an account of an instance in which my anticipatory thinking failed: Years ago my daughters and I took a flight from Dayton to New York. When I left my car in the airport parking lot I tucked my car keys in my briefcase because I wouldn't need them while in New York. For complicated reasons, we were unable to fly back from New York. Instead, we took a train from New York to Toledo, Ohio where we were picked up by my mother-in-law, Bessie. She lived in Detroit and was driving south to my home in Yellow Springs, Ohio, so it worked out for her to meet us at the Toledo train station. A few hours later. Bessie dropped me off at the Dayton airport so I could reclaim my car. As I left Bessie's car, I wondered if I should take my suitcase and briefcase with me but didn't see any reason to do so—she and I were both going to drive to my home; I could get my suitcase and briefcase at that time.

As I approached my car, I realized my mistake. If I had been questioned a minute earlier I would have been able to correctly answer all these questions: Where is your car? (In the Dayton airport parking lot.) Where are your car keys? (In my briefcase.) Where is your briefcase? (In Bessie's car.) Where is her car? (Currently driving away from the airport.) The problem is that all four facts stayed separate until too late. This example shows a failure of anticipatory thinking. I didn't anticipate that I would need the briefcase as I got out of her car.

This trivial example shows how we depend on anticipatory thinking whenever we make adjustments in our routines. Here is a failure of anticipatory thinking that ended in tragedy.

Example 10.5: Friendly Fire   In 1994 two US Air Force F-15 fighter jets accidentally shot down two US Army Black Hawk helicopters over northern Iraq. All of the 26 peacekeepers on board the helicopters were killed. It was clear daylight. No other aircraft were in the vicinity. And the helicopter pilots as well as the F-15 pilots were in radio communication with an AWACS (Airborne Warning and Control System) that was directing all American military air traffic in the area. How could such a thing have happened?

Scott Snook wrote a book titled *Friendly Fire* to explain a number of causes that contributed to the accident. Most of the causes illustrate a failure of anticipatory thinking. I am only going to describe one of them—the failure to anticipate what might happen when two team-mates were separated.

The AWACS carries a team of weapons directors to handle the flow of military aircraft. For the mission in Northern Iraq, the AWACS and other aircraft flew out of Turkey. Once the AWACS was on station, the en route weapons director would track an aircraft through Turkey. Then as it flew into Iraq the en route weapons director would hand off the control/monitoring of that aircraft to a colleague, called the Tacti-cal Area of Responsibility (TAOR) weapons director. The Air Force officers handling these responsibilities on the AWACS sat right next to each other. They were constantly listening to radio messages, making it difficult to talk, so they came to rely on gesture. Over time they had evolved a "nudge and point" coordination routine. As an aircraft was getting ready to cross the border into northern Iraq, the en route weap-ons director would poke an elbow into the ribs of the TAOR weapons director, to get his/her attention, and then point to the blip on the screen that was nearing the border. The TAOR weapons director would nod, and the handoff was completed.

Unfortunately, on the day of the shootdown the radar console for the en route weapons director wasn't working. He had to shift to an extra console on the AWACS, and wasn't sitting next to the TAOR weapons director. No one anticipated how much their separation would inter-fere with their coordination. During the accident, the handoff for the helicopters never got made. Even though the F-15s and the Black Hawks were talking to the same AWACS, they were talking to differ-ent people inside that airplane. The TAOR weapons director, who heard the F-15s announce that they were going to shoot down two "unknown" helicopters,[11] didn't warn the F-15 pilots about the Black Hawks because he didn't know where the helicopters were and wasn't thinking about them. The en route weapons director was still monitor-ing the Black Hawks and didn't know that the F-15s were planning to shoot them down.

Who should have anticipated this coordination breakdown? We can't entirely blame the AWACS crew because it was their very first mission in northern Iraq. They had just flown into Turkey from Tinker Air Force Base, Oklahoma. They weren't familiar with the intricacies of managing the border crossing between Turkey and Iraq, or the tight coordination it required of them. The AWACS did carry a shadow crew of experts on that day to help the new crew learn its duties on its maiden flight in Turkey. I suspect some members of this shadow crew worried when the en route weapons director had to move to a different station after his console failed, but there wasn't much they could do. Besides, the northern Iraq area had been quiet and no one was expecting any difficulties.

In hindsight, someone should have anticipated that the two weapons directors were going to struggle with handoffs. Someone should have helped them work out a new routine. Unfortunately, no one picked up on the ominous intersection of events—the difficult handoff, the new crew, the separation of weapons directors, and many other factors that contributed to the accident.

Anticipatory thinking describes how we actively speculate about what might happen next. The next chapter will describe how we have to actively speculate about what has just happened in order to make sense of feedback.

Why claim 5 matters

It matters because claim 5 (It's bad to jump to conclusions—wait to see all the evidence) can disengage people and create a passive, lazy stance of waiting to receive all the data before doing anything.

It matters because claim 5 encourages organizations to impose bureaucratic procedures for collecting and sorting data instead of helping people engage in anticipatory thinking. This tendency gets stronger after an organization has made a mistake.

It matters because the advice embodied in claim 5 can make people slaves to the flow of information. We always have new information just around the corner that is about to surface. If we follow claim 5, we may never try to synthesize the data. Claims 4 and 5, to collect more data and to resist speculation, are a one-two punch to paralyze any decision maker.

11   The Limits of Feedback

Claim 6: To get people to learn, give them feedback on the consequences of their actions.

"You can't learn without feedback." "Faster feedback is better than slower feedback." "More feedback is better than less feedback." Researchers have demonstrated all these claims. In countless experiments, with animals as well as with humans, feedback is essential for helping people become more skilled.

The people I surveyed strongly lined up with claim 6. The average rating was 5.48, midway between "Tend to agree for most situations" and "Strongly agree for almost all situations." Only seven of the 162 people who responded to this item showed any disagreement.[1]

Disclaimer

I used to believe claim 6 until I noticed all the times when feedback left me confused: cryptic comments on technical reports, general statements in performance evaluations, and so on. I began to wonder why trainees struggle despite getting feedback on their performance.

Before we get too enthusiastic about feedback, we ought to take a look at all its limitations.

Feedback isn't sufficient.

Consider a simple example: I take up archery. In trying to improve, I note how each of my arrows lands—in the bull's-eye, close to the bull's-eye, or missing the target altogether. In this way I can change my technique to get more accurate. Now, if I didn't get any feedback on the accuracy of my shots I certainly couldn't improve. But simply seeing where each arrow lands doesn't tell me what I am doing right and what I am doing wrong. I suppose that over time my style will become more consistent. The more consistent I become, the easier it will be to predict where my shot will land and the more likely it will be that I can get the shot close to the bull's-eye. That's the premise. But I could just as easily get more consistently wrong, picking up bad habits that will prevent me from ever getting very good. As I eliminate the atrocious shots, I may gain a misguided confidence in these bad habits.

Feedback about consequences helps us judge if we are making progress. It can motivate us to do better. However, outcome feedback doesn't help us figure out how to do better. In archery, if a shot continually hits to the left it means I have to aim more to the right, but does that mean changing my aim point, my stance, my shoulder alignment, or the way I lean my head over the end of the arrow? Perhaps the wind is affecting the shots; if so, then I should take it into account. Outcome feedback doesn't help us diagnose what we need to improve.

To improve, we need process feedback about the way we are acting. I need feedback on the way I am aiming and releasing the arrows. What should I be monitoring: the amount I draw the arrow back? my breathing? the way I hold the arrow, or the bow? the angle of my elbows or knees? the steadiness of my wrists?

Researchers[2] have found that outcome feedback—knowledge of results—doesn't improve our performance as much as process feedback, which helps us understand how to correct flaws. But process feedback is harder to come by, and it isn't covered by claim 6 (To get people to learn, give them feedback on the consequences of their actions). Claim 6 refers to outcome feedback.

However, even if we amended the claim to include process feedback, we would still run into trouble.

If we get process feedback, we still have to make sense of it. To learn that a certain set of actions will lead to good outcomes, we have to figure out the cause-effect relationships between the actions we took and the later events.

The archery example was pretty simple. Let's try something more complicated. Imagine that you smile at your boss in the hallway today, and tomorrow you find out that you got a raise. So it worked, no? Of course that's ridiculous. Learning is more than just making connections. Lots of things influenced your boss. We have to tell which were the real causes versus the mere coincidences. We have to infer additional causes we might not have seen. We have to worry about time lags—the time between your actions and the raise, and the time between the decision and its announcement. The paperwork alone may have taken more than a week, and your smile may have been completely irrelevant.

In complex situations you'll never figure out all that is going on. You won't fully understand why you got your raise. Your boss may not even be sure. But it probably wasn't because you smiled in the hallway today.

Compare the notion of feedback in well-ordered versus complex tasks. If I want to improve my accuracy in shooting arrows at a target, I can count on immediate, accurate, clear feedback. In contrast, if I have to write reports that please my boss, I can't count on feedback that is immediate, accurate, or even clear. My boss may not read the report for a week, or may overreact to one statement in an otherwise exemplary piece, or may tell me something like "good job" or those dreaded words, "needs more work." My boss may tell me the report I wrote was fine, but later I might find that it got filed away and was never shown to any of the people who would have benefited from it.

If my boss praises me for showing a lot of initiative, what does that mean? Where did that judgment come from? Which incidents created it? If my boss tells me that I should follow the procedures more carefully and not be a loose cannon, what does that mean? What incidents, what rumors, what interpretations led to this assessment? We have much more trouble figuring out cause-effect relationships when the outcome is ambiguous, and is tied to behaviors like initiative and reliability. We have to contend with all the time lags between our actions, the eventual consequences, and the feedback. These are the kinds of shadows we're often operating in.

Just figuring out if a consequence is good or bad may be hard enough. For example, suppose you are a boss. You give an employee a pay raise, but you also identify an important area that needs improvement. The employee subsequently transfers to another group. Was that because of your criticism? Was it because the raise was too low? How are you going to learn if you can't connect these kinds of consequences to your actions?

The field of cybernetics uses feedback for mid-course corrections. The idea of feedback loops for control works fine for thermostats. But thermostats don't have to make sense of the feedback. Intelligent cybernetic systems can strengthen relationships that are followed by positive feedback, and ignore (or weaken) connections followed by negative feedback. However, that's not how people learn. If we don't get the positive feedback that we expected, we try to figure out what went wrong. When we get negative feedback we try to understand what we did wrong. Cybernetic systems don't do any diagnosis.

It can be impossible to understand feedback if we distort it.
We all simplify the world.[3] We chop events into artificial stages. We pretend that simultaneous events are sequential, that dynamic events are static, and that nonlinear processes are linear. We deal separately with factors that are interacting with one another. It is hard enough to understand accurate feedback. It can be impossible to draw the right lessons from feedback that we have distorted.

Even if feedback is clear, we may distort how we remember it. Think about the typical advice to students taking multiple-choice tests: "Your first impulse is usually correct." Many students interpret this advice to mean that they shouldn't change an answer if they go back over the question and suspect that another answer is correct. The advice is reasonable—first guesses usually are fairly accurate. However, students overdo the advice. They are much too reluctant to change responses. Kruger et al. (2005) investigated why this might be so. They found that when students change an answer that was originally correct, they feel lots of regret because they had gone against the advice. Conversely, when students stuck with an answer that was wrong, well, that was to be expected. Afterward, students recalled more cases where they had shifted and should have stayed than cases where they stuck to their first choice and should have shifted. Not only was regret operating here, but memory was getting in the way. The emotion-laden memories of the erroneous shifts seem to make these cases more vivid, and to strengthen the belief that you shouldn't change your answers.

The day after I met with Justin Kruger at New York University and learned about his research, I attended a retreat with investment managers where I observed the same phenomenon. The investment managers had formulated a strategy for dealing with stocks that went down in price. If the stock was worth buying at the initial price, it was an even better buy when it went down, and they should consider buying more, not selling. When they violated this strategy, the top managers (who had formulated it) remembered the mistake. In contrast, when they stuck with the strategy and lost money, well, that was just part of the risk. The senior managers vividly remembered the times they departed from their strategy and lost money, but they forgot the times when they departed from the strategy and came out ahead. So even trained analysts may run into trouble with the way they remember feedback.

Feedback will not help if people can't detect it.
This is another reason why giving people feedback isn't sufficient—they have to notice it and attend to it. How can we learn from our mistakes if we haven't been watching the right things? In chapter 10, I described a study[4] comparing the eye fixations of novice versus experienced drivers in a computer simulation. The novices were much less likely than experienced drivers to direct their attention to potential hazards. They just didn't know where to look. Not only were they less able to respond to a hazard, they were slower to spot it. That would make it harder to figure out later what caused an accident or even to be aware of near misses. Feedback will not have an effect if drivers aren't looking in the right place to see the critical cues.

Here is another example: Many years ago I purchased a videocassette recorder for my mother-in-law, Bessie, but she couldn't learn to operate it. Before returning it, I watched her try to make it work. She followed the instructions, hit the correct button, and got a feedback message on the screen. But she never noticed the message, because she kept her eyes glued to the remote until she was sure she had pressed the right button. By the time Bessie looked up to the screen, the feedback message had already disappeared. She needed to get ready to press the key and then look up while she pressed, but she was too worried about making a mistake to do that. Today, I think I could have helped Bessie attend to the fleeting screen messages, but at the time I just gave it up as a lost cause.

A further illustration comes from the time a visiting friend whom I'll call Jimmy asked me to help him improve his racquetball skills by playing a few games. Jimmy had never been very interested in athletics, but he had just started dating a woman who liked to play racquetball. Unfortunately, she was much better than he was. He explained to me that he just wanted to give her a good game, and also not be so humiliated. I agreed to try.

Example 11.1: A backhanded compliment   Jimmy and I warmed up a bit. When we started to play, I hit my first serve to his backhand. Jimmy missed the ball completely. I tried a softer serve to his backhand, and again he flubbed the return. I hit another soft serve and

looked back. He lunged at the ball as soon as it got close and mis-
played it.

At that point, I stopped the game. I said we were done playing.
Instead, I was going to hit some shots to his backhand. Whatever else
was wrong with his game, Jimmy seemed to have no backhand skills.
Further, I told him not to swing. I just wanted him to watch how the
ball bounced. We did that for about ten serves. Some of them hit
the back wall and then caromed back to hit the left side wall; others
hit the left wall first and then caromed off the back wall.

Next, I asked Jimmy still not to swing as I hit more serves but to tell
me where he could get a good shot. He dutifully identified all the
points where the ball was easiest to hit. After a while Jimmy asked me
if I would mind if he occasionally swung at the ball. I agreed but told
him not to feel that he had to swing. By this time he really wanted to
hit the ball, and he had little trouble returning my serves to his backhand. When we were done he thanked me for helping him with his
game.

When I first watched Jimmy, I realized that he was having trouble
anticipating the trajectory of the ball, especially when it came off of cor-
ners. He dreaded serves to his backhand, and he lunged for the ball as
soon as it came near him even though it was a tough shot to make, because he didn't want to wait for it to angle off the back wall. Continued
practice wasn't going to help Jimmy, because he wasn't giving himself
a chance to learn how the ball bounced off the walls. He wasn't giving
himself a chance to get feedback. That's why I wanted him to simply
watch the ball. By the time he asked permission to swing, he was eager
to hit the ball instead of dreading it.

Unfortunately, the story had a sad ending. When Jimmy returned
home and resumed his racquetball games with his girlfriend, he discovered that now he had a better backhand than she did. He began to
win regularly. Soon after, they broke up. I guess that provides some
feedback as well.

So far I have been describing the difficulties we have in learning
from feedback in complex situations. Another difficulty is in *giving*
feedback, particularly about subtle cues and tacit knowledge.

It is hard to provide feedback.
It is particularly hard to give feedback on tacit knowledge. If I'm trying
to coach you, and want to build up your expertise, how can I give you
feedback about the accuracy of your mental models, or about your

ability to notice subtle cues, or about your ability to sense what is typical and what is unusual? I'm not likely to even notice these kinds of knowledge. Even if I do give you feedback, you probably won't know what I'm talking about. Notice that I never told Jimmy anything. I never made any suggestions to him, or gave him any feedback. All I did was arrange for him to see the way the ball was bouncing.

Aside from the difficulty of giving feedback about tacit knowledge, instructors who give us rapid and accurate feedback can actually interfere with our learning. Schmidt and Wulf (1997) found that continuous, concurrent feedback does increase our learning curve while we are being trained but that it reduces any performance gains once the training is over. The reason is that we never have to learn how to get and interpret our own feedback as long as the instructor is doing all that work. The performance goes up nicely in the training environment, but then we are at a loss once we move into our work environment. We would be better off struggling to get our own feedback than having it spoon-fed to us by the instructors. The Schmidt-Wulf research involved motor skills rather than cognitive skills, but I suspect that there are times when aggressive feedback gets in the way of learning cognitive skills.

Consider the way we would want someone to coach us to become a better cook. Rapid feedback from a coach (e.g., "no, add more salt") can interfere with our ability to develop a sense of taste that can dictate how to alter the seasoning. We need to learn for ourselves how to evaluate the saltiness of the food.

The very idea of giving feedback suggests a passive learner. Learners are better off seeking their own feedback and asking for advice when they need it.[5] I think there are even times when feedback is de-motivating. The person giving the feedback may feel like a highly competent teacher, expert, or parent, but the recipients feel like dunces becoming stupider by the minute. They are put in a passive role, getting information they haven't asked for and may not be ready to understand. This may be a major reason for the relative lack of success in computer-based Intelligent Tutoring Systems. Giving feedback is probably the most important thing an instructor can do, and even good instructors are often challenged when it comes time to give feedback. A virtual instructor has even less chance of getting it right.

Feedback isn't always necessary.
Feedback applies more to some kinds of learning than to others.[6] It applies to learning about the actions we take. The feedback shows if

our actions were successful (outcome feedback) and perhaps what we were doing wrong (process feedback). Another type of learning is to acquire new facts. If I state that I grew up in the Bronx, you now know something about me. Where is the feedback? Then we have insight learning. When Watson and Crick had their insight about how DNA took the form of a double helix, where was the feedback? They didn't perform any actions. They didn't have anyone around at that instant to applaud them. They looked at the way their new model worked and realized that it must be right. The process of discovering the double helix didn't get reinforced along the way.

We need feedback to learn skills and procedures and routines, not to learn facts or gain insights.

So feedback isn't sufficient for learning, it is often hard to understand in complex situations, and it may even get distorted. People may not even detect the feedback cues. Teachers and coaches may not be good at giving feedback and may even get in the way of learning. And feedback is relevant for learning responses and actions, but perhaps not for other types of learning.

Claim 6 (to get people to learn, give them feedback on the consequences of their actions) holds only when the conditions are very straightforward. In complex situations, learners must interpret the feedback—learn to connect their actions to consequences, learn to sort out the relevant causal threads and the coincidental ones. Sensemaking is at the heart of learning cognitive skills. We aren't just acquiring new knowledge. We are changing the way we see things and think about them. We are making sense of conflicting and confusing data.

Unintended consequences

Let us take claim 6 seriously, and design an organization that trains its workers by giving them feedback on the consequences of their actions.

We will not have to worry about the initiative of the workers. The responsibility for learning is in the hands of supervisors and trainers. They are the ones who will dole out the feedback.

Workers who just don't get it, like Jimmy in the racquetball example, will have to go. They'll get feedback, but it won't do them any good.

If feedback is good, faster feedback is probably better. One of the fastest ways to give feedback is to identify when people depart from the standard procedures.

We probably will de-emphasize tacit knowledge. It is too hard to give feedback about that. We probably will focus only on the actions people take, not the reasons for their mistakes or the ways they are understanding the tasks. We will be setting up a society like the one B. F. Skinner described in his novel *Walden Two*. The *Walden Two* society didn't sound very inviting in 1948, when the novel was published. It doesn't sound any better now.

Replacement

In complex situations, the hardest part of using feedback is understanding it and sorting out the tangle of causes and effects. We have to make sense of feedback in order to learn from it. Sensemaking—that is, seeing what led up to the events that are happening and anticipating how our actions are likely to influence future events—is central to feedback.

For cognitive skills, we want feedback to change the way we think, not just add more facts into our memory.

Consider the case of Doug Harrington, a highly skilled F-4 pilot—in fact, an instructor who taught others how to land on aircraft carriers.

Example 11.2: A hard landing[7]   It is difficult to land an airplane on a stable runway. It is much harder to land when the runway is moving away from you and bouncing up and down with the waves. Aircraft carriers use landing signal officers (LSOs) to guide airplanes in or to send them back up if they aren't lined up well. Harrington had mastered the skill of carrier landings.

The next step in his career was a transition from the F-4 to the A-6. He didn't have trouble learning to fly the A-6. Then came the day when he had to demonstrate that he could do carrier landings in an A-6. He had to do six daytime landings followed by four nighttime landings and he would be qualified. That was when it all fell apart.

On the first attempt, Harrington lined the airplane up perfectly only to hear the LSO tell him "come right, come right." That didn't make sense, but he adjusted a little to the right, only to have the LSO wave him off. Harrington kept botching attempt after attempt, somehow struggling each time to get his plane on the deck. Harrington had lots of feedback that his carrier landings were terrible, but he didn't have a clue what was going wrong. He had outcome feedback but not process feedback.

Harrington's night-time landings were cancelled. He would have to try the daytime landings the next day. If he didn't do well, his flying career in the Navy was over. And he had no idea what was going wrong.

Late that night the Chief LSO came to talk to Harrington about what had happened. He didn't have any advice to give. Instead, he simply asked "Doug, can you describe how you're trying to line up your airplane?" Doug explained that he was doing it the way he always did. He put the nose of the plane on the center line and came in for the landing. The LSO thought about that, and thought about the way the A-6 differed from the F-4 that Doug was used to flying.

There was one relevant difference between the planes. In the F-4, the pilot sits right in the middle and an instructor or navigator sits behind him. Both of them are directly centered. The A-6 positions the two pilots side by side, not front and back. Doug knew that but didn't see how it could make a difference. The cockpit wasn't very large—they were just a few feet apart. So the LSO asked Doug to stretch out his arm with his thumb pointing up, as if he was hitchhiking, and align his thumb with a vertical line such as a door. As you are reading this example you can try this exercise yourself, aligning your thumb with any vertical line in the area. Next, the LSO asked Doug to move his head to the left about 18 inches, and then to bring his thumb back into alignment with the door. Immediately, Doug could see how he was pulling the nose of his airplane off to the left. Now he understood why the LSO kept telling him to come right. The small departure from the center line in the cockpit had a surprisingly large effect on the way he lined up the airplane. His previous strategy of putting the nose of the airplane on the center line of the runway no longer worked. And he understood why.

Doug "nailed" all his landings the next day, and he continued to fly Navy jets.

The LSO was not a coach or a trainer. He didn't give any lectures or offer any advice. He didn't have to add any more feedback. What he brought was curiosity. He wanted to know why a pilot as good as Harrington was having so much trouble. He used Harrington's response to diagnose the flaw in Harrington's mental model. Then the LSO took the interaction another step. Instead of just telling Harrington what was wrong, the LSO found an easy way for Harrington to experience it. Harrington already suspected something might be wrong with his approach. The simple thumb demonstration was enough for Harrington to form a new mental model about how to land an A-6.

This example shows how the impact of feedback depends on the learner. Initially, Doug Harrington got feedback but he couldn't make sense of it.

Therefore, the replacement for claim 6 is *"We can't just give feedback; we have to find ways to make it understandable."* This advice may seem obvious, yet too often we just offer our feedback and don't verify that the person we're trying to help appreciates what the feedback means. If the feedback isn't consistent with the way the person thinks, there is a good chance the person will distort or disregard it. Paradoxically, feedback that challenges our mental models can be the most valuable because it gives us a chance to reflect and even improve.

I am not criticizing the importance of feedback for learning. Just the reverse. I am taking feedback very seriously. Providing useful feedback in complex situations can be very difficult. Lots of trainers and coaches do a poor job. By showing why it is so hard, I hope to encourage people to be more thoughtful about how they diagnose a person's weaknesses and how they frame the feedback so it is effective.

Organizations often provide feedback in the form of metrics, which run into the same kinds of difficulties discussed in this chapter. In my book on intuition (2004) I suggested ways to make metrics more understandable and useful by blending them with stories. Story formats can help people make sense of feedback.

Sensemaking is important even in activities that seem as straightforward as giving and getting feedback. The next chapter examines what is involved in making sense of events.

Why claim 6 matters

It matters because claim 6 (to get people to learn, give them feedback on the consequences of their actions) emphasizes explicit knowledge (facts, rules, procedures) rather than tacit knowledge. People may use this concept to justify programs to deliver more rapid and accurate feedback, without giving any thought to what the learner should change. Systematic approaches to training often buy into this claim.

It matters because feedback is not "fire and forget," that we can just give and walk away. When we are coaching other people, our work is easier if we don't have to worry about their perspective. We may want to offer our wise observations and get on with the rest of our job. We may prefer to be direct and blunt in the feedback we give. But that can be ineffective. Coaching, training, and teaching have to take the learner into account.[8] The learning relationship is just that—a relationship. Coaches have to diagnose what is going wrong; they also have to find ways to get their message across.

It matters because many of us rush to give feedback without first trying to diagnose the difficulty. The Landing Signal Officer who helped Doug Harrington illustrates what can happen by asking a person to explain some puzzling actions. Before we rush to judge and instruct, we should try to understand so that we can help people make sense of feedback and we can offer more useful feedback for them.

12   Correcting the Dots

Sensemaking is the attempt to understand events that have occurred and to anticipate what might happen next. It looks back to sort out the past and forward to prepare for the future. Financial analysts engage in sensemaking to understand why a company performed well or poorly, and to predict how the company is going to do. Meteorologists try to figure out if tropical storms will strengthen into hurricanes. Historians seek to explain the causes of social and political revolutions. Parents rack their brains trying to explain why a child is suddenly getting poor grades in school. Physicians struggle to diagnose unusual symptoms in a patient. Intelligence analysts look for early signs of impending terrorist attacks.

In hindsight, sensemaking seems easier than it was at the time. Once we catalog all the clues to the 9/11 attack, we wonder how the intelligence analysts could have missed it. All they had to do was connect the dots. That attitude leads to claim 7.

Claim 7: To make sense of a situation, we draw inferences from the data.

Some people picture the mind as an assembly line. Data arrive from the senses, then get refined and processed and combined and polished and assembled until we have insights and conclusions. Claim 7 stems from the assembly-line metaphor. It portrays our sensemaking as making more and more inferences from the data we receive.

Figure 12.1 illustrates the assembly line. The data get converted into information, then get further enriched to become knowledge, and finally get transformed into understanding. This assembly-line process illustrates how people and organizations cope with all the data and cues that come at them. We all get more messages than we can possibly sort

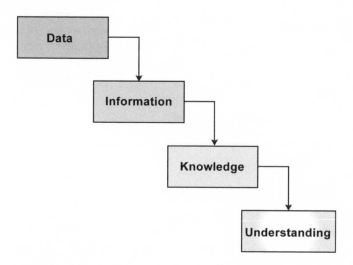

Figure 12.1
Turning data into understanding.

out. We respond by filtering, sorting, and combining all the low-level data to get higher-level cues so that we can reason about a manageable set of knowledge elements. Our organizations assign clerical staff members the job of receiving all the telephone calls, culling all the low-level e-mail inquiries, filtering out the unimportant messages, bringing us only the critical messages. We take this reduced set of inputs and determine what is going on and how to react. Data in, wisdom out.

Sensemaking—the process of figuring out what is going on—is sometimes explained using the metaphor of a picture puzzle; we treat each message and data point as a piece of a puzzle and find a way to put these pieces together.[1]

In the survey, the average rating for 161 respondents was 5.57, between "tend to agree" and "strongly agree." Only two registered any disagreement.

Disclaimer

Attractive as it is, claim 7 runs into several serious difficulties. The assembly-line metaphor fits orderly situations in which you only have to handle explicit knowledge. Once you have defined all the data and described the causes, you can set up filtering rules and do the sorting. All that's left is to connect the dots.

The assembly-line metaphor falls apart in ambiguous settings where you aren't sure what to count as a dot. It isn't that claim 7 is wrong. Like all the other claims, it tells only part of the story. It leaves out what counts as a dot, where the dots come from, how you know that you have finished, and how you suspect that a story is wrong.

What counts as a dot?[2]

In hindsight, when we make sense of a situation it looks as if we just connected the dots. But what counts as a dot? Are these two smudges part of the same dot? Is that smudge even a dot at all?

Once the non-dots are removed, the task of connecting the remaining dots is much easier. Our expertise is as much about *recognizing* legitimate dots as about connecting them. Similarly, the metaphor of sensemaking as putting together the pieces of a puzzle is also misleading. When we assemble a puzzle, we have seen the box cover and know what we are trying to create. The job is much more difficult if we mix five puzzles together, and don't see the cover picture for any of the boxes. Or if we try to solve a puzzle that doesn't have a scene (such as an all-black puzzle) or a shape (such as a puzzle with ragged edges instead of smooth ones). The metaphors of connecting the dots and assembling the puzzle don't do justice to the need to notice and identify the cues in the first place.

Computer programmers define the data elements in advance and then carefully feed data into their machines, being careful to conform to the protocols the machine is expecting. That doesn't sound like the way people get data.

Years ago, when I did my research on firefighters, I noticed that the firefighters and I were seeing different scenes. Looking at a burning building, I was watching the flames. The commander, looking at the same building, was gauging how the wind was spreading the fire—in what direction and how fast. He was also studying the smoke because the color of the smoke yielded clues about what was burning (wood or chemicals) and whether the water sprayed on the fire was having any effect.

In a 1919 book titled *Fighting the Flying Circus*, Eddie Rickenbacker, America's World War I flying ace, described one of his early flights over Germany. When the group returned to their airport, the flight leader asked Rickenbacker what he had seen. Rickenbacker said it had gone very smoothly—he hadn't seen any other airplanes except the ones in their formation. Rickenbacker had seen some German anti-aircraft batteries and found it amusing to watch them waste their ammunition. The flight leader corrected him. A formation of five British Spads had passed under them just before they crossed into enemy lines and another formation of five Spads went by them soon after, neither more than 500 yards away. Plus four German Albatros airplanes two miles ahead of them when they turned back, and another German airplane, a two-seater, later on. Then the flight leader walked Rickenbacker over to his airplane and showed him the shrapnel holes from the German anti-aircraft fire that Rickenbacker found so amusing, including one piece of shrapnel that passed through both wings a foot from his body. Rickenbacker hadn't realized that his plane had been hit. That was the beginning of his real education. The data were there—to the flight leader, but not to Rickenbacker. To survive, pilots had to learn quickly where to look and what to look for.

The people who subscribe to this claim that you begin with the data also buy into claim 2a about logic and analysis we covered in chapter 6. They want to see the objective evidence and not any anecdotes. However, we need stories to put the data into perspective. Without stories, the data don't mean very much. Here is a passage from a textbook on microeconomics by Silberberg and Suen showing how we use our ideas about what is going on to pick and choose which facts to consider.

Example 12.1: Which dots?[3]   What is a theory, and what is the role of theories in scientific explanations? It is sometimes suggested that the way to attack any given problem is to "let the facts speak for themselves." Suppose one wanted to discover why motorists were suddenly waiting in line for gasoline, often for several hours, during the winter of 1973–74, the so-called energy crisis. The first thing to do, perhaps, is to get some facts. Where will the facts be found? Perhaps the government documents section of the local university library will be useful. A problem arises. Once there, one suddenly finds oneself up to the ears in facts. The data collected by the United States federal government and other governments fills many rooms. Where should one start? Consider, perhaps, the following list of "facts."

1. Many oil-producing nations embargoed oil to the United States in the fall of 1973.

2. The gross national product of the United States rose, in money terms, by 11.5 percent from 1972 to 1973.

3. Gasoline and heating oils are petroleum distillates.

4. Wage and price controls were in effect on the oil industry during that time.

5. The average miles per gallon achieved by cars in the United States has decreased due to the growing use of antipollution devices.

6. The price of food rose dramatically in this period.

7. Rents rose during this time, but not as fast as food prices.

8. The price of tomatoes in Lincoln, Nebraska was 39 cents per pound on September 14, 1968.

9. Most of the pollution in the New York metropolitan area is due to fixed, rather than moving, sources.

The list goes on indefinitely. There are an infinite number of facts. Most readers will have already decided that, e.g., fact 8 is irrelevant, and most of the infinite number of facts that might have been listed are irrelevant. But why? How was this conclusion reached? Can fact 8 be rejected solely on the basis that most of us would agree to reject it? What about facts 4 and 5? There may be less than perfect agreement on the relevance of some of these facts.

Facts, by themselves, do not explain events. Without some set of axioms, propositions, etc., about the nature of the phenomena we are seeking to explain, we simply have no way in which to sort out the relevant from the irrelevant facts. The reader who summarily dismissed fact 8 as irrelevant to the events occurring during the energy crisis must have had some behavioral relations in mind that suggested that the tomato market in 1968 was not a determining factor. Such a notion, however rudimentary, is the start of a "theory."

I used to assume that claim 7 was correct before my colleagues and I started to work with skilled meteorologists. In one interview, a weather forecaster described how his computer program identified a strong weather front but he thought a second, smaller front was moving in, just behind the large one. He knew that the computer didn't plot data at a detailed enough level to pick up this second front so he hand-plotted the data in just the small area where he thought he would find it—and there it was.

In judging what counts as a dot we also have to figure out how much detail the dot has to have. It depends on what we are looking for. If forecasters work at too fine a level they'll miss the large patterns. If they choose too coarse a level they'll miss the small fronts and minor anomalies. There is no "right" level and no standard operating definition of a "dot."

If there is no right level, the job of designing displays for forecasters becomes tougher. In one case the developers tried to make it easy for the forecasters to see the patterns and so they smoothed out all the irregularities. However, skilled forecasters need to see these irregularities, because they signal areas where the weather is unsettled. And these are the areas that the forecasters want to watch during their shift because they create a lot of the unpredictability. The problem of the day often emerges from the unsettled regions. The display designers inadvertently smoothed out a critical cue.[4]

It was the less-skilled meteorologists who settled for the official data points shown in the smoothed display. The experienced forecasters decided for themselves what they needed to see. They kept looking until they felt that they understood how the atmospheric forces were playing out. They knew which dots were relevant to the different possible stories.

The data elements that we think are dots may turn out to be irrelevant. The next incident illustrates how we only understand the real dots after we get the better story.

Example 12.2: The helicopter malformation   During an Army training exercise, two helicopters collided. Everyone in one helicopter died; everyone in the other helicopter survived. Our informant, Captain B, was in the headquarters monitoring the radios when the reports came in. (See figure 12.2.)

Because this was a night mission, Captain B suspected that flying with night-vision goggles led one helicopter to drift into the other. Then he found out that weather had been bad, and thought that perhaps the pilots flew into some clouds at night. But a later report showed that weather wasn't a factor, because they were flying below the clouds when the accident happened.

Next he learned that there was a sling on one of the crashed helicopters (helicopter 1 in figure 12.2); it had been in the rear of the formation. He also heard that the helicopter group changed course to an alternate route. Based on these cues, Captain B believed that the last

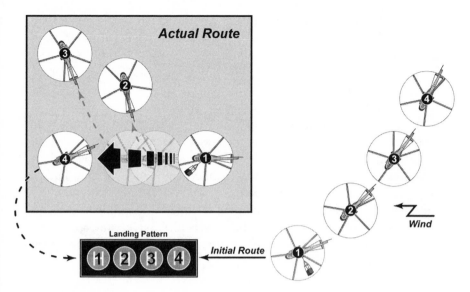

Figure 12.2
The helicopter crash.

helicopter, due to the sling, couldn't slow down properly. The weight of the sling made it harder to stop, to avoid running into another aircraft.

Captain B was puzzled why the sling-loaded helicopter would have been in trail. The standard procedure is to put a sling-loaded helicopter in the lead because it's less agile than the others. Captain B was also puzzled about the route. The entire formation had to make a big U-turn before landing and he wondered if this U-turn might have been a factor.

Eventually Captain B got the real story. The initial route was to fly straight in, with the sling-loaded helicopter in the lead. They needed to deliver the sling load to the far end of the landing zone. But because of a shift in the wind direction the pilots had changed the landing approach to do a U-turn. Aircraft have more control landing into the wind than with the wind at their back. When they shifted the landing approach, they moved the sling load to the back of the formation so that they could still drop off the load in the far end of the landing zone.

The group never had a chance to rehearse the alternate route because of time pressure; the shift in wind direction caught them by surprise. The lead helicopter (number 4 in the diagram) came in fast and then rapidly slowed down in order to make the U-turn. The next two helicopters (numbers 2 and 3 in the figure) bailed out because they couldn't make a safe turn at those speeds and they were afraid to slow down because the sling-loaded helicopter was right behind them. The sling-loaded helicopter couldn't slow down and collided with the lead helicopter.

We can see how Captain B built his story. He started with a single clue, the fact that the accident took place at night. Eventually, he learned the real story. He knew it was the real story because it explained why the sling load was in the back and why they hadn't practiced the new formation. The real story had nothing to do with flying at night. Captain B had dismissed weather as a condition because they were flying below the clouds, but weather really was one of the causes of the accident because of the shift in wind. As the story changed, the dots changed too.

Where do the dots come from?

The notion of connecting dots, deriving inferences from data, conjures up an image of a children's puzzle that displays all the dots; our task is simply to find the right connections in order to see the picture. These puzzles don't have any shadows to complicate the task. But when we make sense of events we usually are seeing only some of the dots that complete the picture, trying to remember others, discarding "wannabe" dots, and adjusting dots that have gotten distorted.

Bill Duggan's 2007 book *Strategic Intuition* is about the way people notice connections. For instance, Duggan explains how Bill Gates and Paul Allen made their initial discoveries. In high school they had programmed BASIC (a simple computer language) onto a PDP-8 mini-computer. Later they noted that the new Intel 8082 chip had enough capacity to contain their BASIC program. Gates and Allen contacted the major computer companies to see if they would be interested in having a BASIC program for this new 8082 chip. None of them expressed any interest. Then, in December 1974, as Allen was walking over to Gates's dorm room at Harvard, he saw the cover of a issue of the magazine *Popular Mechanics* which featured the new Altair personal computer. The Altair, according to *Popular Mechanics*, would run on the 8082 chip and would cost only $397. Instantly, all the connections fell into place. Gates and Allen contacted the manufacturer of the Altair, arranged a demonstration, and were soon on their way toward starting Microsoft. They had a new vision of a software company for microcomputers. Because of their backgrounds, the relevant dots jumped out at them, but not to others. The immediate dot was the cover of *Popular Mechanics*, which linked to their BASIC program and to their enthusiasm for the 8082 chip. Others looked at the magazine and thought that the price of personal computers was coming down. They didn't know about the other dots. You can't connect dots that you aren't able to see.[5]

In a similar fashion, Nate Self (2008) described the connection he noticed as a Ranger captain leading a 13-man team to rescue a soldier in the battle of Takur Ghar in Afghanistan. After his helicopter was shot down, his team was about to be overrun by al-Qaeda fighters. The soldiers were pinned down and getting hit with mortar fire. Then, in the midst of the battle, Self heard a radio transmission with the call sign "Wildfire." He remembered that "Wildfire" was really a UAV (Unmanned Aerial Vehicle), a drone that was controlled by someone who might be in Kuwait, or in Saudi Arabia, or even in Missouri. It didn't matter where the operator was. What mattered was that the Predator UAV was flying overhead to collect imagery of the situation. And Nate remembered from a classified briefing that some UAVs had been equipped with Hellfire missiles. If this was one of those UAVs, then perhaps there was a way out. He quickly checked, found out that his hunch was right, and arranged to use the UAV's missiles against their attackers. Some of the other soldiers involved in this mission knew about armored UAVs, but only Nate Self made the connection that saved his unit. The only explicit dot was the word 'Wildfire'.

Sensemaking seems to depend heavily on seeing such connections. We can't find the connections by exhaustively linking all the elements because we don't know in advance which are the relevant elements, the relevant dots. And we would run into an exponential explosion if we connected every combination of dots. That's where the intuition comes in—to help us recognize which dots are worth connecting and to remind us which dots we need to complete the picture.

When are we finished making sense of a situation?
Claim 7 describes a mindless process of churning out more and more inferences. The number of data combinations grows exponentially as we add more data elements. Surely we aren't randomly connecting data elements and then connecting the connections, expecting to emerge with some insights? We may be able to generate valuable ideas

that way, but the ideas will be buried in useless inferences. Then we will have the enormous task of sorting through all the inferences to try to find ones that matter. No, this bottom-up account of random inferencing doesn't make sense. As Bill Clinton was fond of saying, "That dog won't hunt." Instead, we are directing the way we form connections, just as we're actively searching for data. We are trying to explain what is going on around us. We are looking for the stories. When we arrive at a plausible story, we're done.

Example 12.3: Tom's father   My colleague Tom Miller faced a medical emergency a few years ago. His father was brought to a hospital and then wheeled into surgery to have a pacemaker installed. Tom and his family were very worried about the father's condition. But they couldn't find anyone to spend time with them to explain the problem. They just knew that the father was short of breath. They knew he also had mild congestive heart failure, cardiac arrhythmia, an enlarged heart, mildly high blood pressure, and mild emphysema. He was apparently suffering from fluid buildup in his lungs, and he had had a heart valve replaced 10 years earlier. In short, he sounded like a wreck.

In the hospital, Tom tracked down one of the physicians who was treating his father and asked "Just what is going on here?" The physician tried to deflect Tom, saying that they had installed a pacemaker and he could look up the process on the Web. That might have stopped many people, but not Tom (who at that time headed the Cognitive Systems Engineering Group in our division). "That man is in the intensive care unit recovering from heart surgery," Tom said. "I need you to explain how he got there."

The physician relented. He explained that the heart valve issue was unrelated to the pacemaker. The enlarged heart wasn't very serious itself—except that the place of the enlargement was where some of the nerves connected to the heart to keep it working at a steady beat. Because of the enlargement, the nerves got stretched a little. And that's why the father had cardiac arrhythmia. The heart was fine. But the nerves got stretched. Because they weren't keeping the heart beating as steadily as it should, it wasn't getting the job done to keep fluid levels down in the lungs. That's where the congestive heart failure came in. The pacemaker would take care of that plus they were going to have Tom's father cut down on his fluid intake just to be sure. The mildly high blood pressure wasn't really a problem, nor was the mild emphysema. Neither of these conditions helped any, but they weren't part of this story. And that's what Tom and his family were looking for: a story—an explanation of "why that man got to be in intensive care recovering from heart surgery."

This incident shows how we look for plausible stories that explain how different causes have led up to the situation we are facing. I don't see that in the assembly-line model of drawing inferences from data.

We also engage in sensemaking to question whether a story is plausible. Tom Miller was satisfied when the physician provided a story that accounted for all the data. Other times we don't trust the official story.

What if the stories are wrong?

Claim 7 shows people endlessly generating inferences from data. It doesn't reflect our worries that the data and the stories might be wrong. If you're just looking for connections, then any connections will do. Yet an important aspect of sensemaking is sorting out which dots to believe. A lot of sensemaking is double-checking whether the data are accurate. It's also about judging whether the story rings true.

Example 12.4: The ominous airplanes   After the 9/11 attack, the United States went on high alert. We didn't know what was coming next. In particular, the military and the aviation communities strongly accelerated their scrutiny of potential threats. Then they picked up a frightening sign. After planes were permitted to resume flying, reports came in about small planes circling nuclear power plants all around the country. Our laws prohibit planes from doing this, and the intelligence community worried that these planes were conducting surveillance and getting ready for a different type of attack. But that just didn't sound right to the military officer who was in charge of sorting these reports out. He had read some al-Qaeda manuals that clearly advised terrorists not to draw attention to themselves or unnecessarily break any laws. So the reports about small planes didn't fit the al-Qaeda doctrine. Plus, it was too obvious. One would have to be really stupid to be planning an attack by drawing circles in the sky for anyone to see. Furthermore, some of the pilots had been questioned after landing. They had no idea that they were breaking the law, and they had no terrorist connections.

The officer was an amateur pilot He remembered that his flight instructors had told him to look for some prominent and unmistakable landmark should he ever get lost—something that wouldn't move, such as a solitary mountain, a football stadium, or a nuclear power plant. Was it possible that these pilots simply had gotten lost and were trying to find their way home?

The officer got out a map and plotted all the cases in which small planes had been spotted near nuclear plants. Then he plotted small airfields—the kinds that new pilots might be taking off from. In every case, the nuclear plants being "buzzed" were located between two small airfields. A pilot who was just starting to take solo flights, from one field to another, and was just a bit nervous about being on the right route, that kind of pilot might well find a nuclear plant irresistible.

In this example, the military intelligence officer doubted the obvious story about brazen terrorists. He had a better story—one that accounted for all the same facts plus some additional ones. And he was right.

In the next example, a new pilot could have used a nearby nuclear power plant after he got lost on his first solo flight.

Example 12.5: The misdirectional gyrocompass[6] An amateur pilot, Dave Malek, made a plan for his first solo flight, which was to last 45 minutes. He determined the heading, the course, and the airspeed, set way points for each leg of the trip, looked at a map of the destination airport, and so forth. He performed his pre-flight routine, which included calibrating the altimeter and the directional gyrocompass. He was familiar with the terrain in the area around the airport from which he took off.

After he got airborne, Malek noticed that some of the visual markers did not match the map, but he interpreted these types of discrepancies as the inevitable ways that maps become obsolete. For example, one village extended right up to a small airport—obviously the village had added a new subdivision in the past few years.

Other discrepancies bothered him more. He was seeing trees where he expected farms, and he couldn't explain that discrepancy away because the terrain was hilly—it had never been farmland. About 30 minutes into the flight, he began to feel that he was not on his flight path. However, he didn't have any clear landmarks, because all the small towns and villages looked similar.

Malek's hardest judgment was to determine if he was still on his course or if his intuition was right and he was off course. His instruments had been telling him he was on course. Nevertheless, he decided to check his directional gyro against the magnetic compass. This incident occurred in the late 1990s and Malek's airplane didn't have a GPS system. He hadn't looked at the magnetic compass earlier because it would normally give the same information as the directional gyro. Also, the compass was original equipment on the airplane, dating back a few decades, and the display had yellowed over the years. The black-on-white print was now black on yellow and hard to make out without closely squinting at it for several seconds.

Malek made sure there were no other airplanes near him and then compared the two instruments. He discovered that his directional gyro was about 20–30 degrees off. That shifted him into a different mode of sensemaking. Instead of trying to explain away small discrepancies, he now had to figure out where he was. He had to start over and establish his location. He had a rough idea of where he was because he had been heading south, drifting farther east than he had planned. He knew that if he kept flying south he would soon cross the Ohio River, which would be a clear landmark that he could use to discover his true position.

Once he reached the Ohio River, Malek could see that the configuration of factories on the river did not match the map at his planned crossing point. He flew up the river for a short distance and came to a bend (another good anchor) that had power plants and factories with large smokestacks—still more good anchors. On the map, the high-tension lines intersected with a railroad crossing, and sure enough, that is what he saw on the ground. He then followed the power lines directly to his destination airport.

In the story of ominous airplanes, example 12.4, the data were all accurate but the implications didn't ring true. In example 12.5, Dave Malek had to struggle with bad data when his directional gyro failed. His story—his belief about his location—kept running into discrepancies, but he explained them away. Eventually, he reached a point where the deviation was too great and where the topography was too discrepant from his expectancies.

The assembly-line model of generating inferences doesn't capture the desperation we feel when we get lost and have to sort out where we are, where we want to be, and what data we can still trust.

Dave Malek recovered so well because when he began to doubt the data he devised a test of his navigation equipment. But sometimes people aren't able to recover in time.

In 1988, the USS *Vincennes* shot down an Iranian Airbus on a routine commercial flight. Captain Will Rogers, the commander of the *Vincennes*, had to contend with two pieces of erroneous data. He had been given a mistaken report that the airplane taking off from Bandar Abbas airport in Iran seemed to be a military rather than a commercial airplane. Rogers was also told that the airplane was decreasing in altitude as it approached him, although other crew members correctly argued that it was gaining altitude, as would be expected for a commercial airliner. The entire episode took less than seven minutes, and by the time Rogers heard that the airplane was descending he had less than a minute left to decide whether to fire a missile at it or let it attack his ship. Unlike Dave Malek, Captain Rogers didn't have any quick and easy way to detect or correct either of these errors, and he proceeded to shoot down the Airbus.

When we question the original story, we usually want to hold onto the first story and explain away the discrepancies. The next example is an interview from a study of how nurses in a neonatal intensive-care unit spot early signs of sepsis.[7] It shows the gradual realization that the original story is wrong, and that a baby's life is in jeopardy.

Example 12.6: Watching a baby develop an infection   "This baby was my primary; I knew the baby and I knew how she normally acted. Generally she was very alert, was on feedings, and was off IVs. Her lab work on that particular morning looked very good. She was progressing extremely well and hadn't had any of the setbacks that many other preemies have. She typically had numerous apnea [suspension of breathing] episodes and then bradys [bradycardia episodes—spells of low heart rate], but we could easily stimulate her to end these episodes. At 2:30, her mother came in to hold her and I noticed that she wasn't as responsive to her mother as she normally was. She just lay there and half looked at her. When we lifted her arm it fell right back down in the bed and she had no resistance to being handled. This limpness was very unusual for her.

"On this day, the monitors were fine, her blood pressure was fine, and she was tolerating feedings all right. There was nothing to suggest that anything was wrong except that I knew the baby and I knew that she wasn't acting normally. At about 3:30 her color started to change. Her skin was not its normal pink color and she had blue rings around her eyes. During the shift she seemed to get progressively grayer.

"Then at about 4:00, when I was turning her feeding back on, I found that there was a large residual of food in her stomach. I thought maybe it was because her mother had been holding her and the feeding just hadn't settled as well.

"By 5:00 I had a baby who was gray and had blue rings around her eyes. She was having more and more episodes of apnea and bradys; normally she wouldn't have any bradys when her mom was holding her. Still, her blood pressure hung in there. Her temperature was just a little bit cooler than normal. Her abdomen was a little more distended, up 2 cm from early in the morning, and there was more residual in her stomach. This was a baby who usually had no residual and all of a sudden she had 5–9 cc. We gave her suppositories thinking maybe she just needed to stool. Although having a stool reduced her girth, she still looked gray and was continuing to have more apnea and bradys. At this point, her blood gas wasn't good so we hooked her back up to the oxygen.

On the doctor's orders, we repeated the lab work. The results confirmed that this baby had an infection, but we knew she was in trouble even before we got the lab work back."

Notice the similarity between this incident and example 12.5, the misdirectional gyrocompass. Both people started with a story they felt comfortable with. Both of them noticed some anomalies but explained these away and held onto the original story. The anomalies kept adding up in both cases, and the decision makers discarded their original story because they had a better one.

Example 12.7 recounts another instance in which a watchstander decided not to believe the data. As a result, he prevented a nuclear war.

Example 12.7: False alarm[8] On September 26, 1983, during a tense period in the Cold War, the alarm bells went off at the secret bunker that monitored the satellites that provided the Soviet Union with its early warning system. The bunker received a signal from one of its reconnaissance satellites that the United States had launched five missiles at Russia. Three weeks earlier, the Soviets had shot down a Korean airliner that had blundered into their airspace. NATO had just begun military exercises. It looked like the beginning of World War III.

The duty officer in charge of the bunker, Lieutenant Colonel Stanislav Petrov, had a clear responsibility to alert his superiors. That's why the USSR had set up the early warning system. That's what the bunker was intended for—sounding the early warning so that Russia could retaliate. The flashing electronic maps in the bunker marked the American missiles coming toward him.

But Petrov hesitated. He had a funny feeling in his gut that this was a false alarm. It didn't make sense for the Americans to fire only five ballistic missiles. If they were truly launching a pre-emptive nuclear strike, they would be using many, many ICBMs to prevent the Soviets from re-attacking. Five missiles weren't enough to do anything but provoke the Soviet Union to counter-attack. "I didn't want to make a mistake," Petrov recalled. "I made a decision, and that was it." Petrov also didn't trust the Soviet early-warning system. Therefore, he described the signal to his superiors as a false alarm, hoping that he was right.

Subsequently, the Soviets figured out that the satellite had picked up the sun's reflection off the cloud tops and had interpreted it as a missile launch.

These incidents illustrate how people question the frame despite data that appear convincing. Dave Malek, the nurse in the NICU example, and Lieutenant Colonel Petrov each made sense of events by rejecting the obvious story. In some ways their judgments weren't any different from those of the officer at Pearl Harbor who dismissed the message of unknown airplanes spotted on radar. The mere act of explaining away data doesn't merit our applause. I think the difference from the Pearl Harbor example is that Malek, the NICU nurse, and Petrov, as well as the intelligence officer who explained away the ominous airplanes that circled nuclear power plants after the 9/11 attack, all worried that they were wrong, and worried about the consequences of a mistake. They worried about the quality of the data.

Unintended consequences
If we enforce claim 7, illustrated by the assembly-line model in figure 12.1, we'll filter the data to make sure that decision makers only get pre-digested materials and highly abstracted analyses of the data. However, we use our expertise to see patterns in the data. If we disconnect people from the data, we disconnect them from their expertise.

The assembly-line model takes information search out of the hands of the decision makers. Yet that's another aspect of their skill. Experienced decision makers know how to search for data. Skilled weather forecasters know where to look more closely, and where to conduct a fine-grained analysis. If you hand them a computer-generated forecast, you have taken away their chance to direct the search.

The assembly-line model makes it hard for decision makers to build their own mental models, because they are forced to depend on the dots and the analyses that people at lower levels, with less expertise, are using. Yet experts have to build their own mental models. The skilled forecasters we interviewed wanted to look at the weather data from the past six hours to get a sense of what was happening before they consulted with others or reviewed the computer-generated material. It was the mediocre forecasters who grabbed the computer sheets and worked from there. These mediocre forecasters are comfortable with claim 7.

The assembly-line model obscures the context in which data were collected. This loss of context may not matter to mediocre workers, but experts appreciate the implications of data collection methods. They know that each method has its own limits. Meteorologists know the limits of instruments for sampling wind direction and velocity, temperature, humidity, and so forth. They can take these limits into account. If you give weather forecasters a summary sheet, they can't sort out where the forecast came from.

The assembly-line model builds from data elements—dots—that have been collected. But what about events that didn't happen? These can also be informative. Experts appreciate the significance of these negative cues. But when they are given a set of recommendations and summaries, skilled decision makers don't have any way to notice what didn't happen.

Therefore, the assembly-line model, and claim 7, will disconnect skilled decision makers from their expertise. It will force them to depend on subordinates who have less experience than they do.

Replacement

We aren't passively waiting for data, as claim 7 suggests. We are also defining what counts as data. We are questioning stories that don't seem plausible. We are having insights about ways to connect different types of dots. That's different from drawing more and more inferences in the hope that eventually it will all fall into place. It depends on taking an active rather than a passive stance.

Claim 7 treats people as passively receiving information, rather than actively inspecting situations, probing for features, and testing speculations. The weather forecasters who complained about the smoothed displays wanted to have a picture where they could scan for anomalies, regions where the temperatures were jumbled up, where the wind directions weren't uniform. Skilled hikers aren't just locating coordinates on a map. They are feeling the topography of the land—noting ridge lines they can follow, steep slopes to avoid, distinctive hills they can use as landmarks—and open regions where they'll be able to see those features. If they worked for the forest service, they might be assessing changes in the vegetation or potential for fires in heavy underbrush. The notion that data somehow appear doesn't do justice to these kinds of active searches for meaningful cues.[9] Sensemaking isn't just receiving data and inferences. It also involves knowing how to shake the system to find what you're looking for. Consider the case of Captain Joseph Rochefort, a naval officer working in Pearl Harbor during World War II.

Example 12.8: Japan's next target During World War II, the Japanese followed their attack on Pearl Harbor with additional victories, such as in the Battle of the Coral Sea. Yamamoto, their top naval commander, was obviously getting ready for yet another attack, but the Americans didn't know where it might come. Perhaps Yamamoto would re-attack Pearl Harbor; perhaps he would even attack California.

As Japanese coded messages increased in volume, indicating that an attack was imminent, a US Navy cryptologist had a hunch. He was Captain Joseph Rochefort, an intelligence officer and a cryptologist who had also trained in the Japanese language. Rochefort was the officer in charge at Station HYPO, the cryptoanalysis unit in Pearl Harbor. He and others noticed that more and more of the Japanese messages they could partially decode used the phrase "AF," which seemed to be the code for the next US target. But where was AF?

Rochefort studied a map of the Pacific and decided that if he was Yamamoto, getting ready to stage raids on Pearl Harbor or on the western United States, he would go after Midway Atoll. To test his theory, Rochefort arranged for the small unit on Midway to send a radio message describing a malfunction in their water-distilling plant. Two days later a Japanese cable said that AF was running low on drinking water and directed the AF force to bring additional water desalinization equipment. When Rochefort read this intercepted message, he knew Japan's next target.

Admiral Nimitz then reinforced Midway and sent three aircraft carriers to the island. Nimitz also knew the Japanese order of battle; now that "AF" had been clarified all the previous messages about AF came into focus. Instead of an easy victory over a small garrison in an isolated island, the Japanese lost four of their six primary aircraft carriers and more than 250 airplanes. In one day at Midway they lost twice as many skilled pilots as their training programs produced in a year. The war in the Pacific theatre turned completely around.[10]

Rochefort wasn't waiting for the data to come to him. He wasn't seeing his job as simply deciphering the Japanese messages. His job was to figure out what Yamamoto was planning.

Example 12.9: Refusing to take any scrap   In a factory that produced molds, the workers knew that excessive scrap pushed their expenses up and made them less competitive. The industry standard was about 6 percent, and, at their worst, this factory had a scrap rate of 14 percent. The workers hadn't worried about their scrap rate until the owner lost the company to the bank and the workers took it over. They had to become profitable or they would lose their jobs. They succeeded in bringing their scrap rate down to 6 percent.

The workers wondered if they could get the scrap rate even lower. They questioned what was behind this 6 percent figure and discovered that only a few of the molds accounted for most of the scrap. By redesigning these mold patterns, or by charging more for them, they could become more competitive for the rest of their products. They reduced their scrap rate dramatically, from 6 percent to 2.9 percent. And this reduction took place because they didn't take the scrap rate as firm data; instead they pushed further to investigate where that number came from.[11]

Examples 12.8 and 12.9 illustrate why sensemaking is more than just drawing inferences from the data. The next example contrasts an active stance with a passive one.

Example 12.10: The reconnaissance team   During a Marine Corps exercise, a reconnaissance team leader and his team were positioned overlooking a vast area of desert. The fire team leader, a young sergeant, viewed the desert terrain carefully. He saw an enemy tank move along a trail and then take cover. He sent this situation report to headquarters.

A brigadier general, experienced in desert-mechanized operations, had arranged to go into the field as an observer. He also spotted the enemy tank. He knew, however, that tanks usually don't operate alone. Therefore, based on the position of that one tank, he focused on likely over-watch positions and found another tank. Based on the section's position and his understanding of the terrain, he looked at likely positions for another section and found a well-camouflaged second section. He repeated this process to locate the remaining elements of a tank company that was well camouflaged and blocking a choke point in the desert. The size and position of the force suggested that there might be other elements in the area, and he soon spotted an otherwise superbly camouflaged logistics command post.

In example 12.10, the young sergeant was studying the terrain and reporting on what he saw. The general was speculating about what was out there, and was looking for things that he expected.

We make sense of cues and data by fitting them into frames such as stories. An interesting cue, such as the increased use of "AF" in Japanese messages, may remind us of a frame—a preparation for the next attack. The reverse also happens. The frames we have learned guide our attention and shape what we notice. If we go for a walk in a park, a landscape architect is aware of the way the paths provide interesting views, a tree specialist is distinguishing the different species and how well each is growing, and a maintenance worker is getting a feel for whether heavy lawnmowing equipment might get stuck in the muddy ground. Same park, three different perspectives, three different experiences.[12]

We make sense of cues and data by organizing them into frames such as stories, scripts, maps, and strategies. But the reverse also happens—our frames determine what we use as data. Both processes happen simultaneously, as shown in figure 12.3. This reciprocal action between data and frames is the core of sensemaking. That's the replacement for claim 7. *We make sense of data elements by fitting them*

Figure 12.3
The data/frame model of sensemaking (the process of fitting data into a frame and fitting a frame around the data).

into frames such as stories, but the reverse also happens—our frames determine what we use as data.

The assembly-line model in claim 7 is an information processing account that is consistent with conventional computer programs. If our minds worked the way digital computers do, then the assembly-line model would have more force. Do our minds work like computers?

Why claim 7 matters

It matters because claim 7 (that to make sense of a situation we draw inferences from the data) oversimplifies and distorts the nature of sensemaking in complex settings.

It matters because the claim that all we do is draw inferences from the data or connect the dots trivializes what we do. It ignores how in complex settings we have to decide what is a dot. It ignores the tacit knowledge that it takes to figure out which dots to connect.

It matters because claim 7 can disconnect experts from the data patterns they have learned to detect. People who believe claim 7 are designing decision aids for us, merrily smoothing away the areas of turbulence that we use as landmarks.

13 Do We Think Like Computers?

Ever since the development of digital computers, we have been told that our minds work like computers. Both are machines, both think, both can perform complex operations. It's a perfect match. And the claims that I have surveyed seem to fit into the computer metaphor for thinking.

However, on closer inspection the computer metaphor is misleading. Computers work in the world of clarity rather than the world of shadows. They perform best in well-ordered situations, with explicit knowledge, and clear goals. They struggle with ambiguity. When you enter a data point into a computer program, you don't write "in the vicinity of three or four, but maybe higher." The computer expects a fixed number or range.

Computers solve problems by establishing massive and comprehensive problem spaces and then finding ways to search those spaces. People solve problems by matching them to familiar patterns and spotting leverage points that have been successful in similar situations, forming connections based on previous experience, and working from there to construct a solution. We don't search problem spaces.

Therefore, the computer metaphor for thinking may be part of the trouble with the claims we have been examining. The limitations of machine intelligence mirror the limitations of the claims listed in chapter 1.

Connecting the dots

Chapter 12 explained why sensemaking is more than connecting the dots, but compare the ways computers and people connect a set of dots.

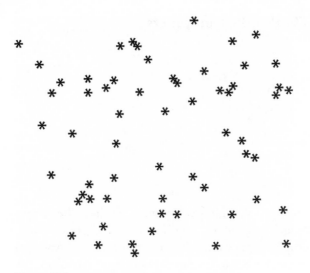

Figure 13.1
The Traveling Salesman Problem.

A leading research paradigm for connecting the dots (we're dealing with actual dots here) is the *traveling salesman problem*. The problem is to find the shortest path that passes through a set of points and returns to the origin. This task is analogous to a salesman traveling to different cities and eventually returning home. Such a salesman would want to find an efficient route so as not to waste too much time driving.

People who are shown a list of cities that a salesman has to visit can easily and quickly find an efficient path. Figure 13.1 shows a set of dots or cities. What route would you plan? Probably it will be close to the route in figure 13.2. This isn't hard, is it?

In fact, figure 13.2. was drawn by a computer that kept calculating and calculating to come up with shorter routes. After 1,500 generations, the computer tour has approximated a reasonable solution similar to what a person would produce. So computers can learn and can improve. But the way they improve is by calculating every permutation and evaluating each result against clearly defined criteria. The computer program that produced figure 13.2 after 1,500 trials actually started with figure 13.3.[1]

No human would start with the random connections shown in figure 13.3. Even infants show more perspective than this.

Some might want to preserve the computer metaphor for thinking and argue that people are just doing the same calculations in their

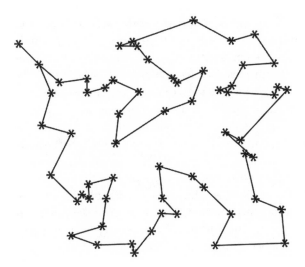

Figure 13.2
A solution to the Traveling Salesman Problem.

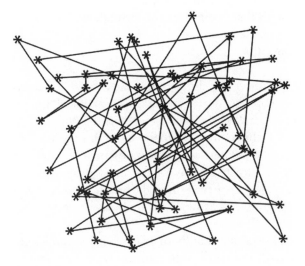

Figure 13.3
An initial computer approach to the Traveling Salesman Problem.

heads. That seems extremely unlikely, but we don't have to engage in speculation to show that such an argument won't work. If you double the number of cities the salesman has to visit, the computer effort goes up exponentially. Each extra city doubles the amount of calculations, and soon you have exceeded the capacity of even the largest and fastest machines. If a computer generated 1,000 solutions per second it would take only 3 minutes to solve a ten-node problem, but that same computer would take almost 4 million years to solve a twenty-node problem (MacGregor et al. 2000).

In contrast, when working with humans, if we double the number of cities in a traveling salesman problem, humans just double the amount of time they take to find a good solution. That's because we don't calculate the answer. We handle the additional complexity by using perceptual skills to *see* the answer. Our minds don't work like digital computers.[2, 3]

There are many tasks that computers can perform better than we can. They can calculate more quickly and accurately. They can search more vigilantly. They can manage more complex simulations. Nevertheless, there are some skills that computers still struggle with.

The magic of human cognition

In 2005 I worked on a project for the Defense Advanced Research Projects Agency to develop the next generation of artificial intelligence (AI). The project was called BICA, which stood for Biologically Inspired Computational Architectures. Its goal was to draw on recent advances in the biology of thinking to radically advance the state of the AI world. The project attracted many of the most prominent AI researchers in the country. My team and I had the job of keeping them honest by designing a "cognitive decathlon" for their new architectures to perform.[4]

Going into the project, I expected that these researchers would exude a confident attitude that AI, the wave of the future, would be able to match and surpass all feats of human cognition. After all, these were the leaders who had already advanced the field of AI during the past decades.

Instead, what I found was modesty and caution. The AI researchers introduced the phrase "the magic of human cognition" to describe all the things that people can do and machines cannot. The AI researchers weren't just voicing opinions. They had spent thousands of hours trying to make their machines smarter and in the process had gained respect for human intelligence and expertise. They shook their heads at all the talents people have and take for granted, talents that resist the best efforts of AI programmers.

My team showed them a standard Dungeons and Dragons–like computer game and also a pencil-and-paper decision exercise that we were thinking of using in our cognitive decathlon. "No way," they protested. "We're nowhere near being able to build machines to perform those tasks. Not now, not in five years, not in any future we can see."

They said it would be impossible to simulate a competent adult. Maybe they might do something interesting if we lowered the bar to the level of a two-year-old, but even that would be a stretch, and language would have to be excluded.

My colleague Don Cox suggested renaming the program TICA (Toddler-Inspired Cognitive Architecture), and for a few months everyone used that new acronym.

I think about the BICA program whenever I hear people who are not AI researchers blithely explain that computers will someday take over all kinds of complex decision tasks. The real AI researchers appreciate how important and difficult it is to describe tacit knowledge, and to design systems that can operate in the shadows as well as under bright lights.

Please don't take these comments as criticisms of machine intelligence. Just because a task has clear goals and reasonably well-ordered situations doesn't mean it is easy. Chess is very difficult to master. Computers approach chess through brute-force methods and lots of "crunching" of different lines of play. In contrast, chess grandmasters rely on the patterns they have learned during many years of practice and playing to recognize good moves.

The defeat of the Russian chess champion Garry Kasparov by IBM's Deep Blue program illustrates another human ability that is difficult for machine intelligence: the ability to diagnose problems. I noted in chapter 11 that cybernetic systems respond to feedback by increasing or decreasing their efforts. They don't try to diagnose why an action isn't successful. Deep Blue, for all its computational power, didn't perform any diagnoses either.

At critical points in the match, Deep Blue's handlers determined that they needed to revise the computer program. They figured out why their program was struggling and made the necessary changes so their program could win the match.

Kasparov also had handlers who gave him advice. But the critical difference is that Kasparov could diagnose shortcomings on his own, without handlers. Deep Blue couldn't. It didn't have a diagnostic routine built into its code. Kasparov foolishly agreed to an arrangement in which both sides used handlers, even though he didn't need his handlers and Deep Blue couldn't have made any adaptations without its handlers.

Playing chess requires more than finding the best moves in various situations; players also have to discover what is wrong with different strategies and plans. The example of Kasparov and Deep Blue illustrates a tendency among computer science professionals to find an aspect of a task that can be reduced to calculations, then arrange for the other aspects, such as diagnosis, to disappear. I am not taking anything away from their ability to beat Kasparov, just using the incident to illustrate how important it is to be able to diagnose from successes and failures. The incident shows how critical and how difficult it is to make sense of feedback. Even though Kasparov lost, the incident further illustrates the magic of human cognition.

III Adapting

In complex situations, our attempts to make adaptations may fail if we persist in pursuing the goals we started with, if we rely too heavily on identifying and minimizing risks, and if we maintain the ground rules we set at the beginning of an activity. Adapting means revising our goals, becoming resilient to threats we cannot predict, and changing the way we work together. To adapt, we have to learn, but we also have to unlearn.

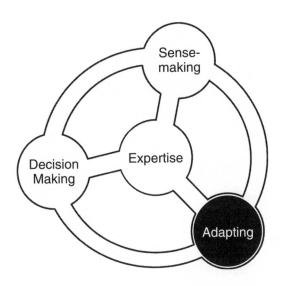

14   Moving Targets

"You have to know where you're going in order to get there." We have all heard this advice our entire lives. We are told that we shouldn't even think of setting out unless we know what we want to achieve.

Claim 8: The starting point for any project is to get a clear description of the goal.

This statement got a higher level of agreement from my sample than any other. The average rating was 5.89, "strongly agree for almost all situations." Out of 163 people, only four indicated any disagreement with this statement; 45 gave the statement the top rating; they completely agreed with claim 8 for any situation.

People definitely want to define clear goals in advance. That way they can set up a schedule and measure if they are making good progress. The more specific the goal, the better.

Many management and planning tools are built around the notion that we first define the goals and then proceed to achieve them. Peter Drucker developed Management by Objectives for managers to help subordinates specify the objectives they want to accomplish in the coming year; then the managers can measure their subordinates' performance using yardsticks they both had accepted.[1] Project managers focus on objectives to set up plans for how they are going to achieve the project goals. Executives regularly announce corporate goals and mission statements to guide the efforts of their employees. The entire system, from personnel management to strategic visions, depends on describing explicit goals at each level.

Disclaimer

Claim 8 is compelling, and I certainly agree that we should try to define the goal at the start of any activity. But claim 8 runs into difficulties when we put it into practice. Claim 8 discourages us from getting started until we clearly define the goal, and it leads us to expect to accomplish that initial goal. The notion of pursuing clearly defined goals can work against us in complex situations. And it doesn't always work so well in stable settings, because it runs up against goal tradeoffs. Let us look at the difficulty with goal tradeoffs first.

Goal tradeoffs

Claim 8 creates the illusion that we have a single goal, but most of the time we're juggling several goals at the same time.

Once, when I was on a private school's board of directors, the school's manager (whose contract we weren't going to renew) started ranting during a meeting: "You say you want me to cut costs and yet at the same time you also say you want a stronger program. Well, you can't have both. Which one do you want? You've got to stop talking out of both sides of your mouth." The manager's grandstanding didn't save his job.

As I walked out of the meeting, I thought that part of his difficulty was that he really believed he could live in a simple world where you had only one goal at a time. Of course we wanted both lower costs and a stronger program. The manager's refusal to keep within the budget was jeopardizing the future of the school, as was his indifference to program quality. We needed to work both fronts at the same time. In a way, he was right—any time we have more than one goal we have the potential for goal conflicts. That doesn't mean we pick the goal we want. Instead, we have to figure out how to trade off the goals so that we can achieve enough of each of them. That's the hard part. No matter how clearly we define our goals we still have to wrestle with goal tradeoffs.

To see how goal tradeoffs work, try the decision-making exercise in the next example.

Example 14.1: Taking a stand[2]   Role: You are a manager at IMPART, a manufacturing company with a diverse range of customers. One of your customers, George Johnson, is way behind on payments for a parts shipment you sent. George's company is fairly large, and so you have been patient about this debt for several months. But Steve, your supervisor, has come under pressure from upper management to clear up the bills. You tell Steve you are going to set up a meeting with George. Steve tells you "I want this paid in full in the next two months."

Steve's instructions couldn't be clearer. You know exactly what you need to bring back. Off you go to the meeting. You present your case forcefully to George.

Here are two counter-offers George might make. Which of these would you accept? You can accept either, both, or neither. Just make sure Steve is satisfied that you followed his instructions.

Counter-offer 1: I'll pay you 80 percent today, but that's it.

Counter-offer 2: I'll pay you half now, the other half in six months.

Which of these offers would you accept, if any? Hmmm. Not so easy, is it? When I give this exercise to leadership workshops, the responses vary greatly. No group has ever converged on a single answer.

What is so difficult here? Steve's goals were clear, but by giving you two goals he created the potential for goal conflicts. George's counter-offers exploit these conflicts. And had Steve prioritized the goals, you would still have had trouble. Imagine that Steve said that getting paid in full took priority over getting the matter resolved in 2 months. If getting paid in full was the top priority, then George might counter-offer to pay in full in 10 years. Steve certainly wouldn't be happy with that. If getting this resolved in 2 months took priority over getting paid in full, George might offer to pay you 10 percent in 2 months, wave you out of his office, and chuckle about how he had outwitted you.

In fact, you need both of these goals. No single goal by itself will be effective. Steve needed to explain how to trade off the goals. You struggle with the two counter-offers because you don't know how Steve sees the tradeoff between the goals. (See figure 14.1.)

Steve could have helped you by explaining how to balance the two goals. He could have said "If we got 70 percent tomorrow I'd be satisfied. If we got 80 percent in 2 months I'd be satisfied." If you could have estimated Steve's tolerance (represented by the "acceptable" line in figure 14.1), anything north of that line would have worked, anything south of the line would have counted against you.

With these instructions, we can see that Counter-offer 1, to pay 80 percent today, would satisfy Steve. Counter-offer 2, half now and half in 6 months, would disappoint Steve.

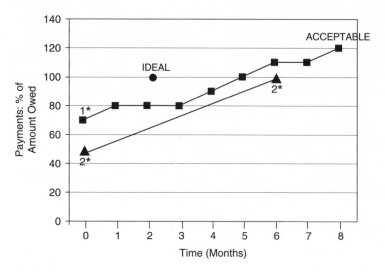

Figure 14.1
Goal tradeoffs.

Very few bosses would try to explain tradeoffs such as those in ex-ample 14.1, because very few bosses even know them. Managers leave the burden on the subordinates trying to carry out the orders.

In example 14.1, Steve probably felt that he had done his job when he said "paid in full in 2 months." After all, he met the standards for claim 8. However, we don't have to accept the ambiguity. In our conversation with Steve we could have probed him with different counter-offers so that we could have gotten a better idea of these trade-offs and learned more about what really matters to him.

We would handle the goal tradeoff more effectively if we knew Steve's motivation—his deeper goals. If Steve was under pressure to build cash reserves because of a credit crunch, that would increase the attractiveness of counter-offer 1 (80 percent payment today). If Steve's bonus depended on the profitability of his division then counter-offer 2 would be more attractive than counter-offer 1. Steve doesn't have to draw a tradeoff curve (not that he ever would); he just has to describe what really matters to him. And if he is uncomfortable talking about his bonus, he shouldn't be surprised if we bring back a deal that he doesn't like.

This exercise shows that even when we have clear goals we can still get befuddled when the goals come into conflict with each other.

Goal tradeoffs matter to paramedics. I recently worked with the British Columbia Ambulance Service, one of the largest and most impressive organizations of its kind. The service was struggling with the aftermath of an accident in which two paramedics died while responding to an unconscious patient. It was determined to establish a safety culture in order to protect its paramedics. As we prepared a workshop on safe decision making, it became clear that the paramedics needed assistance in handling a specific goal conflict: caring for patients vs. protecting themselves. Their work was inherently risky. I heard a story of a paramedic leaning over a semi-conscious victim only to have the man spit blood into the paramedic's mouth. There was another story about transporting a stabbing victim with a possible arterial spurt to a hospital, trying to get an intravenous catheter into the drunken man's arm, only to have him thrash around and inflict a "needle stick" on the paramedic. Then there was the story of a paramedic lowered on a line to a wrecked car teetering on a precipice; the paramedic rescued the children handed to him from inside the car, then, with the car slipping closer to the edge, went inside the car to bring out the children's mother.

The training couldn't be about eliminating risk. It had to be about calibrating the paramedics to the tradeoffs between their own safety, the safety of their partners, their obligation to their families, and the safety of the victims. The challenge was to shift the tradeoff so that paramedics gave highest priority to their own safety. (In these incidents, there was no way to prevent the unexpected blood spitting other than urging the paramedics to keep their mouths closed. The drunken and agitated stabbing victim should have been kept in restraints in the ambulance even if that prevented him from getting an IV. And the paramedic making the car rescue acknowledged that he had been young and foolish—he never should have gone back inside the car.)

Goal tradeoffs are difficult for all of us. Physicians have to wrestle with conflicting goals to restore a patient to health and also reduce the patient's discomfort.[3] Soldiers also struggle with goal tradeoffs. Consider two simple rules of engagement for a young soldier: don't fire at anyone unless that person first fires a weapon at you, and don't inflict casualties on civilians. Both of these are moderately clear. But what happens if an adversary takes a civilian hostage and opens fire? Is it permissible to fire back? Now the situation has become more difficult. The rules of engagement that seemed so clear no longer look straightforward.

Corporations ignore goal conflicts when they issue their famous "corporate values" statements. Top executives spend enormous amounts of time trying to craft these statements, expanding their lists, winnowing them down, trying to get them just right. Quality is #1. The customer comes first. Our people are our biggest asset. And on and on.

Mercifully, most organizations are content to leave these lists alone once they are issued, so their employees can forget about them. I have never seen an organization address the difficulty of goal conflicts. If employees are #1 and customers are #1, what happens when the needs of employees get in the way of the needs of customers? How much will the company raise prices in order to fund better health-care programs? How much abuse are employees expected to take from dissatisfied customers? Organizations prefer to look the other way when their cherished values collide with each other.

The dilemma of goal tradeoffs shows that even clear goals can be ambiguous. And this is the easy case, that involves clear goals in a stable situation. In complex situations our goals are likely to be vague and ambiguous.

Emergent goals

What happens when we *don't* have clear goals? This is the most serious limitation of claim 8. Here we are facing what Rittel and Webber (1973, 1984) described as "wicked problems" in which the goals are incomplete and keep changing, as well as occasionally conflicting. Solutions to wicked problems aren't true or false. Instead, they are judged as good or bad because there is no way to test a solution to a wicked problem. Wicked problems epitomize the world of shadows. When we are faced with a wicked problem—when the goals just aren't clear—there aren't any objective ways to gauge success.

Most of the problems are wicked. Contrast an essay exam and a multiple-choice test. Taking an essay exam is a wicked problem. Midway through the exam, the student may wonder what the teacher really wants to know. Different teachers might give varying grades to the same answer, because essay exams don't have clear criteria and goals. In contrast, multiple-choice exams are easy to grade. The goals are well defined, the questions usually tap into explicit knowledge such as facts, and students usually don't have much to argue about if they don't like their scores.

Claim 8 runs into trouble in complex situations in which the wicked problems prevent us from clarifying the goals at the start. Many of the problems we face are wicked problems in which we may have to re-assess our original understanding of the goals. The goals will become clearer as we learn more. That's why I am calling them *emergent* goals. Let's look at some examples.

Emergent goals at the strategic level

In the earliest days of television, David Sarnoff, the president of both RCA and NBC, had a clear goal: the programs he broadcasted on NBC (the first American television network) should create demand for the television sets RCA manufactured. That was his business model. His company was going to make money by selling television sets. It would appear that he underestimated the revenues he could generate through selling commercials. In those early days of an immature industry, Sarnoff needed some vision to help NBC move forward. Fortunately for him, he didn't get trapped by that vision.

The Sarnoff example shows how goals change dramatically. The next example, the development of the Xerox 914 copying machine, also illustrates the way a company can recover from vague and flawed goals.

Example 14.2: The Xerox 914[4]   Consider how Joe Wilson, CEO of Xerox, evolved his goals for the 914 copying machine in the 1950s. Wilson gambled the future of his company on the success of the new technology embodied by the 914. When he acquired the rights in 1947 to a new method for dry xerography, Wilson's Goal 1 was to forge a licensing arrangement with large companies such as IBM and Bell & Howell so that they could manufacture and sell the machines. Unfortunately, they weren't interested. The IBM executives estimated a market of fewer than 5,000 machines. Kodak's $350 Verifax and 3M's $350 Thermofax were smaller and less expensive to manufacture than Xerox's 914, which was larger than a desk and cost more than $2,000 to produce.

Wilson persisted. He didn't see any real competition to the 914. Carbon paper was cheap but messy and couldn't make many copies. The other copying machines were cheaper, but they were slow, messy, and complicated to operate. Mimeograph machines required special masters; photostat machines were costly and slow. Other devices required special paper and special treatment after the copies came out. The 914 used a dry copying method that needed no chemicals and could duplicate any kind of image onto plain paper with the press of a button.

Wilson had to convince people just to try the new technology so they could see its advantages over the competition. So he identified Goal 2: to manufacture the machines himself and sell or lease them to customers. This goal wasn't realistic either. The lease rate he would have to charge companies wouldn't be competitive with the other, cheaper copying machines. And the machines were much too expensive to sell.

Then Wilson got a better idea from one of the Xerox executives. A Xerox team had been studying people at companies that used the 914 and found that they made many more copies than they realized. And so Xerox shifted to Goal 3: to make money from the *number of copies*, not from the lease.

Xerox offered to lease the 914 machine for only $95 per month, including a 15-day cancellation clause. The lease included 2,000 free copies a month, and charged only a nickel for every additional copy.

This business model seemed highly risky at the time, but it let customers become familiar with the benefits of on-demand copying for all kinds of materials. Customers who might resist buying or leasing an expensive machine couldn't resist the opportunity to make 5-cent copies. Xerox gambled that customers would make more than 2,000 copies per month on the 914. And that's exactly what happened. By 1967 the average Xerox 914 machine made more than 100,000 copies a year. Goal 3 made the 914 a huge success and established our dependence on xerography. Wilson's accomplishment was in diagnosing what was wrong with Goal 1 and Goal 2 and inventing a business model that overcame those flaws.

Wilson's insight was that Xerox should sell copies, not machines. The machines were merely vehicles for getting customers to make copies. When some customers asked to purchase their copiers, Xerox raised the purchase price to exorbitant levels because it didn't want customers to own the copiers. Goal 2, to sell or lease the machines, no longer was attractive. And Goal 1, to license the technology, was overtaken by events. IBM tried to begin negotiations once it became aware of its mistake, but Xerox was no longer interested.

Some might argue that Joe Wilson just shifted his strategy to reach higher goals, such as increasing his company's profits, revenues, and customer base. However, these higher goals can conflict with one another, so the real discovery is in how to trade them off. During the development of the Xerox 914 technology, Wilson primarily wanted his company to survive. He gambled the company's future on Goal 3.

We are told that the goal of a corporation is to make money for its investors. Yet Wilson cared more about keeping his company going. Is that typical? Kaiser, Hogan, and Craig (2008) examined leadership and found that the ultimate goal of organizations was to ensure long-term survival. The slogans about shareholder value and return on investment take a back seat to the more pressing need to stay in business. And companies that are driven to make money for investors have to wrestle with tradeoffs about how much money versus how much risk. The Wall Street investment company Lehman Brothers went bankrupt in 2008 because it had fixated on maximizing profits. Joe Wilson, in contrast, adapted his goals as he went along.

Bill Duggan, in *Strategic Intuition* (2007), describes a number of other instances in which leaders changed their goals on the basis of what they learned. Napoleon went into battle without any firm plans. He maneuvered his forces until he found a match-up that suited him; then he attacked. Bill Gates and Paul Allen, the founders of Microsoft, didn't set out to start a software company. That came only after they failed with their initial ventures and realized the potential for standard software programs. Sergey Brin and Larry Page, the founders of Google, were just trying to find good dissertation topics in graduate school. They tried to sell a patent for their search algorithm for $1 million, but when that was turned down they decided to try to commercialize it themselves. Duggan argues that such breakthroughs depend on the ability to learn by making new connections, not on doggedly pursuing the original goal.

Social service agencies often wrestle with ambiguous goals, particularly when they have to satisfy funding agencies that they are accomplishing the goals stated in a grant application. Typically, an impartial outside evaluator comes in to see how the agency is doing. Often the evaluator meets with the staff at the beginning to make sure everyone knows what the goals are and how success will be measured. Michael Quinn Patton (1978), an experienced program evaluator, describes the process: the agency staff members often have to sit through painful goal-clarification exercises, trying to make their vague goals more explicit or trying to come up with any goals the evaluators can measure. Often the staff just gives up and accepts whatever goals the evaluators think they can measure the easiest. The staff members figure they can deal with the consequences later on. If they don't meet the goals, they can always rely on ploys such as the "goals clarification shuffle," in which they explain that the original goals were never important. For example, in 1969 the program evaluators concluded that the Head Start Program hadn't achieved its stated goals. Head Start hadn't boosted the cognitive and emotional growth of children in the long-term. The Head Start administrators knew that Congress supported the effort to help underprivileged children, so they emphasized health, nutrition, cultural, and community goals rather than cognitive development. An appreciative Congress expanded the program.

Emergent goals at the project level

Perhaps goals are murky when businesses are trying to establish new industries, such as television or computers or photocopiers. If we move down from the strategic to the operational level, where teams are carrying out projects, we sometimes find clear goals. But often we don't. For example, the LexisNexis Corporation spent $80–90 million over three years to prevent any disruption from the "Y2K problem"—the fear that computer programs would fail on December 31, 1999 because some of the computer code only used the last two digits for marking the years. The LexisNexis team worked hard to prevent a Y2K disruption, but even after the program ended, its leaders couldn't describe their original goal. Their job was to ensure that LexisNexis would maintain operations as 1999 shifted to 2000. But if they experienced a two-second delay, would that count as success, or as failure? If 2 percent of their clients lost services for a day but no one else was affected, would that count as success, or as failure? They never knew. More important, it never occurred to them to find out.

The LexisNexis team ran smoothly without specifying the project goals. Here is an all-too-common example of an organization that struggled when faced with ambiguous goals.

Example 14.3: The hard-headed software developers   The vice president of a Fortune 500 company explained his frustrations bluntly: The Information Technology department was at war with the rest of the company. Members of the IT staff showed contempt for everyone who needed their help. People who asked the IT department for support came away frustrated and disappointed.

When we conducted a range of interviews, we uncovered some of the reasons for this impasse. Most of the IT staff members had come to the company straight out of college. They had enjoyed their computer science courses. They had particularly liked the assignments that challenged them to find elegant solutions to different kinds of problems their professors assigned. But here at work, people would bring in fairly mundane problems. And, worse than that, once the IT department delivered the programs that met the specifications, these users would complain—"Oh, that's not what I needed." What a waste of time, trying to help people who didn't even know what they wanted.

The rest of the company held an opposite view. They knew little about software. They brought their problems to the IT staff. The programmers just wanted a specification to work from and showed little interest in what the code was supposed to do. They just wanted to "deliver to the spec." And then they got angry when anyone complained that their code wasn't going to solve the problem.

By this point we could see what was going wrong. The computer specialists had a narrow view of their job. They wanted to continue doing what they had done in college: solve tough problems with elegant techniques. But their customers in the company weren't like their professors. They weren't sure what it would take to solve a problem. They needed a dialogue with the programmers to figure it out. They needed a dialogue even as the code was being written to react to what they liked or disliked and to recognize problems or opportunities they might have missed at the outset. The programmers, locked into their mindset of delivering code to agreed-upon specifications, didn't have the interest or the skills for such conversations.

Once we explained the real problem, the vice president who sponsored our work recognized what he had to do. He decided to identify the programmers who could work with the internal customers, increase their authority, and keep the others isolated from the rest of the company. The VP also initiated a course in collaborating on specifications for anyone in the IT department who was interested. The last we heard, peace was being restored.

Example 14.3 isn't just a cautionary tale about software developers. We see the same pattern in departments of all sorts. People like to pin down their objectives and deliver exactly what was requested. We want to work on well-defined assignments with clear goals. That way, we know what we must deliver, and our bosses can judge our progress. However, we don't always have that luxury.

Alexander Laufer (2009) studied Procter & Gamble, NASA, and other organizations and observed that the managers of successful projects repeatedly started engineering designs before they had finished defining their project objectives. A study of 211 RD projects by Baker et al. (1986) found that the projects that started with well-defined business and technical goals had no greater chance of succeeding than those whose goals were still fluctuating at the start. However, the business and technical goals for the successful projects did become better defined over the life of the project than the goals for the unsuccessful projects. What mattered was eventually discovering goals that were meaningful, not trying to pin these goals down at the outset.

Emergent goals at the individual level

Peter Drucker initially developed the concept of Management by Objectives to help supervisors manage their subordinates. After they agreed on the subordinate's objectives, the supervisor could assess progress toward the objectives in periodic evaluations.

On the negative side, this process can discourage employees from changing their interests and enthusiasms until their next annual personnel evaluation. Surely that is an unintended consequence. Surely most organizations would be better off encouraging employees to take advantage of speculative opportunities instead of keeping on their original path.

Some companies are determined to hold workers accountable for the objectives they announced. And when they try, the difficulties with MBO may provoke a backlash in which divisions and organizations treat MBO directives as merely paperwork or even a system to be gamed.

For example, a former senior manager at Mead Data Central (forerunner of LexisNexis) described how his organization implemented MBO. Mead, the parent company, was a paper and forest products company. Mead Data Central was a fast-growing pioneer in using a computer-based approach to finding information in large text databases. An executive vice president of the unit would come running around announcing that The Mead Corporation needed yearly senior management objectives by 4 p.m. that day. That set off a mad rush to formulate individual objectives because they counted for 50 percent of management bonuses (the other 50 percent was determined by the performance of the unit). Each person generated four to six objectives for the coming year, and assigned weights to these to reflect their importance. Then, after meeting the 4 o'clock deadline, everyone forgot about the objectives.

Many months later, the process would be repeated when the Mead Corporation needed grades for the objectives in order to determine bonuses. Few of the managers could recall what their objectives were, or even find any scraps of paper with the objectives written down. The executive vice president soon learned that he had to give people copies of the objectives they had turned in. The managers would look at their objectives and respond "What were we thinking?" For example, an objective might have been about a licensing opportunity that appeared to be imminent when the objectives were created but then put on hold when a better licensing opportunity arose. Sometimes the managers had to retrofit their activities into the objectives they had specified.

Many effective managers refuse to be confined by the charade of yearly goal reviews. They instruct their subordinates to fill out their objectives in pencil so they can be changed every few months when better goals come along.

Tools for pursuing goals
Another drawback of Management by Objectives is that it calls for objectives that can be measured objectively. It is easier to measure progress if you can count accomplishments, so employees discard any important objectives that they can't quantify, further distorting the evaluation process. Or they propose easy goals with vague deadlines; these will not create much stress or much motivation.

Under well-ordered conditions, we can expect—indeed demand—that the goals be clarified at the start. But complex conditions make for wicked problems that often prevent goal clarification at the outset. Program managers suppress these complications in order to create systematic management strategies. To see how this works, consider a common management tool: the Gantt chart.

Gantt charts illustrate the type of tools that reinforce the managers' rigidity in holding to the initial goals. Gantt charts define tasks, show when each task should be started and when it should be completed, and list milestones. (See figure 14.2.)

Task	2006						
	January	February	March	April	May	June	July
All Projects	1/14 ●———						●— 7/14
Project A	1/14 ●———					●— 5/31	
Task A1	1/14 ●———	●— 2/10					
Task A2		2/19 ●———	●— 3/18				
Task A3			3/26 ●———	●— 4/24			
Task A4				5/4 ●———	●— 5/31		
Project B			3/19 ●———				●— 7/14
Project B1			3/19 ●———	●— 4/14			
Project B2				4/16 ●———		●—6/12	
Project B3					5/16 ●———		●— 7/14

Figure 14.2
A generic Gantt chart.

One multi-billion-dollar project we studied tried to use Gantt charts to keep track of all tasks and all the responsibilities of the prime contractor as well as the subcontractors. Once these Gantt charts were completed, everyone was relieved that the program managers had gained some control over a hectic and complex schedule. They thought they had a roadmap for doing the work. However, once the program was underway some tasks were moved earlier and others were delayed. New tasks were added because of the results of earlier tasks, some old tasks were combined. There were so many changes that by the time each new version of the Gantt chart was officially released, it was already out of date and team members didn't take it seriously.

The limitations of Gantt charts illustrate a basic difficulty of applying analytical methods. Even though more sophisticated scheduling tools are now available, these methods work well as long as the tasks don't change, the schedule doesn't change, the mission doesn't change, and personnel don't rotate in and out. The wonderful economy of communication embedded in a Gantt chart is purchased through all the briefings and project reviews that create common ground among team members. When changes in tasks, goals, and personnel erode that common ground, the shorthand notations on the Gantt chart and the layers of notes and modifications all become barriers to communication and coordinated planning.

Furthermore, Gantt charts depend on accurate estimates of the duration of each task. Often such estimates are fictions. They don't take into account who is leading a task and what other commitments that person has. They don't reflect the pressure task leaders feel to pad their estimates—sometimes by as much as 50 percent—because the task leaders want to be sure they can meet their commitment.[5]

And Gantt charts discourage a team from modifying its goals. In the large project I was describing, once the Gantt charts were constructed and accepted, the customer approved funding for the next phase only if the milestone for the previous phase was reached. Bonuses were linked to the milestones. So no one wanted to move the milestones. And no one dared to think about changing any of the goals of the program. That's another limitation of objectives-based tools such as Gantt charts: they contribute to goal fixation.

Goal fixation

Sengupta, Abdel-Hamid, and Van Wassenhove (2007) identified an "initial goal bias." We can think of it as goal fixation—that is, getting stuck on the original goal. Sengupta et al. studied the way experienced managers handled a computer-based game requiring them to manage a simulated software project. They found that managers failed to revise their targets even when those targets became obsolete. The managers playing the simulation stuck to their original targets and as a result their performance was disappointing. Why did this happen? "Very early in their careers, people incorporate into their mental models the notion that it's important to meet externally set targets. This bias is often reinforced in managerial life. Revising targets is seen as an admission of failure in many companies, and managers quickly realize that their careers will fare better if they stick to and achieve initial goals—even if that leads to a worse overall outcome." (p. 98)

Does goal fixation occur in real corporate situations? I think so. When I explained goal fixation to the chief financial officer of a major corporation, he was very familiar with the idea. He explained why it is difficult for executives to change goals once a program is underway. He could think of many instances in which everyone had signed up to the sales forecast from the marketing department, and bonuses were linked to the degree to which the forecast was exceeded. Tremendous effort went into constructing a management plan to achieve the forecast. Then, when the early data suggested that the target would be missed, no one wanted to face the consequences. Instead, they found ways to explain away the data. They all felt enormous pressure to hold the line. The employees stayed in denial, missing chances to make small

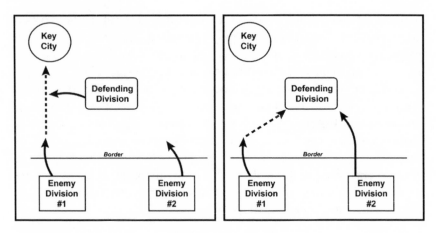

Figure 14.3
Defending against an attack from the south.

adjustments to the goals and plans, until they could no longer ignore the indications. Then they made inefficient and disruptive changes.

Peter Thunholm, a Lieutenant Colonel in the Swedish Armed Forces, has demonstrated goal fixation in a military context (Thunholm 2007).[6] He created a scenario in which teams of military officers role played the headquarters staff for a division, which consists of three brigades. Their division was up against two enemy divisions, each consisting of three brigades. So they were outnumbered 2:1. But they had superior technology. And they were fighting on their own soil, so they had better intelligence. Their orders from higher headquarters represented the situation as shown in the left panel of figure 14.3. The higher headquarters estimated that Enemy Division 1 was going to attack and drive straight north to assault the city. Enemy Division 2 was also going to cross the border, but it didn't have good supplies and so it wasn't going to be able to attack for another 72 hours.

The planning teams worked out how their division was going to sweep to the west and stop Enemy Division 1 before it reached the city, and then be prepared to take on Enemy Division 2. This wasn't a very hard mission. However, the intelligence was wrong. Enemy Division 1 was not headed toward the city. Its real objective was the Swedish defending division being commanded by the planning teams (figure 14.3, right panel). And Enemy Division 2 was not as short of supplies as the intelligence suggested. In fact, it charged north and then swung west. The enemy plan was to catch the Swedish division in a pincer attack.

How did the planning teams respond? Thunholm ran eight teams, each with four to six members, through this scenario. As the exercise unfolded, all the teams could see that Enemy Division 2 was continuing to move. One of the eight planning teams eventually got worried and sent one of its three brigades to set up a defense using the last natural barrier, a river. Six of the eight planning teams watched in dismay. By the time they tried to defend against the attack, it was too late. Enemy Division 2 had already crossed that river.

The eighth planning team never even sent out a defense at all. "Don't pay attention to this," they counseled team members who expressed any worries. They continued their planned attack on Enemy Division 1 and let themselves be hit from the rear. They were good soldiers indeed. None of the eight planning teams showed much talent for renegotiating goals.

Revising goals and objectives is difficult enough. Goal fixation makes it almost impossible for us to adapt to changing circumstances or even to use what we learn as we make sense of situations.

Unintended consequence

Claim 8 states that we should define goals and objectives at the start and then simply proceed toward them. Claim 8 implies that we should not start work unless we can get a clear description of the goal. But if we insisted on clear goals, we simply couldn't get started on most of the important projects in our lives.

Replacement

The replacement for claim 8 is that *when facing wicked problems we have to re-define the goals as we try to reach them*. Most of the problems people encounter have poorly defined goals (Klein and Weitzenfeld 1978). No amount of thinking and analysis will make these goals well defined. In such cases, we are going to have to figure out the goals as we go along. The faster we can learn, the more successful we'll be.

Yet many people take the opposite route. When confronted with complex situations, they try to increase their control over events. They try to increase the details in their instructions instead of accepting the unpredictability of events and getting ready to adapt. They stumble into goal fixation.

Jay Rothman and I have suggested an alternative approach, which we call Management by Discovery (Klein and Rothman 2008). In

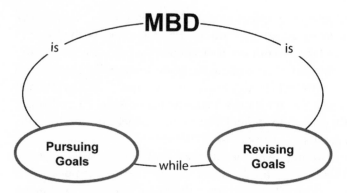

Figure 14.4
Management By Discovery.

contrast to Management by Objectives, Management by Discovery (MBD) says when we face complex conditions we should expect to revise and replace goals on the basis of what we learn.

The military has a slogan that no plan survives the first contact with the enemy, which means that leaders should adapt their plan as the situation unfolds in order to reach the goal. That's *not* what Jay and I mean by MBD. We are not talking about revising the plan to reach the goal. We're talking about revising the goal itself. (See figure 14.4.) That's what happened in the case of the Xerox 914 copier. The Xerox Corporation changed its goals as leaders became aware of the attractions and barriers of their machine.

Jay has plenty of experience with wicked problems and ambiguous goals. He has developed a conflict-management approach based on his experience working on projects such as the Jerusalem Peace Initiative (bringing Jews and Arabs in Jerusalem together for discussions about their disagreements) and performing mediation efforts for international conflicts in Sri Lanka, Cyprus, and Northern Ireland. He also performs mediation efforts in the United States. Example 14.4 describes a project he conducted in Cincinnati.

Example 14.4: Reaching for common goals[7]   In March 2001, Jay Rothman was appointed as a special master for reducing racial conflict in the city of Cincinnati by US District Judge Susan Dlott. Leaders of the city's black community charged that the city's police had long been racially profiling and harassing blacks, particularly during traffic stops and other incidents. The Cincinnati Black United Front and the American Civil Liberties Union prepared a lawsuit against the police department and the city.[8] Judge Dlott wanted to mediate the situation because a lawsuit would deepen the antagonism and further polarize the city, whereas a mediated agreement might be a step toward reducing tension.

The mediation process became more poignant and more critical the next month. Cincinnati exploded in riots after a racially charged incident on April 7, 2001, in which a white police officer shot and killed an unarmed black teenager who was running away but had not committed any crime. (The police officer knew the boy was wanted but didn't know that it was merely for a series of misdemeanors.)

Jay's official task from Justice Dlott was to get the antagonists to agree to a collaborative agreement that would build bridges between the city government, including the police, and the black community. He had to create trust where there was suspicion, and to create a willingness to work together in groups that feared and avoided one another. He had to transform a community. If he failed to get all the parties to agree to a collaborative arrangement, the lawsuit against the city and the police department would go forward.

Jay succeeded. Justice Dlott later stated that Jay and his team had developed the "best police reform agreement in the country." Jay's team obtained questionnaire data from more than 3,500 people and set up a series of meetings for the groups involved in the conflict—the police and their families, the black community, white citizens' groups, youth groups, leaders of religious organizations, social service agencies, business and foundation leaders, and city employees—in order to identify their concerns and their hopes.

Jay was trying to get all segments of the community to coalesce around common goals, but he didn't know what those goals might be. From the questionnaires and the group sessions, Jay's conflict-management team found that all sides had common goals of trust and respect. Members of the black community wanted the police to trust and respect them; the police wanted the trust and respect of the black community. All sides cooperated on a blueprint to move toward those goals, listing steps to be taken and identifying overseers from the city, the US Department of Justice, and the community who would monitor progress. As a result, the lawsuit was dropped. John Ashcroft, then the Attorney General of the United States, traveled to Cincinnati to sign this historic agreement, which he described as a model of reform.

On the one hand, Jay Rothman had a very clear goal: to mediate a settlement so that the lawsuit could be dropped. On the other hand, he needed to help the city, the police, and the black community identify common goals about how they wanted to live together. Before Jay's efforts, no one knew what these goals would be. The participants worked together to discover and clarify goals in order to reach the agreement. The process helped the black community feel less aggrieved and more involved in law enforcement, and it helped change the police culture from enforcement-oriented policing to proactive problem-solving policing. This was truly an MBD process of defining goals as they went along.

In one seminar where I presented MBD, a young military officer expressed some misgivings because he was going to be in situations that required him to act and not wait to make discoveries. I suspect that might be a common concern, so I had better quash it right now.

The Management by Objectives approach sets the expectation that we shouldn't begin executing any plans until we have specified the goals. Management by Discovery encourages leaders to take action rather than sit around waiting for perfect goal clarity. MBD also starts with trying to clearly define goals—how could you ever act if you had no idea about what you wanted to accomplish? The difference is that MBD expects to face wicked problems and complex conditions. Instead of reacting by tightening controls, MBD takes the opposite approach of loosening controls in order to expand the discovery process.

MBD versus objectives-based approaches

Here are the ways in which MBD differs from the traditional objectives-based approach to carrying out work:

Define the objectives at the start. With MBD we still spend time trying to clarify goals at the start. However, we expect to change those goals on the basis of what we learn.

Determine a path to the end state. There are many paths to an end state; if the goals change, so will the path. With MBD we still try to envision a way to reach the end state. That's what a plan does. However, we are also looking for alternative paths we can use when we revise the end state.

Identify the tasks on that path. But if the path changes, so will the tasks. We have to be ready to add, combine, delete, and reshuffle the tasks.

Rather than use a Gantt chart, we should keep track of the options so we can activate one option when another seems to get stuck.[9]

Prepare a schedule showing when each task begins and ends. But if the goals change, the schedule will change. On the basis of what is learned about the connections between tasks, each sub-team can understand how to provide other teams what they need when they need it.

Measure progress in moving toward the goal. But if the goals change, the progress markers will change. So we should prepare ourselves and our clients and supervisors from the start to re-negotiate the goals as well as the schedule and resources.

Jay and I don't see Management by Discovery and Management by Objectives as conflicting with each other. They are two ways to achieve successful outcomes. Each begins with an attempt to define the goals. The primary difference is that in complex situations with wicked problems, MBD recognizes that the original goals may become obsolete. Therefore, the MBD mindset is to move forward even though the goals haven't been specified in detail, and to expect to revise the goals. The MBD mindset is to look for opportunities to figure out better goals than the ones specified at the beginning.

We thought that MBD would be relevant in only a small proportion of situations, perhaps less than 25 percent of the time. However, mid-level managers in the public sector have estimated that 66 percent of their projects involved unclear goals, unpredictable conditions, and lack of agreement with their supervisors about what would count as a successful effort. The higher the management level, the higher the estimations of ambiguous goals.

When it comes to wicked problems and complexity, the standard objectives-based tools, such as Gantt charts, may not be useful.

One strategy is to compile a "goal field" and use it to track what you have learned. You can share this goal field with your subordinates to help calibrate your discoveries. You can ask them to keep their own goal fields so that you can review their progress. Instead of just reviewing dates and budgets and schedules, you can review what they have been learning. A goal field represents the primary goals (there are usually several) and how they relate to one another. The goals usually won't form a neat and simple hierarchy, so it is important to show the interconnections and to highlight areas in which the goals might come into conflict. Finally, you might add some "anti-goals"—that is, things you don't want to happen. If people are engaged in MBD, the goal field should become richer and deeper as they proceed. If that isn't happening, it's a warning sign that they may be fixating on the initial goals.

Why claim 8 matters

It matters because claim 8 (that the starting point for any project is to get a clear description of the goal) prevents people from adapting. MBD isn't a choice. It is what we have to do in unpredictable circumstances when we are faced with ambiguous goals. The choice is whether to do MBD well or poorly. Who is the best manager to lead a difficult project under complex conditions? Is it one who can be counted on to doggedly pursue the initial objectives? Or is it the one most capable of making discoveries?

It matters because too many leaders and managers have only one reaction to adversity: increasing the controls. Many people try to tame turbulence, ambiguity, and complexity by redoubling their efforts to specify the goals and detail the plans. That strategy works well for managers early in their careers, when they are assigned projects with clear goals. But later, as they get assigned to programs with wicked problems, this can be the wrong approach.

It matters because most management tools and training programs assume that goals are clear and stable.

It matters because people are highly vulnerable to getting fixated on goals.

It matters because commercial, military, and government organizations are run by precise objectives leaving them inflexible when they have to pursue ambiguous goals.

15   The Risks of Risk Management

We spend a lot of time worrying about how to avoid risks. We buy cars with extra airbags. We read the latest news about which foods to eat. We invest our money in balanced portfolios. We deliberate about which sports to let our children play, and when to let them drive at night. We have ethical, legal, and financial responsibility for managing risks. If we loan our car to a neighbor who drinks, and that neighbor gets into an accident, we may be liable because we failed to protect against the risk.

Organizations have turned risk management into a specialty. They develop safety programs to reduce the chances of accidents. They hire lawyers to make sure their contracts and policies don't have any loopholes that could get them sued. They announce regulations designed to limit their responsibility for injuries. They take out insurance policies for further protection.

But it isn't possible to achieve perfect protection. So we have to make choices. We have to decide which risks to worry about and how to protect ourselves. Fortunately, there is a basic type of risk-management strategy[1] that lets us do just that.

Here are the basic steps in effective risk management:

1. Systematically identify the risks that might affect our plans.

2. Focus on the most worrisome risks. We can do that by estimating the likelihood and the impact of each of the risks. Then we can calculate which risks pose the greatest threat.

3. Develop risk-mitigation plans to reduce the biggest ones and/or minimize their potential damage. These risk-mitigation plans can set milestones for progress, and can alert us when our safety margin is getting too small.

4. Implement these plans.

5. Track whether the risk-mitigation plans are working. If a project begins to run into trouble, we increase our monitoring. We identify new risks and iterate the process.

These five steps promise to help us manage the risks to which we are exposed. They are the basis for the risk-management claim that will be examined in this chapter.

Claim 9: Our plans will succeed more often if we identify the biggest risks and then find ways to eliminate them.

In the survey, respondents agreed with claim 9, giving it a 5.22 rating. Eleven out of 164 respondents disagreed. The majority of respondents believed that we can systematically control risk.

Disclaimer

You know the drill by now. The risk-management strategy works effectively in well-ordered industries that have enough experience to reliably identify the risks in advance. Mature industries have already encountered the major risks and worked out procedures to deal with them, so the advice is least valuable where it is easiest to apply. In contrast, we struggle to apply these five steps to risk management in complex projects, for which we need the most help.

Let us now review the five steps of risk mitigation.

Step 1: Systematically identify the risks that might affect our plans.
Nothing to it. Just jot down all the ways the plan or program can fall apart. That's fine in a mature industry or activity. But if we have never carried out a plan of this kind before, or worked in this kind of setting before, how successful can we be in anticipating all the risks? Working in well-ordered situations in mature industries, risk analysts can use historical data to compile lists of risk factors, making step 1 go more smoothly. In complex situations, in which context affects what can go wrong, these lists become less helpful.

When we look at projects that failed, the most devastating risk factors often turn out to be things no one expected or was even thinking about. The high-powered managers at Long Term Capital Management (see chapter 5) never expected the kinds of financial turbulence that followed the Russian default in 1998. The admirals at Pearl Harbor never expected to be a Japanese target; Pearl Harbor was supposed to be the hammer, not the nail. Before 9/11, the Federal Aviation Administration never seriously considered that large airplanes are themselves bombs.

Nassim Taleb makes the point in his 2007 book *The Black Swan* that risk equations are built around the history of what has happened in the past and therefore don't include unexpected events that are rare and have a great impact. He calls these black swans because these events aren't supposed to exist. Yet they do, they don't figure in anyone's calculations, and they throw all the estimates out the window.

Life insurance companies are able to calibrate risk assessments and spread their risks across large numbers of policy holders. Imagine a life insurance company operating in Botswana just before the AIDS epidemic. Life expectancy in Botswana dropped from just over 60 years in 1986 to under 40 years in 2003. AIDS is the type of black swan event that makes a mockery of precise calculations of risk.

Furthermore, we can't will ourselves to be smart. Baxter et al. (2004) demonstrated this in a study they ran with Marine officers.

Example 15.1: Ambushed   To help young Marine platoon leaders learn to set up an ambush, the research team gave them a series of difficult and unexpected challenges using a desktop simulation. Each lieutenant was asked to set up an ambush to stop enemy reconnaissance teams that were infiltrating from the north. These teams were expected to come down from the north on routes 7, 31, and 75 (figure 15.1). Each lieutenant who was tested had the assignment of blocking the infiltration along route 31, in the center of the map. Each had to figure out how to position his fire teams to get the job done.

The researchers changed the scenarios from one trial to the next. A lieutenant would start out expecting the enemy to move methodically into the "kill zone" where the ambush was set up, only to find that the enemy vehicles had spread out and weren't all in the kill zone at the same time. On the next trial, the enemy sent a small force behind the ambushers, to ambush them. Next, the enemy mixed their soldiers in with civilians traveling south in trucks. Each trial presented a different complication.

The training worked very effectively to teach the platoon leaders the dynamics of an ambush. When the platoon leaders were given the same types of problems a second time, using different terrain, they did

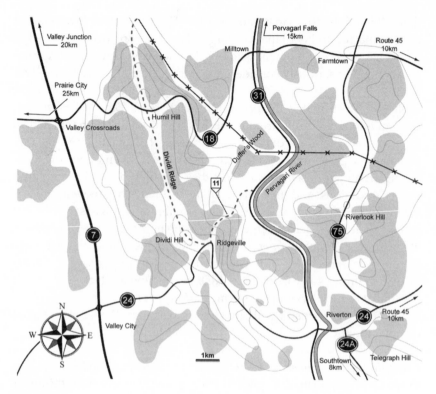

Figure 15.1
Ambushed.

much better. Their performance improved from 13 percent to 83 percent. So they learned from their experience. The platoon leaders later said that this experience was one of the most valuable opportunities for learning they had at their school.[2]

However, the platoon leaders never got any better at anticipating what the trainers were going to throw at them from one trial to the next. They couldn't see what was wrong with their mental models of an ambush until after the scenario exposed the problem. The platoon leaders knew that they were being tested. They knew that the scenarios were going to contain unexpected challenges. They knew something was coming. But they couldn't will themselves to spot the risks.

And the researchers gave them hints! In the first scenario, the five enemy vehicles were about to enter the ambush zone but then a few vehicles slowed down so that they spread out. They weren't all in the ambush zone at the same time. The platoon leaders suddenly realized that an ambush isn't so simple. Do they spring the ambush to hit the lead enemy vehicles? That just leaves the vehicles at the end to counter-attack. Do they wait to ambush the last vehicles? But that lets the lead vehicles through. The hint here was a set of radio messages from the platoon to the east, on route 75, that had sprung its ambush too quickly and was now being mauled by the rest of the enemy formation. The controllers sent those radio messages just before posing the same dilemma to the platoon leaders—but the platoon leaders never connected that message with their own situation. They never wondered why the platoon on route 75, might have sprung the ambush too soon.

In another scenario, the enemy sent a unit down a path (along Dividi Ridge, on the map) behind the platoon's position in order to ambush the platoon. The hint was a radio call from the platoon on the west, covering route 7, asking "What's that movement on the ridge line?" The platoon leaders radioed back that it wasn't them—never pausing to wonder just who it might have been.

If we had asked these platoon leaders to identify the risks in their ambush plans, they would have missed each one. When people are unfamiliar with the landscape—which is inevitable when facing unpredictable situations—we shouldn't have high expectations for this first step of the risk-management process. None of the scenarios in this study involved a black swan, but they felt like black swans to the young officers.

Sometimes, what seems like a risk depends on our perspective. It depends on where we are standing.

Example 15.2: Anchor and adjust During the Iran-Iraq War (1980–1988), the United States sent out ships to protect the sea lanes in the region. One Aegis cruiser stayed anchored off the coast of Iran. Each day the cruiser watched an Iranian patrol airplane take off and follow the exact same route down the coast, turn around, and return.

Eventually, the Aegis cruiser had to leave its position to rotate some of its crew members, including a new commander. As soon as the cruiser completed its transfer, it returned to the same location. But not exactly the same location. The new commander anchored the cruiser in a slightly different place. This new position shouldn't have mattered, except that it put the cruiser directly in the usual path of the Iranian patrol.

The next day, the Iranian patrol took off, flying the same route it always used. As it headed straight for the Aegis cruiser, the new commander became alarmed. Without any sense of the history of this airplane, the new commander saw an Iranian military airplane coming straight toward his ship. He made preparations to shoot it down. Only with great difficulty did his crew manage to convince him that they weren't under attack.

The new commander perceived a definite risk. The crew saw little or no risk. What we experience as a risk depends on us, and not just on the external situation.

The risks of speaking out

One of the barriers to carrying out step 1 of the RM process is that people are often unwilling to publicly describe potential problems. Even when organizations have people who notice the early signs of problems, they may be unwilling to speak out because they are afraid of disrupting the harmony of the team. And they are afraid of being ostracized and marginalized.

Perhaps we can overcome people's reluctance to speak out by appointing "devil's advocates" to critique plans and find weaknesses. Unfortunately, that strategy doesn't work either.

Example 15.3: The myth of the devil's advocate   One suggestion for identifying risks at the start is to use "devil's advocates." Most people have heard of the notion of a devil's advocate, and most people think it is a good idea. My survey included this statement: "Organizations should appoint devil's advocates to review their plans." The average rating of 5.11 showed that the respondents agreed with the statement. Fewer than 10 percent disagreed—14 out of 161.

However, the research doesn't back up our faith in devil's advocates. Charlan Nemeth and colleagues found that when devil's advocates were appointed in a group they created the paradoxical effect of creating more support for the orthodox position, rather than increasing doubt (Nemeth, Connell, and Rogers, and Brown 2001; Nemeth, Brown, and Rogers 2001). The experiment tested teams of college students on how well they could design a plan to satisfy the vacation requests of employees in an organization. The devil's advocates didn't improve performance even if the group knew who was taking on this role, or even when the devil's advocates were assigned to champion a view with which they agreed.

Nemeth et al. speculated that the devil's advocates weren't helping because people can't have a meaningful argument with a devil's advocate whose task is to present a one-sided opinion. Devil's advocates can't change their minds, appreciate the force of a rebuttal, or be a real partner in discovery-oriented debate. Therefore, groups may simply stop having debates with the devil's advocate. They may stop engaging in any kinds of debates because, having an official devil's advocate, they may feel confident that they have officially considered all sides of the issue.[3]

The one thing that did improve the group's performance was having a person engage in authentic dissent with the group's views. The groups that included an authentic dissenter produced the best solutions, compared with groups that had devil's advocates.[4] Trying to "clone" authentic dissent didn't work, even if the "clone" was arguing for a position that he or she actually held. The dissenter had to speak out spontaneously.

Authentic dissenters may be disliked even when they have helped the group do a better job. Typically, the dissenter's morale suffers. That's one reason organizations have tried to use official devil's advocates to ritualize the dissent role so the group cannot reasonably get angry at the person playing the role.

When an organization doesn't want to hear about a risk, it explains the risk away. Woods (in press) has described how NASA dismissed fears of the foam debris strike that resulted in the *Columbia* disaster. One method NASA used was "discounting through differencing," focusing on the differences between the current situation and the ones that gave rise to the worries.

I am not saying we shouldn't identify risks at the start. That clearly is a prudent step to take, as long as we don't over-analyze or delude ourselves into thinking that we have captured all the threats. But how to do it without getting the authentic dissenters in trouble?

The PreMortem method I described in chapter 4 encourages team members to identify risks at the beginning of a project to get all the concerns on the table.[5] The PreMortem method asks the team members to imagine that a plan or project has failed—this is certain—and to try to explain why it failed. The PreMortem doesn't ask anyone to take on the role of a devil's advocate. It doesn't try to quantify the overall risk level. Everyone on the team contributes his or her reasons why the project failed. Team members gain respect by suggesting reasons that are more insightful and non-standard. The PreMortem method shows the team that authentic dissent is valued, and that everyone can contribute by flagging potential problems. This way of trying to identify risks at the start seems to keep the project team alert and to prevent the team from fixating on a plan it may have to change or fixating on goals it may have to replace. However, the PreMortem method cannot identify all the major risks a new project faces.

One reason many of us have a misplaced faith in our ability to identify potential risks is that when we look at failures, even cases like Pearl Harbor or 9/11, we see that the cues were there in the first place. If only we hadn't been so blind. If only we had compiled lists of leading indicators and applied them diligently, we might have noticed the signs. However, the signs are clear to us only after the event, after we have had our eyes opened by the breakdown or accident.

Step 2: Focus on the most worrisome risks.
Estimate the probability and the impact of each risk, then calculate which risks pose the greatest threat. The formal way to carry out this process is known as Probabilistic Risk Assessment. It lets you enter objective judgments of the probability and the impact of each risk you have identified and then calculate the risks you most need to worry about. All good, if we are actuaries working for a life insurance company. Not so good otherwise. That we can assign a single number to a risk doesn't mean that the risk is a simple property. Suppose that you have a plan to open a restaurant in a promising neighborhood. The risks will change depending on your skills (how much experience you have in running restaurants, adapting menus, and replacing staff members), your resources (savings, time, and energy), and similar factors. What constitutes a risk for one person, starting his or her first restaurant, may not be as great a risk for someone else who has started several restaurants, succeeding in most and failing in others. As was pointed out in chapter 5, when we try to make decisions purely on the basis of statistics drawn from previous events, it's like driving while looking only through the rear-view mirror.

You could find a generic checklist of risks in opening restaurants, and the base rates for success. But probabilities aren't stable and past data aren't necessarily relevant. Conditions change. True, the last three restaurants at this site all went out of business. But an upscale movie complex just opened next door. A lengthy street-repair project, right in front of the restaurant, is now completed. These events might make a difference.

Even without all these complications, step 2 of the RM process depends on accurate estimates of probabilities and impacts. But we are notoriously bad at generating these kinds of estimates, particularly in ambiguous situations. And besides, how can we assign probabilities to risks that we haven't identified? The concept of black swans is that we can't imagine them in advance. Therefore, our risk assessments are bound to be inaccurate.

Here is an example that Taleb used to illustrate the concept of a black swan.

Example 15.4: The real gambles[6]   The owners of a Las Vegas casino were determined to cut down on the amount of money they lost to cheaters. The casino bosses installed sophisticated surveillance gear and used statistical models to keep on top of events.

However, the real risks lay elsewhere. The highest risks and losses didn't agree with the risk-management calculations. The casino lost approximately $100 million when Roy Horn, one of its star performers in the popular Siegfried and Roy show, was mauled by a white tiger. Another risk came from a contractor who had been injured in a construction accident and was angry about the small settlement the casino/hotel offered him; he made an unsuccessful attempt to dynamite the casino by placing explosives around pillars in the basement. A third risk was the casino's potential loss or suspension of its gambling license owing to an employee's failure for several years to file the forms the IRS requires that document high profits achieved by lucky gamblers. (The casino considered itself fortunate to get off paying a very large fine.) Then there was the time the casino owner's daughter was kidnapped. To pay the ransom, the owner took money from the casino's reserves, which violated the state gambling laws.

The casino hadn't included any of the highest risks into its RM calculations. It had no way of anticipating any of these events, so how could it prioritize them?

Methods of risk and reliability analysis assume[7] that a system can be described as parts, or subsystems, that can each fail with a certain probability. Although this bottom-up approach to risk and reliability analysis has been highly successful for technological systems, it is ill-suited to understand failures of humans or socio-technical systems. These systems cannot meaningfully be decomposed into parts. Their parts interact strongly, and they interact differently depending on context.

RM calculations reassure us because they are so quantitative and official looking. However, numerical calculations can disguise overconfidence. Before NASA decided to launch the space shuttle *Challenger* in very cold weather, the official launch estimate was that there would be one catastrophic failure per 100,000 launches.[8]

Even when the warning signs are clear, the risk calculations can be terribly inaccurate and deceptive. The global financial crisis that began in 2008 was triggered by miscalculations about the risks of sub-prime mortgages and the risks of various financial instruments based on these mortgages. For years, people had been warning about a housing bubble, about excessive leveraging, about inappropriate policies at Fannie Mae and Freddie Mac. Warren Buffett, one of the richest men in the world, had referred to credit default swaps as "weapons of financial mass destruction."

All five of the major Wall Street investment banks were battered. Two were sold off and one slipped into bankruptcy. No one could accuse these banks of ignoring risk. They all had risk analysts and they used state-of-the-art risk-calculation methods such as Value at Risk (VaR). JPMorgan had spent seven years developing the VaR method and had been proud to see VaR gain widespread use in the financial community. VaR was highly accurate at making short-term analyses but was insensitive to extreme events that could dramatically reduce financial liquidity. No one had envisioned a liquidity risk.

Few communities focus as much energy on risk management as Wall Street. Methods such as VaR failed to identify the major risks, step one of the risk management process, and to accurately prioritize them, step two.

Bear Stearns, the first investment bank to fall, had a close view of the collapse of Long Term Capital Management in 1998. Bear Stearns had been the broker that cleared LTCM's trades. Bear Stearns had also argued, unsuccessfully, against the rescue of LTCM by the Federal Reserve Bank of New York. LTCM had brought its failure on itself—it had deliberately reduced its equity to only 3 percent of assets. Yet when Bear Stearns collapsed in 2008 its equity-to-assets ratio was also 3 percent.

So we had a predictable contraction in the housing market (predictable in the sense that many observers publicly predicted it), more sophisticated and powerful methods for calculating risks, and the specter of LTCM a decade earlier. Yet the risk-management process failed and as of 2009 the global economy is still reeling. I don't see these events as a strong endorsement of risk management.

Taleb believes he is a pessimist because his descriptions of black swan events show the limitations of analytical risk-management methods. I think Taleb is too optimistic. He is just arguing that we can't predict black swans. I am suggesting that even when they appear in front of us we may refuse to believe in them. By definition, these kinds of events are hard to comprehend and so we explain them away.

Step 3: Develop risk-mitigation plans.
The risk-mitigation plans should protect us by reducing the main risks and/or minimizing their potential damage. These plans describe what we should keep an eye on, when we should sound an alarm, and how we should react in case of a problem.

Paradoxically, in unpredictable environments the risk defenses can become part of the problem. Mintzberg (1994) points out that planning reduces commitment and reduces flexibility. Once a plan is developed, the managers relax because they have safeguards in place. People in the organization may lower their guard, believing that the risk-mitigation plans have ensured their safety.

Along similar lines, Weick and Sutcliffe (2001, p. 66) note that "plans create mindlessness instead of mindful anticipation of the unexpected." Weick and Sutcliffe identify three ways that plans, such as risk-mitigation plans, can reduce mindfulness. First, plans sensitize us to expect some things, but that can mean ignoring other things that we don't expect—precisely the kinds of black swans that can catch us off guard. Second, plans tell the people in an organization how they are supposed to react, so they may not notice how their organization's capabilities have eroded. Third, routines can't handle novel events, but plans are built around routines.

These limitations don't mean that we should stop making any plans but rather that we should realize that planning will not guarantee success and may actually increase the risks. RM plans are built to counter the previous threats that were encountered, but may get in the way of noticing and reacting to the next threats.

RM plans can themselves introduce risk. Pre-nuptial agreements are a form of risk mitigation, but I doubt that they increase the chances for happy and long-lasting marriages. Full-body computer scans to screen for cancer create their own side effects from the high levels of radiation. So does screening for lung cancer.

Example 15.5: Early cancer screening can be hazardous to your health   It doesn't take much for us to worry about whether we are developing cancer. It just takes a bout of constipation (is that colon cancer?), shortness of breath (lung cancer?), or hearing about an old friend or relative who just got diagnosed too late for treatment. Suddenly we want to be secure. We want to know about any little cancers just starting to grow inside of us.

Bach et al. (2007), who studied the effectiveness of early screening for lung cancer, advise us to do away with it. They argue that our mental model for cancer screening fits cancers like cervical cancer. "Pap" smears work for cervical cancer because the screening can identify the aberrant cells that grow into malignant tumors; surgeons can remove these cells before they grow and spread. The fact that nearly all cases of cervical cancer are caused by human papilloma virus (HPV) infection simplifies detection. Because of "pap" smears as an early screening method for these pre-malignant changes, the rate of invasive cervical cancer has dropped dramatically since it gained widespread acceptance.

But lung cancer is different. Most of the anomalous cells caught by a CT (computerized tomography) screen don't ever develop into lung cancer. Bach et al. suspect that the real precursors of lung cancers are very fast-growing, so the chances of finding them in time are very low.

Bach et al. studied a sample of patients who had died of lung cancer and reviewed the results of the CT cancer screening these patients had received six months earlier. The majority of patients who died from lung cancer showed *no* signs of lung cancer in the CT screens conducted six months earlier. The CT screening was worse than useless. The CT screening resulted in more people being diagnosed with possible lung cancer. But Bach believes most of these small cancers aren't serious and aren't worth treating. Still, once the CT screening identifies a small tumor, surgeons will have to remove it. Thus, the screening increased the frequency of lung surgery tenfold, even though it didn't lower the risk of dying from advanced lung cancer.

Unnecessary lung surgery is a health hazard. The biopsy itself is risky, and the post-operative risks of complications (20–44 percent) and death (5 percent) are fairly high, all for a screening procedure that doesn't reduce the risk of dying from advanced lung cancer.

Risk-mitigation plans also create difficulties in nuclear power plants. Jens Rasmussen, one of the fathers of cognitive systems engineering, asserts that the more technological and procedural safeguards that are built into a plant, the more confused the operators get when an unexpected risk does appear. The "safeguards" add complexity to an already complex system. Faced with a malfunction, the operators have to cope with the built-in safeguards while trying to diagnose and manage the malfunction.

Remember the Gimli Glider incident, in which an airliner ran out of fuel. The initial failure stemmed from having a second, redundant fuel monitoring system plus a computer program to choose which was most accurate. The safeguards just added more things that could go wrong and added confusion about how to work around the fault.

Back to Wall Street. Many investors hoped that by diversifying, they could protect themselves from anomalies, but that doesn't take into account more systemic failures that affect the entire portfolio. Thus, today the "safe" strategy of bundling lots of sub-prime mortgages together to reduce the risk in a financial portfolio doesn't seem like such a great idea, because the entire sub-prime industry collapsed.

Step 4: Implement the risk-mitigation plans.
What happens each time the project plan itself changes? Does the risk-mitigation plan have to be reviewed and revised? The discussion in chapter 14 on emergent goals showed that project plans are likely to change as new tasks get added, other tasks get deleted or combined, and schedules slip or get accelerated. Each of these alterations can change the risk profile. Must risk managers continually revise their mitigation plans?

RM plans still rely on safety officers, who tend to become co-opted by the managers simply by working together harmoniously. Most attempts to set up alarm systems fail, because the alarms get ignored. Even sophisticated alarm systems in hospitals get ignored (Xiao et al. 2004). People have a talent for explaining away inconvenient data— recall the case of Lieutenant Colonel Tyler dismissing the radar signals of Japanese aircraft attacking Pearl Harbor, and the case of Lieutenant Colonel Petrov ignoring the satellite signals warning of an American ICBM attack.

Example 15.6: One Meridian Tower[9]   In Philadelphia, the developers of a 38-story office building arranged for a private service to monitor the fire alarm system in the building, and to call the fire department in case an alarm was activated.

On February 23, 1991, a fire started at 8:40 p.m. in a vacant office on the 22nd floor, and activated a smoke detector. The building's engineer and its two security guards chose not to notify the fire department. They reasoned that some workmen who had been on that floor earlier in the day probably hadn't cleaned up properly, and that dust particles were setting off the smoke detector. No reason to make this into an emergency—it would misuse the resources of the fire department and might even reduce their responsiveness in the future when they might really have to rush over. Instead, the engineer went up to investigate.

The private service received the fire alarm. Instead of calling the fire department, it called the building to make sure the people there knew about the alarm. By the time the building's employees got the call, they were already checking the alarm.

The engineer took the elevator to the 22nd floor and was trapped amidst heavy smoke and heat. He used his portable radio to call the security guard in the lobby, who recalled the elevator to the ground floor.

Once the engineer and the security guards were safely outside the building, they realized that no one had yet called the fire department. In fact, the first call to the fire department came from a passerby who used a pay telephone to call 911.

By the time the firefighters arrived, the fire had spread out of control. It burned for the next 19 hours. Three firefighters died fighting the blaze; another 24 were injured. At the time, it was the largest high-rise office building fire in American history.

After 11 hours of attempting to control the fire, the commanders worried that the structural damage might cause the building to collapse. They consulted with a structural engineer, who confirmed the possibility of a "pancake" structural collapse of the fire-damaged floors. They ordered all firefighters to cease their efforts and withdraw.

The fire went out when it reached the 30th floor and triggered the automatic sprinklers on that floor. The building was a total write-off, at a cost of more than $1 billion.

The type of dereliction recounted in example 15.6 is fairly common. The person responsible for sounding the alarm decides to investigate first. The person responsible for providing an independent assessment gets co-opted.

Step 5: Track whether the risk-mitigation plans are working.
If a project starts to run into trouble, we increase our monitoring. We also identify new risks and iterate the process.

Our tracking will necessarily increase as the plan itself runs into difficulty. We would be negligent if we constructed RM plans and didn't use them when they were most needed.

But look at the effect this increased tracking can have. If we are managing a project that is having trouble, we need our energy to recover. However, if the RM overseers redouble their scrutiny, that means more meetings. Quarterly review meetings turn into monthly meetings, which metastasize into weekly meetings. These meetings aren't simply 90-minute affairs. We have to prepare for them. We have to gather data, formulate project briefings, orchestrate the schedule, and make other preparations that take their own time and impose their own burden on attention. Just when we need to concentrate on recovering the project, we're hit with a growing distraction. Some people refer to step 5 as the "death spiral," because troubled projects that enter the stage of heightened management scrutiny rarely recover.

The successes of RM are in well-ordered projects, in mature industries. Risk-management specialists get angry with me for questioning their methodology. They point to all the places that use risk management, but they haven't shown me any data demonstrating that the methods do any good under complex conditions. RM specialists argue the importance of taming the complex projects by imposing some of their analytical discipline.

I agree with RM specialists that people should try to identify risks at the start. I just wonder how complete these lists can be in complex and changing situations.

Reviewing these drawbacks to risk mitigation, we can see a parallel to the deliberate planning concepts discussed in the last chapter. When working in an unfamiliar and shadowy landscape, we can't neatly identify, prioritize, and cauterize all the risks in advance.

Now that we have covered some of the limitations of risk management, let's take a step back and examine different perspectives on risk. The RM approach in claim 9 applies to only the first of these.

Three different concepts of "risk"

We can distinguish at least three different ways people think about risk, exemplified by the safety officers who use a prioritize-and-reduce strategy, the investors who use a calculate-and-decide strategy, and the program managers who use a threat avoidance strategy.

Prioritize and reduce

The discussion of risk management in this chapter only applies to people such as safety officers and risk managers. They are the ones who try to carry out the five-step strategy and who use Probabilistic Risk Assessment to quantify the risks they face. Here, a risk is a potentially adverse event that has a given probability of occurring and an impact that can be estimated. The RM approach estimates probabilities and impacts in order to prioritize which risks to worry about the most. The prioritize-and-reduce approach comes into play when we need to preserve assets that may be jeopardized, or when we need to safeguard project plans. The risks are events that might destroy an asset or derail a plan. Prioritize-and-reduce makes the most sense for well-ordered domains.

Calculate and decide

Decision researchers define risks in terms of gambles.[10] When you flip a coin, you know the chance of it coming up heads is 50 percent, and when you wager money on that outcome you can calculate the chances of winning. If you invest that money in a Treasury bill, the rate of return is much smaller than the gamble on the coin flip but the chance that you will lose your money is also much smaller. In this sense of risk, actions lead to known outcomes that occur with specific probabilities.

Investors rely on the calculate-and-decide framework. They are happy with risk as long as it has the appropriate potential for reward. The goal of investors is to make good gambles in relation to the level of risk they accept. Some of the best gambles, such as acquiring a company or investing in a dramatically different kind of product, come with high risks. Paul Schoemaker, a noted decision researcher, defines risk as the potential for loss and gain, given that we know the outcomes and probabilities. Decision researchers are fond of constructing decision trees to appraise the likelihood and the desirability of various courses of action.[11] In the cases of gambles, investments, and sometimes even life choices, we can calculate the odds because we know the critical factors and how they work. The calculate-and-decide approach to risk works best in well-ordered situations.

Anticipate and adapt

Chief executive officers view risks as threats. They want to avoid threats, but they know that they will have to take some gambles in order to reap rewards. Therefore, they try to manage the risks, but in a different way than the risk-management school describes.

Zur Shapira, a professor at New York University's Stern School of Business, studied several hundred top executives to see how they thought about risks.[12] He found that they had little use for probabilities of different outcomes. They didn't find much relevance in the calculate-and-decide or the prioritize-and-reduce schools. Probability estimates were too abstract for them. They preferred to think about specific scenarios and the worst possible outcomes. Shapira described their strategy as a two-stage process. The first stage was to consider the worst plausible case and see if it was tolerable. If it wasn't, the executives would avoid it and reject the option. They wouldn't pursue a course of action if they didn't think they could manage the threat. If the threat seemed manageable, the executives moved to the second stage, in which they examined the benefits of that course of action to see if it was worth pursuing.

The CEOs' methods of approaching risk are different from the calculate-and-decide methods that decision researchers use. That explains why CEOs don't listen to the researchers. The CEO approach to risk is also different from the approach of the risk-management school, which advocates the prioritize-and-reduce strategy, with its emphasis on quantitative prioritization. That strategy may be relevant for some mature industries, but not for the complex challenges Shapira's CEOs faced. Their anticipate-and-adapt perspective fits complex, ambiguous, and unpredictable situations.

Shapira describes a vice president for finance in a large corporation who did prepare quantified estimates of risk dimensions for meetings of top management: "In particular, he recalled one meeting where the board was considering the purchase of a subsidiary in a foreign country. He brought to the meeting numerical estimates of risk, but the board members were not interested in them. Rather, they spent most of the meeting talking about the need for 'developing a sense of the volatility of the political situation in that country.' The senior vice president of the construction company observed: 'You don't quantify the risk, but you have to be able to feel it.'" (p. 51)

How do executives deal with risk? Shapira asked them to rank their strategies. The most common strategy was to collect more information, which often meant changing the odds, finding an angle that was less pessimistic. Most of the executives seemed to believe that they could do better than the estimates showed, by really applying their energies. The executives didn't trust the estimates they got from others. They needed to understand what went into the estimates; they also needed to get a feel for the risks. What is risky to one person may be less so to another. The executives needed to judge if they would be able to adapt to potential risks associated with a course of action.

Unintended consequences

Claim 9 (that our plans will succeed more often if we identify the biggest risks and then find ways to eliminate them) will make us overconfident when we are in complex and ambiguous situations and we are unlikely to identify the biggest risks in advance and unlikely to be able to eliminate them.

If we enforce traditional RM practices in complex situations, we run the risk of imposing additional procedures and constraints that reduce flexibility.

Replacement

In complex situations, we should give up the delusion of managing risks. We cannot foresee or identify risks, and we cannot manage what we can't see or understand. Furthermore, the bag of tricks we have developed from past incidents probably will not help us in the future. We have learned a lot about disaster relief from the mistakes made in New Orleans after Hurricane Katrina, and communities will do a better job in the future, but some critical features of the next disaster are bound to be different. Not many American cities are located below sea level. And despite its risk-management plans and its awareness of its vulnerabilities, New Orleans was unable to cope with the crisis.

Too often risk management gets aimed in the wrong direction. It gets aimed at what can happen out in the world that might affect us. In his 1983 book *Fundamental Surprise*,[13] Zvi Lanir showed that in many dramatic cases the surprises were inside, not outside. The people caught napping were aware of what an adversary wanted to do but had stopped attending to their own abilities. They gave themselves too much credit for being able to detect the early signs, to absorb a first strike, to have the resources to battle back. They missed the slow erosion of their own strengths. The fundamental surprise was about themselves, not about the external world.

The nuclear power industry, one of the greatest consumers of risk management, has had too many surprises. Managers in that industry are diligent in identifying risk factors. But even they never predicted the sequence of events that led to Three Mile Island or to Chernobyl. Those accidents were caused when operators made mistakes because their control room displays were confusing (Three Mile Island) or because of pressure to get tests completed quickly (Chernobyl).

Weick, Sutcliffe, and Obstfeld (1999) contrasted the culture of high-reliability organizations to the culture of organizations that suffer higher accident rates. The high-reliability culture prefers to learn from the near-misses rather than wait to learn from accidents. Their culture expects all workers to stay alert for any anomalies. The difference in mindset gives them a greater ability to anticipate, avoid, and manage risks.

The concept of an adaptive mindset has given rise to a new discipline of *resilience engineering*. Woods and Hollnagel (2006) and others have described resilience engineering as a means of designing projects, organizations, and systems to be adaptable and to withstand unpredictable risks. Instead of investing in safeguards against previous threats, resilience engineering seeks to improve an organization's ability to reconfigure in order to manage unexpected disturbances. Resilience engineering can be thought of as risk management by discovery.

The replacement for claim 9 is that *we should cope with risk in complex situations by relying on resilience engineering rather than attempting to identify and prevent risks.*

Resilience engineering seems to be the type of approach that would suit the senior executives that Zur Shapira studied. This approach matches their anticipate-and-adapt strategy. The following example shows how a resilient organization responds to a crisis.

Example 15.7: Crisis management at Toyota   In 1997, one of Toyota's major factories burned to the ground. Because the factory was the sole source of a specific valve essential to the braking systems of all Toyota vehicles, Toyota lost nearly all the specialized tools, gauges, and manufacturing lines for this valve. And because Toyota used the "just-in-time" inventory method, it only had three days' supplies available in its pipeline. After it used these up, its production of 15,000 cars a day would come to a complete halt worldwide. Toyota would need six months to build a new factory.

Toyota didn't have a plan to respond to this emergency. It didn't shift to a centralized control mode. Instead, it left the problem to the local plants to figure out. Each of them had formed strong working relationships with their vendors and suppliers. Each of them had different resources.

More than 2,000 companies reorganized themselves. They developed at least six different production processes, each with different tools, engineering approaches and organizational structures. Even firms that were competitors joined in for this just-in-time adaptation. As a result, production of the valve resumed in three days. Within a week, production levels had regained their pre-disaster levels.

Toyota didn't depend on risk-mitigation plans. Instead, it relied on informal relations that had built up over the years. No one could have predicted or planned for the solutions. By giving individual workers rapid access to information and resources, Toyota enabled this network to do its job. A risk-mitigation plan that was developed years earlier wouldn't have been sensitive to the different conditions in 1997.

In complex settings, the notion of a "substance" called "risk" that can be quantified and controlled seems misguided. In complex settings, risk isn't a quantity we can manage and reduce. Instead of trying to predict and control unpredictable risks, resilience engineering prepares managers to expect to encounter unpleasant surprises.

Resilience engineers don't wait for accidents, or for black swans. Instead, they assess the way the organization responded to small disturbances in the past—its "stretchiness." Did the organization adapt smoothly, or was it brittle? As Dave Woods put it (2007), resilience is "the potential for future adaptive action."[14]

Adaptive functions such as managing by discovery and resilience engineering, usually get carried out by teams and organizations. These functions depend on smooth team coordination, which depends on common ground.

Why claim 9 matters

It matters because the five-step process that works nicely in well-ordered settings is usually not effective for managing risks in unpredictable settings. Worse, such a process can lull an organization into complacency.

It matters because organizations that try to eliminate risk are playing so as not to lose, which increases the chances that they will lose.

It matters because we need to develop resilience as a tactic for protecting ourselves against risk. We need to engage in Risk Management by Discovery.

16 The Cognitive Wavelength

In a college relay race, when one runner approaches the next one and says "Stick," the second runner knows just what this means. The first runner doesn't have to waste breath explaining "I am now almost close enough to hand you this baton I am holding, and by the time you hear me and reach back I will be able to place it in your outstretched palm."[1]

Common ground is the knowledge, beliefs, and history we share that let us coordinate smoothly with one another. In a relay race, the runners know what to expect from one another. They are on the same wavelength.

If you and I are having a conversation,[2] you will make assumptions about what I already know so that you will not have to explain everything you say. The more accurate your assumptions, the easier our conversation will be. You won't be telling me things I already know, and you won't be mystifying me and forcing me to stop you and ask for clarifications. These shared beliefs let us make accurate assumptions about other people. More important, they let us make accurate *predictions* about what others are going to do. Teams do better when the members can predict one another's actions more accurately.[3]

Example 16.1: Predicting your partner's actions Anyone who has played a team sport, such as tennis doubles, knows the importance of predicting a partner's actions. Blickensderfer, Cannon-Bowers, and Salas (1998) put this to the test. They gave tennis players a battery of decision-making exercises right before a big doubles tournament. Each exercise showed a diagram with the four players on the court, and showed the shot that one of the opponents had just made. The players had to describe what they would do in reaction to this shot, and what they thought their partner would do. The questionnaire showed diagrams of a few options; participants indicated the likelihood of each one. Blickensderfer et al. tabulated the scores showing how much the partners agreed about how they would react to each situation. Some teams had much higher levels of agreement than others.

The teams with the highest degree of agreement also did the best in the tournament. The correlation was −0.69,[4] which was statistically significant ($p = .01$). If we knew the test scores of a team, we would have a very good idea of how successful that team would be.

We don't know what caused what in the study by Blickensderfer et al. Maybe the teams that practiced more together came to share the same mindset and coincidentally had also become more skilled. Or perhaps the ability to predict a teammate's reactions increases coordination. Most likely both explanations are at work here. Either way, if we find that a team has greater common ground, we can expect them to do better than other teams.

We need to predict in order to coordinate with others, even if the others are complete strangers. For example, we coordinate our driving with people in other cars whom we will never meet. We count on them to follow rules and to behave sensibly.

Our cars are equipped with a special button that announces to the world that we are no longer predictable. Every car has to prominently display the button for activating the hazard flashers. That's how important predictability is for common ground and coordination.

Claim 10: Leaders can create common ground by assigning roles and setting ground rules in advance.

Claim 10 asserts that we can create common ground. Good leaders prepare the members of their team to build and use predictions about one another. They carefully and clearly explain what each person should do. They explain how the team is going to work. They try to eliminate any ambiguities that may create confusion. This process will strengthen team coordination, because coordination depends on interpredictability. Everyone on a team tries to predict and anticipate how the others are going to act.

I studied good leadership in action almost 20 years ago at the Army War College in Carlisle, Pennsylvania. My research colleagues observed a number of small teams simultaneously tackle the same difficult project. We wanted to size up the quality of teamwork at the college, which trains high-ranking Army officers. The project goals were well defined so that evaluators could compare the team outputs, but the teams were under great time pressure. Most of the teams dove right into the work, usually went off track, and had to retrace their steps. Our observers were having a great time documenting all the tumult. Except for one observer who got assigned to a group whose leader started off slowly. This leader explained the roles and functions of each member, and described the project goals in some detail. He took about 15 minutes, ignoring signs that the other teams had already started working. Finally he released his team to get underway. The frustration with observing this team was that they didn't go off track. They didn't make mistakes. The time invested at the start more than paid for itself in reduced confusion. As a result, our observer came back empty-handed, without any good examples of coordination breakdowns to share with us.

I saw the same phenomenon during a training exercise at the National Defense University in Washington. The participants were Army and Air Force colonels, Navy captains, and senior civil servants. On the first day of a three-day exercise, the team leader spent about two minutes explaining his intent. Predictably, the team members misunderstood critical details and wasted their time until the leader could redirect them. On the second day, the leader spent 5 minutes describing his intent. The problem persisted, but not as severely. On the third day, the leader spent 10 minutes describing his intentions. He was learning the benefits of setting up common ground at the start.

The survey participants gave claim 10 an average rating of 5.21 (with 11 out of 160 disagreeing). They tended to agree with this claim in most situations. They believed that they could create common ground in a team by briefing everyone at the start about roles and ground rules.

But what does it mean to "create common ground"? How can we ensure good common ground? Before we try to create common ground, we should see how it works and why it fails.

Disclaimer

Common ground is never as good as we think it is, and it is always eroding. We can't prevent its erosion, especially under complex and changing conditions. Runners on a relay team find it easy to maintain common ground because there is very little variation in their actions.

When goals, roles, and abilities change, we can't count on sustaining common ground. The following example shows a bad handoff between air traffic controllers, rather than runners on a relay team.

Example 16.2: Handing off an airplane[5]   The flight plan that an airplane follows can change for many reasons, such as when the weather conditions change unpredictably. To change a plan, the flight crew works with the airline dispatchers and also with air traffic controllers (ATCs).

During a flight from Dallas–Fort Worth to Miami, a dispatcher noticed a dangerous line of thunderstorms. With the agreement of the airplane's captain, the dispatcher rerouted the airplane. The ATC approved the new route. The dispatcher then turned his attention to the dozens of other airplanes for which he was responsible.

The Miami-bound flight progressed from one ATC sector to another. The ATC in the new sector rejected the reroute and put the airplane back on the original flight plan. The captain assumed that this ATC also knew about the weather front, which must have weakened, and so he didn't object when he was reassigned to the original route. That was his mistake. The new ATC had not been watching storm systems in that area. As a result, the airplane got trapped by a line of thunderstorms. The captain circled, waiting for a break. As he ran short of fuel, he decided to fly through the storms and land in Miami, the only usable airfield at the time. It was a tense approach and landing, but the airplane made it.

What went wrong? The dispatcher spotted the thunderstorms and made a course correction. The captain was agreeable—too agreeable. He knew about the weather and assumed the second ATC also knew about it. That's where the common ground fell apart. Each of the three parties—dispatcher, captain, ATC—believed that they were all seeing the situation the same way. They didn't appreciate how badly their common ground had eroded. The new ATC didn't wonder why the flight plan had originally been changed, and didn't check on the larger weather picture. The captain believed that the new ATC had a better understanding of the weather conditions than he did. And the dispatcher assumed the thunderstorm problem was resolved when he originally re-routed the airplane. The common ground eroded without anyone realizing it. They only figured out afterward what had happened—after it was too late.

Claim 10 asserts that giving clear instructions can provide common ground. And it's true that clear instructions at the start are one basis for common ground. Certainly, clear instructions are better than vague ones, clear procedures are better than confusing ones. But giving clear instructions and having standardized procedures at the start can't protect us. The next example shows how everyone followed the rules and a woman died as a result.

Example 16.3: A hospital is a dangerous place to get sick   A young woman with an unexplained high blood pressure in her lungs was admitted to a hospital for diagnostic tests. The medical team suspected she suffered from primary pulmonary hypertension, but they didn't have any way to directly confirm that diagnosis. Instead, they had to rule everything else out—and there were more than 25 alternate explanations. Their strategy was diagnosis by elimination, which is why they had her in the hospital for five days, undergoing lots of tests.

Ordinarily, venous blood returns via the veins to the right half of the heart and flows easily through the lungs, where it picks up oxygen and then goes to the left half of the heart. The left half of the heart does the heavy pumping, shooting the blood through arteries out to the rest of the body. The right half of the heart has the easy job, because the pressure of the returning blood is usually enough to keep the circulation going. However, in patients with pulmonary hypertension the resistance to blood flow through the lungs builds up. These patients need the right side of their heart to keep the blood moving.

When first admitted to the hospital, the woman mentioned that she had had seizures, but the staff couldn't be sure if these were true seizures or if she had just passed out because of her blood pressure/pulmonary hypertension condition. They figured that if she had a seizure while she was in a hospital, they would be able to treat her.

And then she had a seizure in the middle of the night after spending five days at the hospital, when no one on the diagnostic team was around. An intern rushed in, saw the seizure, and knew exactly what to do: give her Dilantin in an IV, the standard first step for a patient in the hospital having seizures.

Unfortunately, Dilantin doesn't only prevent seizures. When you give the medication in an IV, it also dilates the venous blood system. For most patients the dilation of the venous system poses no danger. But because of the resistance to blood flow in her lungs, this woman needed the venous blood to return to her heart under high pressure.

Otherwise, the right half of her heart wouldn't have enough boost to get the blood through the lungs. When the Dilantin was given and dilated the venous blood system, the pressure of the venous blood returning to the right half of her heart basically disappeared, which meant that blood flow through the lungs also stopped. Then she stopped getting oxygenated blood to the left side of her heart. And the left heart stopped feeding oxygenated blood to itself. Her heart was immediately starved of oxygen. That's what killed her.

The intern didn't know about the diagnosis of primary pulmonary hypertension because the diagnosis hadn't gotten pinned down yet. Under the emergency conditions, the intern didn't have time to read through her charts and test results.

Hospitals can't document everything about each patient and expect every person treating that patient to be aware of the patient's entire history. Every time a hospital moves a patient from one ward to another, risk goes up because common ground is disrupted. Following the rules will not always protect patients. In this case, it killed the patient.

There is no magic formula to guarantee common ground. Some leaders are better than others at strengthening common ground at the outset, but that can't prevent its erosion during dynamic and unexpected events.

The next example describes a loss of common ground between two software teams that never met. When we hear about a software failure, we may wonder "How could they be so stupid?" The actual stories, however, are usually more complicated.

Example 16.4: Crashing into Mars   One well-publicized failure happened in September 1999, when the $125 million Mars Climate Orbiter crashed. According to the *Washington Post*, "NASA's Mars Climate Orbiter was lost in space last week because engineers failed to make a simple conversion from English units to metric units, an embarrassing lapse that sent the $125 million craft fatally close to the Martian surface."[6] But that's not exactly what happened. Engineers do appreciate the difference between feet and meters.

What really happened is that the team that developed the software for the Mars Climate Orbiter re-used a lot of software from a previous project, the Mars Global Surveyor spacecraft. They didn't know that, buried within that earlier program, in the thruster equation, was the conversion from feet to meters. That's how the earlier software made sure that there wouldn't be any confusions about feet and meters, leaving it safe for engineers from different countries to use any standard they wanted. But the earlier software didn't document this conversion, so it was well hidden inside the thruster equation.

The developers of the Climate Orbiter had to make some minor changes to the thruster equation because one of the systems on the Mars Climate Orbiter was a different size than the comparable system on the Mars Global Surveyor. When the software developers made this change, they didn't suspect that they were leaving out the conversion factor from feet to meters. And that's what doomed the Mars Climate Orbiter.

The context of an entire software program can affect each module. Simple actions such as re-using a module become risky because the software developers don't know about the rest of the program, which can run into millions of lines of code. To be careful, every time they made a change, the programmers would have to read through every line and consider its relationship to all the other lines of code.

Many software experts sadly acknowledge the hazards of re-using code from one program to another. The original programmers working on the Mars Global Surveyor couldn't document everything, and a trivial feet-to-meters conversion wasn't worth their time. How could they know that the Mars Climate Orbiter software team would not only re-use their thrust equation but alter it? This little gap in common ground between the two sets of programmers cost $125 million.

We can re-use this incident to illustrate how easy it is for common ground to get degraded, and how even a small degradation can result in a large failure.

These examples—one in a hospital, one in an Air Traffic Control handoff, and one in a Mars mission—all involved breakdowns of common ground. In each case, people didn't get the information that they needed from others in their organization who had that information. Similarly, in the case of the Gimli Glider, the Edmonton mechanic, Conrad Yaremko, never recorded his rationale for marking channel 2 of the Fuel Quantity Indicator System as inoperative. As a result, the Montreal mechanic didn't understand why it was important to leave channel 2 turned off.

More worrisome are the common ground breakdowns[7] in which team members hold *mistaken* beliefs about what others know. The next example illustrates such a breakdown by showing how easy it is for e-mail to confuse us.

Example 16.5: Mailadaptive communication Consider a case in which Joe sends an e-mail message to Steve, the leader of his team. Steve likes the e-mail and forwards it to Andy, copying Joe. So now everyone on the team has received the e-mail and knows that everyone else has received it. Right?

Not always. Imagine that Steve's e-mail never got through to Andy—perhaps Andy's mailbox was full or his server was down for periodic maintenance, or his new spam blocker was hyperactive. The system sends a message to Steve saying that the e-mail didn't get through. But it doesn't send a message to Joe or any other people copied on Steve's e-mail to Andy. Therefore Joe still believes that Andy got the message. Steve knows Andy didn't get it. And Andy doesn't even know there was a message. Three people, three different beliefs.

If Andy and Joe run into each other, Joe may make comments based on his assumption that Andy got the message, and Andy may play along, trying to make sense of Joe's remarks. It may take them a long time to realize what has happened.

If this example strikes you as fanciful, let's change the names. Let's change Joe to Jack, Steve to Nikita, and Andy to Valentin. And let's dial the calendar back to October 1962, the Cuban Missile Crisis. Jack Kennedy has ordered a naval blockade of Cuba. Ships that might be carrying weapons to Cuba are going to be intercepted and turned back. Soviet submarines in the area are going to be hunted, forced to surface, and sent away. To make sure that Soviet submarine commanders aren't provoked into doing anything stupid, Jack has sent a message to Nikita Khrushchev explaining how the submarine procedure will work: the US Navy will drop live hand grenades into the ocean to let the submarine know it has been spotted. Then, if there is no response, practice depth charges will be dropped, signaling the submarine to surface. These are just signals—they won't damage the submarine. But Nikita (or, rather, his staff members) has not relayed this message to the Soviet submarine commanders in the vicinity of Cuba. Therefore, Valentin Stavitsky, one of these commanders, is surprised and then outraged when he is subjected to these actions, which he takes as an American assault.

Valentin hasn't checked in with Moscow in many hours. He thinks it is possible that hostilities have broken out. He interprets the hand grenades and depth charges as ways of tormenting him. Rather than submit without a fight, he orders his crew to fire its nuclear torpedo at the American warships, an act that might well have triggered World War III. Fortunately, his fellow officers convinced him to hold his fire. (For a fuller description of this incident, see Dobbs 2008.)

Example 16.2, the flight to Miami, also illustrated a corrupted common ground breakdown. The pilot mistakenly assumed the ATC knew about the bad weather and interpreted the ATC actions to fit that assumption.

Common ground is always imperfect and continually eroding. Some of the reasons for this erosion are that we aren't very good at taking the perspective of others, we get tripped up by ambiguous words, and we have different life experiences that color our understanding.

Self-centered attention[8]

We aren't always able to take someone else's perspective. We may assume that if we see or hear something, then others will see and hear it and understand it the way we do. We don't appreciate that they may be focusing on something else because their different goals and priorities affect how they look and listen. I used to believe that common ground could be firmly established in stable work settings, such as commercial aviation, until I encountered examples such as the following.

Example 16.6: The fuel leak[9]   Many years ago I was a member of a research team that studied the decision making of commercial pilots, using a NASA B-737 simulator. We inserted a malfunction into an otherwise standard scenario: the fuel tank in one of the wings was leaking. The fuel gauge for that tank showed the drop. This malfunction had actually happened once but was very unusual. One of the aircrews we observed doubted that the fuel was leaking. They thought the fuel gauge was malfunctioning.

The captain reasoned that if fuel really was leaking from the tank on that wing then the wing would be getting lighter, which would change the way the airplane handled. He turned to the first officer, who was flying the plane, and said "Are you having any trouble?" The first officer answered "No." That argued for a gauge problem. It took another 10 minutes for the captain and the flight engineer to conclude that fuel really was being lost.

Afterward, during the debriefing, the crew watched the videotape of their attempts to diagnose the malfunction. Upon seeing the first officer say "No," the captain and the flight engineer thought they found their culprit. But the first officer asked us to rewind the tape. He argued that the captain's question wasn't clear. Yes, the airplane was handling poorly. He was so busy trying to keep it straight and level that he lost track of the conversation between the captain and flight engineer. He assumed they both knew about the leak—it was obvious. So, when asked if he was having trouble, he answered honestly that he wasn't. He was able to keep the plane level. The captain should have asked him if the plane was imbalanced—that's what the captain really wanted to know.

Common ground got corrupted here because the captain assumed that the first officer understood the reason for asking "Are you having any trouble?" The captain assumed that the first officer was gripped by the problem-solving dialog going on right next to him. The first officer assumed that the captain was aware of how much he was struggling to keep the plane level. Neither appreciated the perspective of the other, even though they were sitting side by side, and as a result the captain misinterpreted the answer and wasted 10 minutes verifying the fuel leak. In some circumstances, those 10 minutes could have been critical.

The ambiguity of words

Even if we try to take another person's perspective, we can't be sure we mean the same thing by the same words. For example, Los Angeles erupted in riots after the acquittal of police officers who had been videotaped while brutally beating Rodney King. During these riots, the Los Angeles Sheriff's Department prepared to assault a house in which a small group of suspects were hiding. The Sheriff's Department directed a National Guard unit to "cover us" while the police officers ran up to the house. The Guardsmen agreed. The Sheriff's officers signaled that they were going to start their assault. At that, the National Guard troops started firing their weapons at every window in the house.

The police officers quickly stopped the assault. They couldn't believe what they had just witnessed. In reviewing the situation with the National Guard officers they learned that "cover me" means "pin the enemy down" to a soldier, whereas it means "protect me in case you see anyone threatening me" to the police.

'Risk' is a word that can lead to confusion. The preceding chapter contrasted the way decision analysts, risk managers, and top executives use the word 'risk'.

A college professor told me about a student who was trying to do the right thing for his six-year-old son. Their pediatrician had diagnosed the child with "attention deficit disorder." The student explained to my friend that after hearing this diagnosis he went home each day to spend several hours with the boy. It took my friend a few minutes to realize that her student hadn't appreciated what "attention deficit disorder" meant. He was interpreting the words to mean that his son wasn't getting enough attention.

The word 'teamwork' gets tossed around a lot, such as the importance of coordinating global teams. People from different countries will all agree that they have to show strong teamwork in order to be successful. But if we scratch beneath the surface, we usually find that 'teamwork' means different things in different cultures. No wonder so many global teams run into trouble.

Western assumptions about teamwork emphasize a few concepts: Team members should be interactive and should monitor and help one another. Workers should identify with the team and its success. The leader should create a climate of openness, encouraging everyone to challenge ideas, and should collaborate in arriving at new ideas. Conflicts should be confronted so the team can move forward.

Such advice actually runs counter to the ways that teams function in many non-Western nations (H. A. Klein and McHugh 2005). Teamwork traits that we expect in the United States, such as mutual support and open dialogue, create discomfort in many people from India, the Middle East, and East Asia. Some workers expect to interact directly with their supervisors on their tasks. They don't expect to interact with their co-workers. They are offended by and suspicious of the practice of mutual monitoring and support. They don't want their co-workers "spying" on them. They are put off by the Western expectation that they should identify with their work team—their primary identification is with their extended family. Workers from many Asian countries are troubled by the open airing of conflicts and critiques of ideas that Westerners associate with a creative environment. They expect the good leader to work out conflicts behind the scenes. For them, the purpose of meetings is to find out what the leader has in mind, not to engage in rude give-and-take.

'Teamwork' doesn't mean the same thing all over the world. Western managers can't simply announce a set of best practices for the multi-national team to follow and assume that they have created common ground.

Another word that creates confusion is 'leadership'. In one meeting I attended, a senior person explained that poor leadership was a big problem in his organization. Everyone else nodded. The senior person complained that many leaders turned out to be incompetent and had to be replaced. Everyone nodded more vigorously. Then the group started to discuss different training approaches that might improve leadership. I interrupted the discussion to ask why the leaders had to be replaced. Had anyone gone through all the records to identify the weaknesses? No, no one had done that. This group was going to fix a leadership problem without ever clarifying or diagnosing it.

We all have different experiences with leadership problems. Even when people within the same organization agree that they have a leadership problem, they are likely to mean different things, some remembering incidents of micromanagement, others recalling unfair or unethical acts, leaders who took too much credit, disorganized leaders, indecisive leaders, leaders who were afraid of being unpopular, or leaders who failed to provide the necessary guidance.

One antidote to the slipperiness of words is to make better use of examples. This method, defining by example,[10] can reduce the ambiguity of words and terms such as "leadership problem."

Not only are words ambiguous, they also change meaning over time. I can now e-mail you a paper without any paper being involved.[11] You can start your own list of ambiguities, particularly during long meetings. See how often people talk past one another using the same words and terms. And don't even ask about contranyms.[12] Perhaps we should marvel at how well we do communicate despite the barrier of having a "common" language.

Different life experiences

Common ground also erodes because we have different life experiences that affect how we see things. Teams that have worked together for a while[13] have shared working experiences and precedents about how to handle situations. That's why bringing in new team members creates risks. The new members don't have the shared experiences of the rest of the team. Foushee and Helmreich (1988) unintentionally demonstrated the importance of shared experiences in their study of how fatigue affects the skills and decision making of commercial pilots. They ran a number of cockpit teams through a demanding eight-hour flight simulation. The simulation scenarios included some challenging malfunctions at the start and other malfunctions at the end of the test session. Then Foushee and Helmreich analyzed the data to see if they got any statistically significant findings. They did, but in the wrong direction. Their shared experiences during the eight hours increased the teams' ability to predict their reactions, and improved their coordination. The pilots did better at the end than at the beginning.

The examples of the airplane that had to fly through thunderstorms to reach Miami and the woman who died in a hospital after a seizure illustrate how easily common ground is lost and how devastating the consequences can be. I suspect that many accidents stem from a failure of team coordination brought on by a breakdown in common ground. Claim 10 provides false assurance that we can set the team's common ground as we would set a clock.

Claim 10 (that leaders can create common ground by assigning roles and setting ground rules in advance) is necessary but not sufficient. It suggests that we can improve common ground by preparing a team more carefully. It certainly makes sense to prepare a team by explaining everyone's roles and functions, going over the ground rules, and describing the goals. But claim 10 goes too far in suggesting that we can rest easy once we have completed the preparation. As the examples illustrate, common ground is never perfect and is always eroding.[14]

Unintended consequences

If we took claim 10 seriously, we might spend less time watching teammates once a project gets underway. We would assume that we were all "on the same wavelength," so we wouldn't have to check out any anomalies.

We would put our faith in the roles and instructions set up at the beginning, which would make us less flexible as we discovered what the project really required, who was stepping up, and who was getting pulled off in another direction.

Common ground is much easier to establish in well-ordered, stable situations. When a situation changes rapidly, we can't count on common ground. Furthermore, we shouldn't want to box ourselves in to the roles and goals described at the outset.

Replacement

Common ground is never perfect and is always eroding, particularly when teams have to work in the shadows. We have to continually monitor and repair it, not just calibrate it at the beginning.

The replacement for claim 10 is that *all team members are responsible for continually monitoring common ground for breakdowns and repairing common ground when necessary.* Once we have finished preparing the team we should still be on the lookout for breakdowns. We should continually monitor common ground, staying alert for early signs of confusion.[15] That requirement holds for the team's leader and also for everyone on the team.

In complex situations, the original plans, goals, and roles are likely to change, degrading the team's common ground. Instead of trying to increase control, we should expect common ground to erode and then repair it on the fly. When facing unpredictable crises, a group can't get trapped by the original roles and goals. The Apollo 13 manned lunar-landing mission provides an example. Two days after launch, an explosion crippled the spacecraft. The controllers in Houston cancelled the mission to land on the moon; they would be lucky to get the three astronauts back alive. Gene Kranz, the lead flight director, faced an unprecedented emergency. He pulled one of the four controller teams, the White Team, out of the rotation, called them his Tiger Team and gave them the task of figuring out how to get the astronauts back alive. Kranz also added another person to the team: a controller who was renowned for his cool thinking under pressure. This 15-person team had to figure out how to keep systems running, how to best use the limited battery power available, how to conserve water, and all the other challenges. The Tiger Team didn't appear on the original organization chart. Their new assignment didn't appear in their job descriptions. They didn't have any procedure guides for their work. They exemplify a self-organizing team. The success of NASA's Mission Control organization in bringing back the Apollo 13 astronauts illustrates the process of resilience that was covered in chapter 15.

When people agree to be members of a team, they take on a responsibility to fix any important common ground breakdowns they spot, in order to increase predictability and team coordination. When team members shirk that responsibility, the results can be tragic.

Example 16.7: The **Vincennes** *shootdown*   On July 3, 1988, the USS *Vincennes*, an Aegis cruiser, mistakenly shot down an Iranian airliner, killing everyone on board. The *Vincennes* had been patrolling the Straits of Hormuz to keep ships safe during the Iran-Iraq War. The airliner took off from Bandar Abbas airport in Iran, on its way to Dubai International Airport just across the Straits. The crewmembers of the

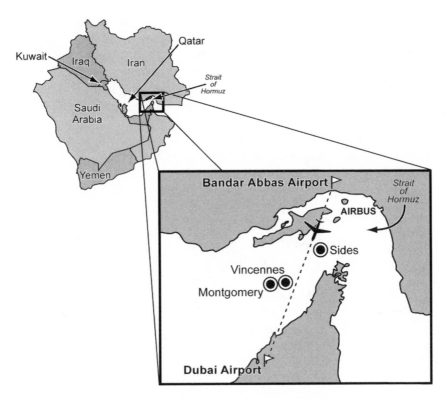

Figure 16.1
The *Vincennes* shootdown.

Vincennes, who were fending off an attack by Iranian gunboats at the time, viewed the airliner as a threat because it was flying directly toward the *Vincennes,* because it had not taken off at a scheduled time, because it ignored radio warnings to change course, and because it had (erroneously) been detected using a military identification code.

The final straw for Captain Rogers, the commander of the *Vincennes,* was that the airliner was reportedly descending as it approached his ship rather than continuing to climb as a commercial airliner would do. Some people in the Combat Information Center on the *Vincennes* did report that the airplane was climbing, but others claimed that it was now descending. Why did Rogers get these different reports? (See figure 16.1.)

When the airliner first took off, the radar operator on the *Vincennes* assigned it the track number 4474. But another US Navy ship, the *Sides,* picked up the same radar track and gave it the number 4131. A few minutes later (and the entire flight lasted less than 8 minutes), the computer system coordinating track numbers figured out that the tracks numbered 4474 and 4131 were the same and assigned the airplane the track number 4131. The computer then reassigned track number 4474 to another airplane, a US Navy A-6 that was more than 100 miles away.

In the confusion about the Iranian gunboats and the approaching airplane, Captain Rogers asked "What is #4474 doing?" This turned out to be a very bad question, because he used the original, obsolete track number. Some of the crew members in the *Vincennes*'s Combat Information Center punched that number into their computers and saw that the aircraft was descending. But they also should have seen that it was located more than 100 miles away, and that it was a US Navy A-6. They reported that the airplane was descending, but they never asked Rogers why he was curious. They were in a position to repair the breakdown in common ground, but for some reason (perhaps time pressure, perhaps because they didn't think it was important, perhaps because they were afraid to correct their captain) no one raised the issue.

Other crew members in the Combat Information Center realized that Rogers meant 4131, and they found that the plane was ascending. But they never told Rogers that he was using the wrong track number.

Everyone in the *Vincennes*'s Combat Information Center was culpable—the crew members who passively used Roger's mistaken track number, the crew members who realized what he meant, and Rogers himself for creating a climate in which not a single crew member raised the alarm about confusion over the track number of the airplane they were getting ready to destroy. Members of a team take on the obligation to correct confusions about critical beliefs that can result in common ground breakdowns.

Good teams are proactive, alerting everyone to unexpected events that might catch people by surprise. Studies of highly reliable organizations, such as power plants and aircraft carriers, show that good teams spot potential confusions and repair them.[16] They also take advantage of slow times to re-calibrate common ground, because they know from experience that once they are in the middle of a crisis it may be too late.[17]

One of the clues that common ground is breaking down is when we say "How can they be so stupid?" in regard to some of the actions taken by our teammates. People usually aren't stupid. If they seem stupid, then maybe we don't understand what is going on.

I suspect that effective teams also learn to anticipate when and how common ground may degrade. They may make extra effort to connect with team members who are at different locations.

Common ground typically suffers during transitions. The handoff of the airliner from one air traffic controller to another created the confusion about the line of thunderstorms. The failure that doomed the Mars Climate Orbiter stemmed from programming changes made by software specialists working on a new system who hadn't written the original code. The woman who suffered a seizure while she was in the hospital for diagnostic tests was treated by an intern who wasn't familiar with her condition. The potential loss of common ground occurs all the time during shift rotations in hospitals and utility companies and many other kinds of industries.

If we know that handoffs are points of vulnerability, why not prepare standard procedures so that the people going off shift will systematically go through all the relevant events with the people just coming on shift? Well-structured settings might benefit from having routine scripts for making handoffs.

Complex settings, on the other hand, wouldn't benefit from routine handoff scripts. Emily Patterson (2008) studied the handoff process in a hospital setting and found that the people on the shift that was ending started their handoff by going over the most important issues. However, what was most important changed from shift to shift, depending on what was happening. If we tried to force each handoff into a routine script, the outgoing shift might run out of time before they could talk about the most urgent topics. Better they should prioritize their conversations.[18]

Why claim 10 matters

It matters because we take common ground so much for granted that we don't appreciate how fragile it is and how easily disrupted. Claim 10 (that leaders can create common ground by assigning roles and setting ground rules in advance) can give teams a false sense of security.

It matters because many leaders like to issue directives and then consider their work done. They blame subordinates for anything that might go wrong instead of accepting their responsibility for monitoring and repairing the common ground in their organizations.

It matters because performance depends heavily on common ground. When we trace back a variety of accidents, the failures at the team level seem to outweigh failures at the individual level. Most of the team failures involve breakdowns in common ground. Team coordination depends on predictability; without adequate common ground we can't reliably predict one another's actions.

17 Unlearning

Filling a mental storehouse

Much of the training and guidance that we receive relies on the store-house metaphor: our minds are storehouses to be filled, and as we grow up and gain experience we add more and more information into them. With the storehouse metaphor, formal education becomes a matter of loading up with the necessary facts and rules. Teachers and trainers become inventory managers. Their job is to tally the contents of a student's storehouse, notice any important items that are missing, and fill the gaps.

The storehouse metaphor assumes that we can organize our knowledge into explicit facts, rules, and procedures, also a comforting notion. As inventory managers we can easily check whether the trainee's store-house contains a certain fact, rule, or procedure. We can test a person before and after a lesson to make sure that the new units of knowledge have been successfully stored. Evaluation becomes easy.

The storehouse metaphor works best in well-ordered domains that have neatly sorted out the concepts, principles, trends, and dynamics. Once we have put all the relevant knowledge into the appropriate forms, we can construct well-organized training programs. We can evaluate performance by seeing how well workers conform to the rules and procedures, and how many of the facts they know. We can perform quality reviews to see if people are doing the job the right way. And we have a strategy for building experts: just feed people more facts and rules.

Disclaimer

The storehouse metaphor doesn't work as well in complex situations as in well-ordered ones. It ignores tacit knowledge—perceptual skills, workarounds, pattern matching, judging typicality, mental models. As we saw in chapter 3, tacit knowledge is hard enough to describe, let alone to inventory.

Look back at the example of the horse-race expert in chapter 7. The expert, MM, knew a lot of facts about races. The interview uncovered just a small portion of his knowledge, but MM's skill went beyond the mere accumulation of facts. His skill was to visualize the races from the racing program. Having seen many thousands of races and then looked at the way each race was recorded, he had learned to animate the written record, to replay the races in his mind even if he hadn't been there to watch the action. You don't find that kind of tacit knowledge and ability in a storehouse of facts.

The storehouse metaphor runs into another problem in complex settings: fixation. The metaphor is all about getting knowledge into the storehouse. What happens when we have to get knowledge out?

Cognitive rigidity

A married couple flew down to Florida on a vacation. They rented a car at the airport. After they got to their hotel, the husband decided he needed to run an errand. He wasn't exactly sure of the directions but he knew he needed to find an exit off Interstate 75. While he was gone, his wife turned on the TV in their room. She saw a news bulletin about a car going the wrong way on I-75. Being a good wife, she called her husband on his cell phone to alert him: "Be careful—I just saw an announcement that there's a car going the wrong way on I-75." "One car going the wrong way?" he responded. "There are hundreds of them!"

"Cognitive rigidity" refers to fixation—holding on to our initial explanations even in the face of contrary evidence.[1] We don't have much trouble explaining away contrary data: the data may be flawed, or irrelevant, or ambiguous. Fixation isn't a type of defective reasoning.[2] It's a natural outgrowth of the way we use our mental models to guide our attention and make sense of events. If we discarded our mental models at the first hint of anomalies, our comprehension would likely be worse, not better.[3]

Scientists fixate in the same ways as ordinary people. Scientists don't readily give up their theories in the face of contrary data. They adapt and modify their theories.

Example 17.1: Students and scientists Chinn and Brewer (1993) examined the way people reacted to anomalous data that contradicted some of their beliefs. They compared science students with actual scientists, and found that both used six common strategies to explain away discrepancies:

· They ignored the data. Scientists don't pay attention to new claims for perpetual-motion machines or extra-sensory perception.

· They found something wrong that allowed them to reject the data. When Galileo, using telescopes, made findings that contradicted Aristotle, rival scientists argued about the reliability of the telescopes.

· They found a reason why the data didn't really apply. It wasn't clear if the phenomenon of Brownian motion (the random movement of particles suspended in a liquid or gas) was in the realm of biology, in the realm of chemistry, or in the realm of heat theory in physics, so scientists whose ideas were challenged by Brownian motion simply explained that one of the other fields would have to figure it out.

· They came up with a reason to hold the data in abeyance until some time in the future. When astronomers found that the orbit of Mercury was inconsistent with the Newtonian view, they just expected that someone eventually would reconcile the anomaly.

· They reinterpreted the data to make them less problematic. When a scientist speculated that mass extinctions in the Cretaceous era were caused by a meteor or comet, citing layers of iridium at a site in Italy, rivals argued that the iridium might have seeped down from layers of limestone above it.

· They made a small, peripheral change in their theories and models that seemed to handle the data without having to re-conceptualize anything. Galileo's opponents believed that the moon and other heavenly bodies were perfect spheres. When Galileo persuaded one critic to look through a telescope and see mountains on the moon, the opponent countered that these mountains must be embedded in a transparent crystal sphere. When Copernicus suggested that Earth was rotating around the sun, astronomers who disagreed pointed out that the position of the stars stayed the same throughout Earth's putative orbit around the sun each year. Surely during a six-month period when Earth would be moving from one side of the sun to the other, the stars should change their positions. Copernicus responded, not by giving up his ideas, but by making a peripheral change in his theory. He suggested that the stars must actually be very far away, and thus Earth's orbit wouldn't make much difference. This *ad hoc* explanation seemed feeble when Copernicus first voiced it, but we now know it was correct. So fixation isn't always a weakness. It can help people mature their ideas.

Physicians exhibit cognitive rigidity. Feltovich, Coulson, and Spiro (2001) showed that pediatric cardiologists had difficulty getting off the garden path.[4] Once they formed an impression of what was wrong with a child, contrary evidence didn't make them rethink their diagnoses. But how did that happen? Weren't the cardiologists noticing the contradictions? Feltovich et al. identified more than 20 different strategies that the cardiologists used to dismiss the contrary evidence so they could hold on to the initial diagnosis. They referred to these strategies as *knowledge shields* because the cardiologists used them to shield their initial beliefs. The strategies described by Chinn and Brewer are all examples of knowledge shields. They are all ways that we maintain our fixations.

The storehouse metaphor fails to take fixation into account because the metaphor focuses on adding more knowledge into the storehouse. When we begin to work in an area, we tend to oversimplify matters in order to gain some initial understanding. Later we have to abandon these oversimplifications—another way we adapt.

The need for unlearning[5]

To learn better mental models, we may have to unlearn some of our existing ones.[6]

Example 17.2: Time slices   In the Cold War era, US Air Force pilots prepared to fly into communist countries at very low altitudes, using the terrain to mask themselves from enemy radars and surface-to-air missiles. This is called "nap-of-the-earth" flying, hugging the ground to fly below radar and to use valleys and hills for cover.

During nap-of-the-earth flight, the airplanes often are only 200 feet above the ground, sometimes only 50 feet. But the lower the altitude, the greater the risk of an accident. Flying fast at low altitudes, pilots don't have much room to recover from slight errors. At these altitudes, power lines pose a hazard; pilots have to look for pylons or poles, because they won't be able to see the lines in time and their terrain-following radar won't detect them. Although the Air Force regularly conducted low-altitude flight training, pilots were crashing too frequently.

One unit decided to try a different approach to training. Previously, pilots had been trained to lower and lower altitudes, which only encouraged them to hold on to their old mental models. This unit treated low-altitude flying as a new skill. The pilots' experience was working against them; too many of their normal routines and habits were inappropriate in the low-altitude condition. The pilots needed to learn a different way to fly.[7] The instructor for this group started them right away at a very low altitude, only a few hundred feet above the ground. This made the pilots fairly nervous, but they did their initial nap-of-the-earth flying over flat terrain and without having to do other tasks. As they became skilled and comfortable flying at the low altitudes, the instructor added more tasks. Critically, the pilots learned the time slices when they could safely divert their attention to fiddle with their radios or make turns. They didn't have to worry about diverting their attention when they were flying at 1,000 feet or higher. At the very low altitudes they had to anticipate where they would have the time to perform tasks other than flying their aircraft. The new training concept dramatically reduced the number of crashes.

The preceding example shows how important it is to jettison old mental models that may get in the way. But we don't have to only look at specialized tasks such as nap-of-the-earth flying. Think back to when you made the transition from hunt-and-peck typing to touch typing. You could have been content with speeding up the hunt-and-peck style, and some people are still using that technique. Others have made the transition, are resisting the temptation to backslide, and are keeping their eyes focused on the computer monitor instead of their fingers. Touch typing isn't exactly like nap-of-the-earth flying—we can walk away from our computer crashes—but the analogy gives you some flavor of what it feels like to relearn a skill you felt comfortable with. And compare your fluency in typing with hitting the number and symbol keys on the top row, where many of us still hunt and peck.

Doug Harrington's struggle to re-learn how to land an airplane on an aircraft carrier (chapter 11) provides another example of unlearning. Harrington wanted to do better. He was getting feedback about his poor performance, but the feedback wasn't working. Feedback doesn't get any more direct than being waved off from an aircraft carrier as you get ready to land, believing you are perfectly lined up. Despite getting immediate and accurate feedback, Harrington still didn't learn what he was doing wrong. Because he didn't understand what was wrong with his mental model, he was unable to give it up.

Harrington's failures that day prepared him to change his mind—to change the mental model he had used successfully. His failures were clear, public, personal, and emotional. When we agonize over a failure, we feel lost. We aren't sure what we could have done to make the outcome better. The process of unlearning seems to work best when we go through this type of emotional process. Losing confidence in our mental models permits us to entertain new beliefs.

Now let's try a demonstration using the Monty Hall problem. If you have looked into this problem in the past and gotten frustrated, or even decided that it was incomprehensible, perfect. That's exactly the attitude I want.

On Hall's television show *Let's Make a Deal*, contestants had to guess which of three doors to open. There was something valuable (often a car) behind one of the doors. Each of the other two doors opened to reveal a goat. But there was a gimmick. After the contestant picked a door, Hall would open one of the other doors, invariably revealing a goat. The contestant then had a choice: either stick with the original door or switch. On the surface, this seemed like a 50/50 bet. Two doors remained, behind one of which was a valuable prize. However, it turns out that the odds are much better if the contestant switches.

Most people can't see why, and they reject arguments trying to explain the advantage of switching. Even prominent mathematicians insist that the odds are 50/50. As far as I can tell, Leonard Mlodinow, in his 2008 book *The Drunkard's Walk*, has provided the best explanation about why one should switch. Until now.

Example 17.3: Explaining the Monty Hall problem   We are going to make three passes at the problem. The first pass uses an exercise that relies on experience, the second exercise relies on a question, and the third exercise uses a new frame.

The experience   Place three similar objects in front of you, as shown in figure 17.1. They can be coins, ashtrays, sticky notes, or whatever is handy. These objects represent the three doors on *Let's Make a Deal*. (Please do the exercise instead of just reading about it. It makes a difference.)

Your initial choice:

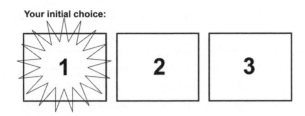

Figure 17.1
The Monty Hall Problem.

We're going to go through this two times. The first time, you will stick with your first choice and we'll see what happens when the prize is behind each of the doors. The second time you will shift from your first choice, and again we'll see what happens when the prize is behind each of the doors.

To save time, throughout this exercise you are always going to pick door 1 on the left. (See figure 17.1.) It's easier to explain this way rather than doing all the permutations.

Let's start the first set of three trials, where you stick with your initial choice, door 1.

For the first trial, find another object, perhaps a small packet of sweetener, to represent the prize, and put it on door 1. Now, you picked door 1 and the prize is behind door 1. As a stand-in for Monty Hall, I open one of the other doors (it doesn't matter which, because neither has a prize behind it), you stick with your original choice, and you win. Congratulations.

In the second trial, the prize is behind door 2. Move the marker behind door 2. You pick door 1, I open door 3 (showing that there isn't a prize behind it), you stick with door 1, and you lose. Too bad.

In the third trial, the prize is behind door 3. Move the marker over there. You pick door 1, I open door 2 (no prize), you stick with door 1, and again you lose. So by sticking with your original choice you win one out of three times. Those are the odds you would expect.

Now let's go through the drill a second time. This time, you are always going to switch.

In the first trial, the prize is behind door 1. Move the marker back. You pick door 1, I open one of the others. It still doesn't matter, but suppose I open door 2. You switch. You aren't going to switch to door 2, because I've already shown that the prize wasn't there, so you switch to door 3. I open all the doors, and the prize is behind door 1, your original choice. You lose, and you feel like a chucklehead for switching.

In the second trial, the prize is behind door 2. Move the marker over. You pick door 1. I open door 3, which doesn't have a prize. You switch. Obviously you won't switch to door 3, because I've already shown that the prize wasn't there. So you switch to door 2 and you win.

In the third trial, the prize is behind door 3. Move the marker over (this is the last time, if you're getting tired). You pick door 1. I open door 2. You switch to door 3, and you win again.

Thus, when you stuck with your original choice you got the prize one out of the three trials. When you shifted you got the prize two out of the three trials. If that doesn't convince you, we'll go to the next exercise.

The questions   The first question in this exercise is "Why was switching successful two out of three times, whereas sticking with your original choice was successful only one out of three times?"

Here is another question: With three doors available, I am giving you a lot of information by opening one of them before you make your final choice. In the experience we just went through, when you stuck with your original choice did you make any use of that information?

If after pondering this question you still aren't convinced, we'll continue to a third exercise.

The new frame   Let's change the set-up. Suppose that after you chose door 1, I offered you *both* of the remaining doors. If the prize was behind either the middle door or the door on the right, you would win. Would you stick with door 1, or would you take the two remaining doors? (Hint: Your odds seem much better if you can choose two doors than if you choose just one.) Now, is there any difference between an option in which I offer you two doors versus an option in which I open one door that doesn't have a prize behind it and offer you the remaining door?

I find that these three exercises convince most people, even skeptics who had announced that nothing was going to change their mind. Notice that I began with the experience. The purpose of the experience is to force you to doubt your mental model about the 50/50 odds. As long as you still have some faith in that 50/50 model, you are going to be hard to convince. So I need the experience to get you to give up faith in the 50/50 mental model. You have to unlearn your initial mental model before you can adopt a better one.

And also notice that I haven't provided any explanation at all. That's why my approach is so convincing.

When the *Parade* columnist Marilyn vos Savant pointed out that switching made more sense than sticking with the initial choice (1990, p. 13), she explained that if you switch then you win if the prize is behind door 2 or door 3. You will win either way, because of the hint. But if you don't switch, you will win only if the prize is behind door 1. This succinct explanation left Marilyn vos Savant's readers unconvinced.

Complex learning isn't simply a matter of adding additional beliefs, as in the storehouse metaphor. Rather, we have to revise our belief system as we experience failures and admit the inadequacy of our current ways of thinking. We discover ways to extend or even reject our existing beliefs in favor of more sophisticated beliefs. That's why it might be useful to replace the storehouse metaphor for learning with the snakeskin metaphor.

The snakeskin metaphor

In a complex world, the snakeskin metaphor may be better than the storehouse metaphor. Snakes continually shed their skin. Every growing organism must shed its skin, or else the old skin would trap it. But snakes shed their skin in a very visible way. As they grow a new skin they wriggle out of the old one and leave it behind. The snakeskin metaphor suggests that we outgrow our initial mental models and have to shed them as our beliefs become more sophisticated.

Now, when we adopt richer mental models we aren't entirely forgetting our old ones. Doug Harrington would still use his old strategy if he were flying a single-seat airplane. Rather, we suspend our belief in the old mental models so that we can learn new ones. Our content knowledge is reorganized or "re-deployed." Then we may compartmentalize the different mental models, or abandon the previous one, or we may even find a way to blend them.

Ways to unlearn and re-learn
How can we get people to abandon old mental models so they can grow into new ones?

To overcome fixation, one thing we can do is spot when it is happening to us, or to others. To do that, we can ask this question: What evidence would it take to change your mind? (It is easier to spot fixation in others than in ourselves.) If someone can't think of any evidence, that is a sign that he or she may be fixating.

A second suggestion is to keep an eye on how much contradictory evidence we need to explain away in order to hold on to our beliefs. If we are mistaken about what is happening, the contradictions should mount and we should be explaining away more and more discrepancies. We will reach a point where we realize that we are wrong. The sooner we get to that point, the better.

Third, we can look at some comparable cases to see what typically happens; if our estimates are much different we better have a good explanation.[8]

Fourth, we can bring in a person who doesn't have much history with the issues at hand and who thus will have a fresh perspective. That's what happened in the example of the UAVs in Kosovo (chapter 10). The officer who figured out that the staff members were watching their own team and not a gang came in after the staff had been working the problem. He wasn't in the room when they got on the garden path or when they became increasingly committed to it.

Doug Harrington was fortunate. If the LSO hadn't visited him on the fateful night, he would have ended his aviation career in the Navy without understanding what went wrong. Instead of waiting for failures, as in Doug's case, we can manufacture them, maybe using exercises and simulations that prepare learners to absorb feedback. That's a fifth suggestion. We can use these exercises to create a conflict and show people that their old beliefs don't work very well.

Example 17.4: Going against the flow   My colleagues Danyele Harris-Thompson, Dave Malek, and Sterling Wiggins once did a research project to train operators who control the movement of petroleum products in pipelines that can be hundreds of miles long. The operators had been trained on the various pumping stations along the route and on the ways to control each pump to keep the product flowing. Danyele, Dave, and Sterling found that the highly skilled controllers had developed a feel for the movement of product inside the pipeline. They had learned to "play" the pumping stations almost as one would play a musical instrument.

Danyele, Dave, and Sterling built a set of decision exercises to present the operators with dilemmas. In one exercise, the technicians at one of the pumping stations had asked permission to shut their station down for 20 minutes for routine maintenance. This simple request, had the operators honored it immediately, would have reduced pressure down the line, triggering a chain reaction of pump shutdowns due to low pressure. In fact, the entire line was going to get shut down if that pump was turned off for maintenance.

The skilled controllers immediately saw the consequences. They delayed the shutdown until they found a way to re-jigger the other pumps to keep the line flowing. In contrast, I watched a new controller, with just a few months of experience, give permission to turn off the crucial station without thinking of the consequences.

The control room operators soon realized that these dilemmas really helped the rookies to think about the flow inside the pipeline rather than just follow rules for operating the equipment. Instead of memorizing each of the pumping stations and the features of the pumps (which had been their formal training), they learned more by working out the connections between the stations and the ways they interacted in keeping the lines flowing. The exercise showed them that their mental models were too shallow, and helped them achieve a new way to think about the capabilities of each of the pumping stations along the line and how it interacts with the other pumping stations.

People usually have to lose faith in their old mental models before they can seriously consider new ones. When the operators in the preceding example saw that their intuitive reaction would have shut down the entire line, they knew that they needed to find a richer perspective. Similarly, in example 17.2 the pilots suddenly forced to fly at low altitudes knew that their usual routines wouldn't work anymore. As a result, they become more receptive to new routines. In the Monty Hall problem, the first pass, the experience, was designed to force you out of your original viewpoint.

A sixth strategy to overcome fixation is to use analogies and metaphors. For example, high school physics students are initially skeptical when shown a book resting on a table and told that the table is pressing upward on the book. That just doesn't make sense to them. To shake them free, some teachers asked the students to imagine balancing a book on their outstretched hands. Obviously they would have to press upward to support the weight of the book. Next, they imagined placing the book on a spring, first pushing it all the way down and then having the spring rebound a bit. Obviously the spring is pressing upward against the book. Then the students imagined the book on a springy plank of wood, weighing it down but then having the plank rebound. Eventually, some of the students accepted that the solid table must be pressing upward against the book. By gradually introducing alternative analogies, the teachers helped the students arrive at a better understanding.[9]

Feltovich et al. (1984) gave pediatric cardiologists a garden-path scenario in order to study their reasoning strategies. The experts (two medical school faculty members each with more than 20 years of active practice plus two fourth-year follows, each with more than 400 patients with congenital heart disease) relied on "logical competitor sets." Even if the cardiologists didn't believe in these competitors, they had the discipline to identify and test them. In contrast, the students (four fourth-year medical students just completing a six-week course in pediatric cardiology) rarely considered a logical competitor set of plausible alternatives.[10] Watson and Crick showed some of that discipline when they investigated a double-helix structure even though they didn't think it was right. Using logical competitor sets is a seventh strategy to overcome fixation.

An eighth strategy is the crystal ball method (Cohen et al. 1997). This method is to have someone explain what he or she thinks is happening, then say that a crystal ball shows that the explanation is wrong, even though the facts are correct. The person has to come up with a different explanation for the same facts.

A ninth strategy is simply to be curious when we encounter anomalies. Instead of explaining them away, we sometimes wonder about them. Anomalies only seem anomalous because our mental model is limited. For example, in 1900 the physician and bacteriologist Walter Reed was sent to Havana and put in charge of a special Yellow Fever Commission to try to determine what causes the disease, how it spreads, and how to control it. We now know that yellow fever is caused by a virus and spread by mosquitoes, but at the time viruses were unknown and undetectable, and the notion that a tiny mosquito could kill a man seemed ridiculous. Most thought the disease was caused by filthy conditions. Then Reed heard about a curious case in which an unruly soldier had been put in prison for a month, at which time he contracted yellow fever and died. Yet none of the other eight convicts in his cell contracted yellow fever, even though they shared the same conditions and one later slept in the dead man's bunk. All of them had been sealed in the prison cell. But the cell did have a window. Reed wondered about that window, and speculated that some-thing tiny—perhaps a mosquito—flew in, bit the one convict, and flew out again. Because of this natural experiment, Reed arranged for systematic tests of the mosquito theory of how yellow fever spread, and he was soon able to cut yellow fever deaths in Havana from 500 per year to zero.[11]

All these methods have some value in helping people shed out-moded mental models and learn new ways to think and to transform their mental models.

Notice that each type of method for breaking free from fixation involves an activity. The pilots unlearn by actually flying differently in simulators or airplanes. The physics students construct a new under-standing through various activities.

Similarly, activities can help us understand the mental models of subordinates and teammates. We can watch them as they engage in activities. Many years ago, my colleagues and I prepared some decision-making games to help young Marine squad leaders get ready for an upcoming exercise. The company commander selected one of his three platoon leaders to run the squad leaders through these games. He left the other two platoon leaders free to work on other things. The platoon training officer assigned to run the games had a chance to watch how all the squad leaders thought about tough dilemmas. He observed the squad leaders in his own platoon as well as the ones from the other two platoons. Pretty soon the other two platoon leaders started showing up for the training. They noticed that these exercises were a rare opportunity to watch the thinking processes of their squad leaders. They could note the kinds of cues they noticed and the cues they missed, the kinds of actions they considered and the kinds they ignored. The decision exercises gave all the platoon leaders a unique opportunity to take stock of their squad leaders' mental models.

The storehouse metaphor isn't wrong. It is useful for teaching ex-plicit types of knowledge and new procedures in stable environments. However, when we apply the storehouse metaphor to complex settings and to tacit forms of knowing, we have taken it past its boundary con-ditions. Training developers who rely on the storehouse metaphor will design courses that cover the explicit knowledge needed to perform tasks, but those courses usually won't address the tacit knowledge that is also necessary to do the work or the flawed mental models that have to be adjusted.

The storehouse metaphor will also affect hiring and promotion decisions because it undervalues the expertise, the tacit knowledge, and the rich mental models of skilled workers. The notion that expertise depends on facts, rules, and procedures offers false optimism about the ease of creating experts. It encourages trainers to stuff employees with facts, rules, and procedures more quickly and efficiently. That's why we need a different metaphor and different methods for learning cognitive skills.

IV Finishing

I am no lover of disorder and doubt as such. Rather do I fear to lose truth by this pretension to possess it already wholly.

—William James, *The Varieties of Religious Experience*

We are now ready to review the ten claims, put them in a different perspective, and see what that process tells us about finding our way through complexity.

18   Reclaiming Our Minds

I promised in chapter 1 that I would review the claims at the end of the book. Here is that review.

Claim 1: Teaching people procedures helps them perform tasks more skillfully.

Think about the manager who rejected the standard procedure for handling a bubble of natural gas in the pipe leading to his oil rig. He merely prevented the rig from exploding and killing everyone on board.

Disclaimer
Following procedures can reduce flexibility. For many skills, teaching procedures can interfere with learning. Procedures aren't sufficient to get complex tasks done, they may need continual updating, and they can make it harder to develop and apply expertise.

Replacement
In complex situations people will need judgment skills to follow procedures effectively and go beyond them when necessary.

Claim 2: Decision biases distort our thinking.

People use heuristics that generally work well but aren't perfect. Few of the so-called biases seem to have any substantial effect in natural settings. For example, Gerd Gigerenzer showed that AIDS counselors didn't know how to interpret the results of HIV tests, but by giving them frequency data instead of probabilities Gigerenzer and his research team could make decision bias disappear.

Disclaimer
People use heuristics that generally work well but aren't perfect.

Replacement
Decision biases reflect our thinking. Rather than discouraging people from using heuristics, we should help them build expertise so they can use their heuristics more effectively.

Claim 2a: Successful decision makers rely on logic and statistics instead of intuition.

Patients with brain damage that blocks them from using intuition and emotions in making decisions become paralyzed for even simple choices. Shoppers made better decisions about complex choices when they were prevented from analyzing the situation.

Disclaimer
The idea of relying on logic and suppressing intuition has led to its share of blunders.

Replacement
We need to blend systematic analysis and intuition.

Claim 3: To make a decision, generate several options and compare them to pick the best one.

The Recognition-Primed Decision (RPD) model describes how people actually make decisions, not by generating and contrasting options, but by recognizing a reasonable action as the first one considered and then evaluating it by imagining how it will play out. People are more likely to use this strategy as they gain experience.

Disclaimer
We rarely use formal methods of decision making.

Replacement
Good decision makers use their experience to recognize effective options and evaluate them through mental simulation.

Claim 4: We can reduce uncertainty by gathering more information. Too much information can get in our way.

The historical examples of Pearl Harbor, 9/11, and Enron illustrate we don't need to gather more information as much as we need to make sense of the information we have.

Disclaimer
Gathering more data will help us to solve puzzles, but not to solve mysteries. Mysteries require sensemaking more than data.

Disclaimer
More information helps with some types of uncertainty but not with other types. More information can increase uncertainty and reduce performance (because the marginal value of additional data points keeps getting smaller, while the interconnections and the complexities keep increasing). Excessive data can push us past a saturation point.

Replacement
In complex environments, what we need isn't the right information but the right way to understand the information we have.

Claim 5: It's bad to jump to conclusions—wait to see all the evidence.

Another passive view. The anesthesiologists who actively generated and tested speculations were the ones who figured out why the simulated patient was having trouble breathing; the ones who tried not to speculate until they had all the data didn't figure out what was wrong. Watson and Crick actively explored their erroneous triple-helix model and discovered how DNA is the structure of genetics. In complex settings, engaging in anticipatory thinking is better than stifling one's speculations.

Disclaimer
We can't follow the advice to keep an open mind—and we shouldn't follow that advice, because it will make us passive.

Replacement
Speculate, but test your speculations instead of committing to them.

Claim 6: To get people to learn, give them feedback on the consequences of their actions.

But what about the case of Doug Harrington, the Navy pilot who thought he was perfectly lined up to land his A-6 on the aircraft carrier? He sure got clear and direct feedback. The Landing Signal Officer basically told him: "No, you're not going to land on this carrier. Maybe another carrier or some other landing strip. You're not even close to being lined up." That feedback didn't enable Doug to learn what to do. He ended his day sitting bewildered in his room until the LSO came by to help him figure out what was going wrong.

Disclaimer
Feedback is hard to understand in complex situations, and it won't help if the learner doesn't understand its implications.

Replacement
We can't just give feedback; we have to find ways to make it understandable.

Claim 7: To make sense of a situation, we draw inferences from the data.

That's one of the things we do, the assembly line in the mind. But it's too passive a view. We also use our understanding to figure out what counts as a data point. And we're trying to fashion a coherent story, not just churn out more and more inferences. The general in the desert was looking for enemy units and found a lot more than the young sergeant.

Disclaimer
You can churn out inferences forever without understanding what is going on. Sensemaking is more than just a long list of inferences. It's about forming a story to explain events.

Replacement
We make sense of data by fitting them into stories and other frames, but the reverse also happens: our frames determine what counts as data.

Claim 8: The starting point for any project is a clear description of the goal.

But in complex settings, and with ill-defined goals, we would never get started. Joe Wilson was able to create a business around the Xerox 914 copier because he kept re-defining the goal as he went along. We need Management by Discovery more than Management by Objectives.

Disclaimer
In complex settings, most of the goals are vague and ambiguous rather than clear-cut. Goal fixation—that is, continuing to pursue goals that have become irrelevant—affects too many managers.

Replacement
When facing wicked problems, we should redefine goals as we try to reach them.

Claim 9: Our plans will succeed more often if we identify the biggest risks and then find ways to eliminate them.

Executives show little patience for formal risk analyses. Instead of trying to quantify the risks at the start, they want to ensure that they will be able to manage the risks that might arise.

Disclaimer
In complex situations, we should give up the delusion of managing risks. Managers reject mechanical strategies for identifying, quantifying, and prioritizing risks. Instead, they want to understand situations so they can be alert to new problems they may have to handle.

Replacement
We should cope with risk in complex situations by relying on resilience engineering rather than attempting to identify and prevent risks.

Claim 10: Leaders can create common ground by assigning roles and setting ground rules in advance.

Cases like the woman who died in the hospital while being diagnosed illustrate the fragility of common ground and the importance of continually monitoring and trying to repair it.

Disclaimer

We can't set a team's common ground as we would set a clock. The faster the situation changes, the more rapidly common ground erodes.

Replacement

All team members are responsible for continually monitoring common ground for breakdowns and repairing the breakdown when necessary.

Re-testing the claims

Table 18.1 lists all the beliefs that I have discussed. It is the same as table 1.1 in the first chapter. What are your opinions about each of the beliefs? If you filled out both table 1.1 and table 18.1, compare your responses.

As I stated in chapter 1, the right answer for all the statements is "It depends." It primarily depends on the complexity of the situation.

I think some readers will agree less with the statements now than they did in chapter 1. They will still see merit in the claims, but they'll also be aware of the limitations.

Some readers may hold to their original ratings, or may even agree more strongly with some of the statements. If they have learned more about what they value in the claims, then I am satisfied. The purpose of this book is to open a dialog about the boundary conditions for the claims.

I don't want to see a shift from strong agreement with the claims in chapter 1 to strong disagreement here. I don't think the claims are wrong, and I don't intend to convince you to move from one extreme to the other. I just want to help you explore the implications of the claims.

What I am really hoping is that you are looking at these statements and appreciating that the issues are much more complicated than you originally thought. By now you should have a deeper understanding of how we make decisions, how we make sense of events, and how we adapt.

The ten claims are myths. I don't mean that they are false. By 'myth' I mean "a belief given uncritical acceptance by the members of a group, especially in support of existing or traditional practices."[1] For example, many organizations have a myth that they practice open communication and welcome criticism. Newcomers shouldn't accept such myths until they have had a chance to see for themselves how the

Table 18.1

Scale

Claim	1 Completely disagree for any situation	2 Strongly disagree for almost all situations	3 Tend to disagree for most situations	4 Hard to tell	5 Tend to agree for most situations	6 Strongly agree for almost all situations	7 Completely agree for any situation
1. Teaching people procedures helps them perform tasks more skillfully.							
2. Decision biases distort our thinking.							
2a. Successful decision makers rely on logic and statistics instead of intuition.							
3. To make a decision, generate several options and compare them to pick the best one.							
4. We can reduce uncertainty by gathering more information.							
5. It's bad to jump to conclusions—wait to see all the evidence.							
6. To get people to learn, give them feedback on the consequences of their actions.							
7. To make sense of a situation, we draw inferences from the data.							
8. The starting point for any project is to get a clear description of the goal.							
9. Our plans will succeed more often if we ID the biggest risks and find ways to eliminate them.							
10. Leaders can create common ground by assigning roles and setting ground rules in advance.							

organization responds to criticism. The ten claims are cognitive folk myths that have enjoyed routine acceptance. What I've tried to do is present a critical appraisal of the claims so we can understand them better, understand where they don't apply, understand how they can get us in trouble, and more fully understand ourselves.

Why did the claims arise?

One source of these claims is that we like to imagine that we live in a simple and orderly world. Simple messages travel better and resonate more effectively. We prefer simple explanations over complicated ones. We can construct more impressive tools for well-ordered situations—for searching under the streetlight—than when we have to pick our way through the shadows of a complex world.

Another source of the claims is a systems-engineering mindset. We all like puzzles—problems that are solvable. We like to examine the connections between a small set of variables to figure out what is going to happen next. Norman and Kuras (2006) assert that systems engineers embody this type of puzzle-solving mentality—they specify the requirements, then analyze the initial conditions and the resources available, then design processes to transform the initial conditions into the desired outcomes. "A hallmark of the process," Norman and Kuras write, "is the ability to justify everything built in terms of the original requirements. If requirements change, it dislodges the careful scaffolding upon which the system rests. . . . The specific desired outcome must be known *a priori*, and it must be clear and unambiguous." (p. 212) Norman and Kuras point out that traditional systems engineering doesn't work with complex systems.[2] The ten claims in the survey all fit nicely into the way systems engineers view the world.

We are also attracted by analytical tools that accompany the claims. Why take responsibility for making our own decisions if we can follow a formula instead? Who wants to entrust subordinates with decision authority if instead we can direct them to follow a set of explicit decision rules? Who wants to depend on unpredictable human beings who come and go? The claims help us to ensure consistency even as people rotate through an organization.

Despite their limitations, the ten claims have important strengths. They reflect our desire to unscramble complexities by imposing various forms of discipline that include procedures, rules, and forms of analysis. These kinds of tools have shown their value in well-ordered settings, and they may well let us make some progress in managing complex situations. The systems-engineering mindset can oversimplify complex problems and often gets applied to projects that are beyond its scope, but we should encourage such efforts, although cautiously and skeptically. We have much to gain when they work.[3]

Deliberate analysis

By this point, I hope, you will react with suspicion when you hear simple advice on how to conduct analyses to solve complex problems. "Make sure you pin down the goals in advance—otherwise you'll be chasing after shadows." "Nothing to it—just break the project down into stages, estimate how long each will take, and you've got your plan." Situations aren't often this simple. We can't calculate our way through life.

Don't get me wrong. I am addicted to analysis where I think we can make some discoveries. I admire the way the New York Police Department started using crime statistics in the 1990s to anticipate where crimes were likely to happen. I have enjoyed Bill James's books on baseball statistics, and since reading *Moneyball* I have been hoping the Oakland Athletics will win a World Series. I have been playing fantasy baseball for more than 15 years, and I'm still looking for some statistical edge. I have great respect for economists, operations researchers, and other types of analysts

I draw the line at analyses that don't dig very deep, stop with shallow answers, and pretend that they are sufficient. I'm worried about analyses that carefully avoid the tacit knowledge that might muddy the picture. I'm disappointed when researchers describe elegant analyses that work only in well-ordered situations and gloss over how brittle these methods really are.

Think back to the example of my daughter Rebecca in a rowing competition (chapter 5). The objective data showed that by mid-point Rebecca had an uphill battle to win her match. But these data didn't take Rebecca's race strategy into account. In fact, Rebecca had the race sewed up.

Most of the debates I see center on this topic of analysis. Some communities prefer a more extreme statement that we should rely on intuition instead of analysis. Others claim just the reverse: that all modern accomplishments come from analysis. I don't have much sympathy for either type of extremist.

That I have described some of the limits of analysis doesn't mean that I am taking an anti-rational stance. And if the hard-core analysts can't tolerate any question about their methods, all the more reason to be skeptical. Recall the example in chapter 1 about how our eyes have two separate systems, one for focusing in bright light and one for orienting in dim light. We need both of these systems—foveal vision and peripheral vision. We think both intuitively and analytically. Psychology researchers mostly study the reflective mode of thinking. Consequently, we don't know as much about intuitive thinking. We don't know as much about how people think under complex and ambiguous conditions.

19 Getting Found

We think and act differently in the shadows than under bright street-lights. We make our way using a sense of orientation rather than pin-point navigation. We can't base our judgments and decisions on crisp logical arguments, assign numbers to the strength of evidence, or apply the strong types of analyses that are the standards for rationality.

Complexity, emergent goals, and tacit knowledge

We have to search for the keys to adaptive decision making in the shadows. We have to appreciate the way people think when faced with complexity, with wicked problems, and with tasks that require tacit knowledge. These three themes guide each of the chapters in this book. They are the conditions that overwhelm the ten claims.

The first theme contrasts well-ordered settings with complex, ambiguous, and unpredictable settings. If you look back at the survey, you'll see that most of the claims assume that the world is well ordered. The claims express faith in procedures, in logic, in structured methods for decision making, in using information to heal uncertainty, in clear and immediate feedback, in setting up clear goals, in eliminating risks, and in fixing roles and rules. Many of the tools and guidelines about how to think more effectively are designed for well-ordered situations.

Our greatest challenges, however, are complex and unpredictable conditions. Admittedly, there are pockets of regularities within complex conditions, and there are pockets of ambiguity even within well-ordered situations. Nevertheless, well-structured tasks (such as designing a bridge or an airplane) are different than complex tasks (such as formulating a new health-care program, a new policy toward a semi-hostile country, or a marketing strategy for a new product). Designing bridges and airplanes isn't easy. The reasons I see them as less complex than some other tasks are that we have been designing and building them for a long time, we have methods and tools to help us, and we have rigorous standards to gauge whether the designs are good. We have immediate feedback. In 1628, when the Swedish ship *Vasa* sank after sailing less than a mile on its maiden voyage, it was pretty clear that something was wrong with the ship's design. In contrast, we often don't find out about flaws in health-care strategies, foreign policies, or marketing strategies for years if not decades, and even then people disagree about the nature of those flaws.

The second theme contrasts clear goals against ambiguous ones. Many of the claims I have covered presuppose clear goals. Yet in complex situations we usually can't pin the goals down in advance. They are emergent. We have to clarify and re-define the goals as we proceed, learning from mistakes.

The third theme contrasts explicit and tacit knowledge. A number of the claims focus on explicit knowledge. That's the easiest form of knowledge to manage and to proceduralize. The claims about teaching procedures, giving feedback, and setting roles and rules in advance work best with explicit knowledge. Many professionals are still wary of tacit knowledge. Businesses that pride themselves on running by the numbers tend to overlook tacit knowledge; as a consequence, they consider their employees as costs, not as assets. However, skilled performance depends primarily on tacit knowledge.

Most of what we hear about the way people think under conditions that involve complexity, wicked problems, and tacit knowledge is negative—it emphasizes what people can't do. We can't use the strong analytical reasoning strategies that work so well with clearly defined tasks.

As long as we view intuition as the absence of conscious, deliberate analyses, we aren't going to get very far. This perspective would be like studying peripheral vision by cataloguing its sins—we can't read with it, it fades out in daylight, and it doesn't record color. Yet without peripheral vision we couldn't navigate our way through the shadows.

By examining the limitations of the ten claims, we can begin to appreciate how we decide, make sense of situations, and adapt when all the evidence isn't in, the goals are ambiguous, and the situation is unfamiliar. We can appreciate how we draw on our experience.

Experience-based thinking is different from analysis-based thinking. The two aren't opposed to each other; they are complementary, like daytime vision and night vision. Experience-based thinking isn't the absence of analysis. It's the application of all that we have encountered and learned.

Expertise cannot be replaced.

Contrary to the popular view of experts as walking encyclopedias, we would do better to regard experts as detectors. They have spent many hours tuning themselves to notice cues that are invisible to the rest of us.[1] They can make discriminations that most of us can't make. Just as we need special devices to detect radon in our homes, or radioactivity levels near a nuclear power plant, or oxygen levels in a stream, experts pick up cues, patterns, and trends that otherwise go undetected. Think back to some of the cases that we examined in previous chapters—the gerontologist who was sensitive to the problems of an elderly patient; the racetrack expert breathing life into a racing form; Rocky Rockwell, with his ability to detect landmines; the sports announcers who see the gap in a diver's ankles upon entering the water; the graduate students at Cornell who discovered that Enron was financially unstable; the oil rig manager who became nervous when told about a blocked pipe; the Navy landing signal officer who wondered why Doug Harrington couldn't get his airplane lined up straight; the Marine general who found an enemy command post during an exercise; even Jack Aubrey, the fictional British Navy captain. Each of them could see things that others couldn't.

The ten claims put us on the defensive. They discourage us from relying on our own judgment, our own mental models. They make it seem as if there is a right way to think—by calculating—that doesn't take tacit knowledge into account.

Several claims suggest ways that we can replace expertise—with procedures, with explicit knowledge that can be added into mental storehouses, with methods to calculate the best decisions, with emphasizing logic and analysis over biased intuitions, with systematic steps to convert data into knowledge, with computational decision aids, with sufficient data, with managing by objectives, with strategies for controlling risks.

As we have seen, the different ways of replacing expertise will not work very well in the shadowy world of ambiguity and complexity. These claims can get us in trouble, particularly when we most need guidance.

And while I'm on the topic of expertise, I hope you have gained some useful expertise about the way you think in complex and ambiguous situations. I have tried to help you "unlearn" the ten claims, or, rather, to modulate your trust in them. Even if you accept some, most, or all of the claims, I hope that you now look at each of them and appreciate its limitations. That would mean that your mental models about the claims have gotten richer.

I also want to create a different mindset. We are often encouraged to control conditions as much as possible. This control-oriented mindset is best suited for well-ordered situations. In ambiguous situations, in the world of shadows, we aren't going to be able to control everything that matters. We're going to adapt. We should *expect* to adapt.

The mindset I want to foster is to expect to run into problems and to prepare ourselves to recover, to be resilient. Instead of putting all our energy into preventing problems—which is unrealistic—we need a mindset of recovering from problems.

Navigating through the shadows

Imagine that you and I are hiking through a wilderness area. We'll be hiking for several days, and we don't want to carry extra batteries for a GPS system. We begin our journey in the conventional way. We plan each leg of the trip, identify the points where we have to change direction, and perhaps add some landmarks to help us recognize those choice points. We may draw a map showing the segments of our trip, maybe the distance for each segment, and the extra details around each shift point. Navigation means traveling each segment and changing direction at the right places.

This concept of navigation fails to capture the adventures we have when something goes wrong. It ignores our growing doubts about whether we made the correct turn, or whether we missed the turn altogether.[2] It slides past our worries that the map might be wrong. It misses the fear we experience when we realize that we are lost.

Some people deny that they have been lost, lest it be taken as a sign of weakness. Late in his life, Daniel Boone was asked if he had ever gotten lost during all his explorations and wanderings. "No," he replied, "I can't say as ever I was lost, but I was bewildered once for three days."[3]

In his 1976 book *Analysis of Lost Person Behavior*, William Syrotuck summarized 229 cases in which people got lost in wilderness areas. (In the United States, rescuers conduct about 50,000 search and rescue missions a year.) Many who get lost are hunters who concentrate more on the game they were tracking than on their location. They get disoriented in the midst of indistinguishable tall trees, fog, and overcast skies. In the excitement of the hunt, they became exhausted amidst broken rock, dense underbrush, or deep snow. Hikers get disoriented when detouring around rockslides or poorly maintained trails; they miss obscured trail junctions.

"People who are lost," Syrotuck writes, "may experience different types of reactions. They may panic, become depressed, or suffer from 'woods shock.' Panic usually implies tearing around or thrashing through the brush, but in its earlier stages it is less frantic. Most lost people go through some of the stages. It all starts when they look about and find that a supposedly familiar location now appears strange, or when it seems to be taking longer to reach a particular place than they had expected. There is a tendency to hurry to 'find the right place.... Maybe it's just over that little ridge.' If things get progressively more unfamiliar and mixed up, they may then develop a feeling of vertigo, the trees and slopes seem to be closing in and claustrophobia compels them to try to 'break out.' This is the point at which running or frantic scrambling may occur and indeed outright panic has occurred. Running is panic!" (p. 11)

We don't get lost only in forests. We also get lost while driving on paved roads in cities and suburbs.[4] The directions may be faulty (right-left reversals, inaccurate scale, wrong street names). Construction or accidents may block the streets on our route. Signs may prohibit us from making left turns that are absolutely necessary. Landmarks may be invisible at night or in fog or snow. Street signs may have been turned around by vandals, obscured by snow or fog, lost in glare, or hidden behind large trucks or trees. Neighboring communities may use the same names for different streets. We may see the correct name but in reference to an avenue or road rather than a street (e.g., the various Peachtrees in Atlanta). We may have gotten disoriented by a diagonal street, such as Packard Street in Ann Arbor.

Boston is notorious for having discontinuous street numbers where a street runs through neighboring municipalities that have grown together so we don't realize that we have moved from one to another. The streets may not be at right angles, or even straight, making it hard to keep heading in the right direction. Perhaps we know the route number, but the street signs tell the names of the roads instead. Or they tell us the final destination of a highway but we don't know where on the map to look to find this city and so we don't know which highway we're on. There is a vast potential for getting lost any time we move away from familiar terrain, any time we leave the streetlights and move into the shadows.

Global Positioning System devices can overcome many of these problems. I have one, and I like it. But a GPS device won't help with highways blocked by accidents or construction. It won't help if we decide to change our route and can't re-program the device while moving. It doesn't give us the rationale for its suggestions, leaving us wondering about how much to trust it. If we expect to continue on a road and it tells us to turn off we don't know what it is thinking and we can't ask it for an explanation. It can make us vulnerable if we have become so passive that we're just waiting for the next direction and don't have any idea where we are. It will keep us from getting lost most of the time, but when we do get lost we can be in worse trouble. Any time we are in an unfamiliar place, even when we have a GPS system, we risk getting lost.

Now let's take a different perspective on navigation, a recovery-oriented mindset rather than a follow-the-steps mindset. In traveling over complicated terrain, whether in the woods or in a city, we can assume that there is a reasonable chance that we'll make some kind of error. Our recovery-oriented mindset is to look at a map to see where we are likely to get confused. How will we know that we have gotten off track? How can we find our way? Even if we don't get lost, we may at least get bewildered. Think back to all the times you wondered if you had driven too far and wanted to turn around, only to come to the next landmark shortly thereafter.

A map looks different when we adopt a recovery-oriented perspective. New features draw our attention—roads that will show when we have gone too far, streets that resemble the ones onto which we want to turn, confusion zones where we're likely to go the wrong way. By reviewing a map this way, we may prevent some of the mistakes. But the point of the recovery-perspective exercise isn't to eliminate mistakes. That's the control mentality at work. Rather, the point is to assume that we will get disoriented. When disorientation happens, we want to understand the map to more easily recover from our mistakes.

The notion of a recovery perspective grew out of a project I did in 1990 at Fort Campbell, in Kentucky, with Steve Wolf and Marvin Thordsen. We watched UH-60 Blackhawk helicopter teams in a high-fidelity simulator. Their mission for the exercise was to convey soldiers into drop zones deep in enemy territory. The helicopter pilots had to deliver the soldiers during a pre-determined time; artillery barrages would be suppressed during this time window so that the helicopters could safely land and then take off. The mission sounded simple when it was briefed to the teams.

During their planning sessions, most of the teams concentrated on the checkpoints listed on their maps. They would start out flying north, following a road past the first checkpoint, which was where the road crossed a stream. The second checkpoint was at a T intersection where another road dead-ended into the road they were following. Then they would come to a range of hills and turn left. In all there were ten checkpoints on their way to the drop zone. The helicopter crews figured out the average flying speed they had to sustain. They even jotted down the time they would have to hit each of the checkpoints in order to get to the drop zone. It was like watching dispatchers file a schedule for a bus route.

None of the missions followed the script. Only one of the ten crews made it to the drop zone during the period when artillery was suppressed. The others were usually too late but sometimes too early. All the helicopters were detected by enemy radar at some point and had missiles fired at them. The helicopters immediately went into evasive maneuvers and dropped below the tree lines to break the radar lock. Then they had to figure out where they were. They may not have been lost but they certainly were bewildered. With the clock continuing to run, they had to change their routes and fly faster than they wanted, which reduced their chances of picking up landmarks.

We had watched the crews spend their planning time studying the checkpoints and calculating the time at which they would reach each one. During their planning period they hadn't looked at the confusion zones—the areas where they might have to scramble for their lives. The checkpoints were based on prominent landmarks, but the teams didn't anticipate when they would leave relatively safe areas and become vulnerable to enemy radar and missiles.

For all their navigation training, the crew members had never learned how to get found. Emerging from the tree lines, they often went in the wrong direction or else wandered aimlessly until they lucked into a landmark and could continue on their way.

Navigation is easy when we know where we are and where we are heading. It becomes much more difficult once we have gotten lost.

Whenever we work on projects in complex conditions, there is a reasonable chance that at some point we'll get lost and have to recover our bearings. We'll have to get found.

This is where the two mindsets diverge. When a project runs into trouble, people with the control mentality get frustrated and discouraged. However, when the routines break down, those with a resilience mindset switch gears. Now they are going to improvise, to discover workarounds. They are going to have a chance to explore the shadows.

Acknowledgments

I want to thank everyone who helped me produce this book. Dave Artman and Tom Miller, my Division Managers at Applied Research Associates, gave me full support and encouragement even though they knew the book would take me away from other responsibilities. I am grateful for their trust and their patience. Tom Stone, my editor at the MIT Press, continually fueled my energy with his enthusiasm for the project. Diane Chiddister and Paul Bethge provided very thorough editorial reviews, making useful suggestions about how to express ideas with greater clarity. Terry Blessing, Emily Rougier, and Christina Gabbard helped me with final production of the manuscript. Kevin Jones designed several of the graphics and modified others.

Veronica Sanger was my primary production support person for the book. I have been enormously lucky to be able to depend on Veronica for so many things during the ten years we worked together. She has spoiled me by responding to e-mail requests for assistance in the evenings and on weekends, and I appreciate her loyalty and her professionalism.

I also want to thank all the friends and colleagues who reviewed a chapter—in some cases two or three chapters. The book covers a lot of territory, and I depended on the criticisms and advice of others who knew more than I did about the specific topic and research literature in any particular area. I didn't always take the advice of my reviewers, but I was always grateful for it. Some of the reviewers took strong exception to the draft I showed them, and I expect that they won't be much happier with the final version. So please don't take any of the names below as endorsing any of the ideas or conclusions I've presented. Instead, take these names as people who responded quickly and forcefully and constructively to my draft chapters. In all cases, the final version took on a new and better shape because of the ideas that these reviewers offered. They are Dee Andrews, Max Bazerman, Herb Bell, Lia DiBello, Paul Feltovich, Rhona Flin, Keith Holcomb, Robert Hoffman, Greg Jamieson, Danny Kahneman, Alex Laufer, Raanan Lipshitz, Jo McDermott, Chris Miller, Jay Rothman, Jenny Rudolph, Mike Shaler, Zur Shapira, Peter Thunholm, Beth Veinott, Karl Weick, Dave Woods, and Yan Xiao.

I also drew on the assistance of Peter Bach, Patti Bellinger, Stuart Donn, Steve Gabbard, Jack Harrald, Peter Ho, Lam Chuan Leong, Bill Long, Dave Malek, Laura Militello, Shane Mueller, Bruce Pease, Mike Vidulich, and Laura Zimmerman for assessments and/or suggestions regarding specific examples. Jason Riis provided me with invaluable assistance in collecting the survey data for each of the claims.

And then there are the reviewers who read and commented on the entire manuscript. Steve Wolf brought the perspective of a serial entrepreneur. My brother Dennis Klein read the book through the eyes of a professional writer. Jesse Rothman helped me understand how an undergraduate would view the book. Buzz Reed helped me to try to make this book a worthy successor to my first book, *Sources of Power*. Susan Praeger offered her judgments and impressions as a professional who works outside of my research community. Each of them made valuable suggestions about how to frame the ideas and the material.

Patrick Lambe is in a class by himself. Patrick offered to look at the manuscript and then made comments on each of the chapters. But he also wrote an eight-page memo offering ideas about how to re-shape and re-organize it. I have adopted many of Patrick's suggestions, and I am tremendously grateful to him.

Finally, I would like to thank my wife Helen and my daughters Devorah and Rebecca. I thank them for the usual reasons—their acceptance of my preoccupation and distractedness, their encouragement and support, their tolerance for an endless stream of book-related questions, their willingness to have their own incidents used as object lessons. However, I have another reason to thank them. After I had been working on the manuscript for a year, it was time to get reactions. I naturally turned to my family. They were the first ones to read the manuscript. They were the only ones I trusted to see it in its roughest form. I expected candid and critical comments from them because my family has learned to be skeptical of anything I propose. I also knew that their reactions would be motivated by their desire to help me and to improve the book. They didn't disappoint me. They never do.

Notes

Chapter 1

1. In Norse mythology, 'Gimli' means a place of peace, or paradise.

2. Hoffer and Hoffer 1989; Stewart 1992.

3. The conceptual framework is described in greater detail in Klein et al. 2003. We use the term *macrocognition* to describe the way people think in complex situations.

4. Orasanu and Connolly 1993.

5. These are the claims that run counter to the macrocognitive perspective described in Klein et al. 2003.

6. I created negative statements to mix in with each version of the questionnaire because otherwise people would be filling out the scale using the same ratings for each question, which could affect their choices. I have also changed the order of questions shown in chapter 1 from the order I used in the survey because of the way I wanted to sequence the chapters.

7. I used a seven-point scale because some people don't like to assign extreme ratings and I wanted to see how many would at least give a rating of 5 or 6.

8. The topic of complexity has become its own discipline with its own conferences and books. It can be a fairly slippery topic. It seems to have one meaning for mathematicians, another for biologists, another for engineers, and another for philosophers. I am not going to wade into these waters. I am going to contrast a complex domain with a well-ordered one. Complex domains are difficult to predict for several reasons—they have lots of interconnected causes, the situation keeps changing rather than being stable, and we haven't figured out all the variables we need to track. I find that people like to propose their own personal definitions: Complexity is measured by the number of parts. Or by the interconnections between these parts. Or by the ways these interconnections change over time. I am not inclined to try to tease these apart. I just want to distinguish complex from well-ordered situations.

Chapter 2

1. Gawande 2007b,c.

2. Despite their success, these checklists have aroused some backlash, and their use has been rescinded in several instances because innovative checklists are, in a sense,

experimental procedures and, according to the Office for Human Research Protections, require the patient to give informed consent for their use.

3. Pronovost et al. 2006. See also Haynes et al. 2009.

4. Klein 1979.

5. Dreyfus 1997; Dreyfus and Dreyfus 1986.

6. There are times when a skilled player can sacrifice a queen in order to win the game. One of the most famous examples is a game in which Bobby Fischer, at the age of 13, beat a leading American chess master 20 moves after sacrificing his queen.

7. Dreyfus and Dreyfus 1986. Bert and Stuart Dreyfus include additional development of expertise beyond Stage 5 in the 1988 edition of their book.

8. It actually happened another time, to a Japanese Airlines flight.

9. Johnston, unpublished.

10. See Langer 1989; Weick and Sutcliffe 2001; Weick and Sutcliffe 2006.

11. See Morris and Rouse 1985; Patrick and Haines 1988; Kontogiannis 2000.

12. Sauer, Hockey, and Wastell 2000.

13. Vicente 1999.

14. DiBello 2001, p. 80.

Chapter 3

1. Hoffman and Nead 1983.

2. Here I am paraphrasing Orr (1990), who stated that tacit knowledge is "the ability to do things without being able to explain them completely and also the inability to learn to do them from a theoretical understanding of the task."

3. Polanyi 1967.

4. Readers in countries where drivers stay to the left should substitute "right turn."

5. Vanderbilt 2008.

6. Making a left turn against oncoming traffic is not a trivial decision. A large proportion of accidents and injuries occur at intersections where drivers made the wrong decision about when to turn left. The current enthusiasm for traffic circles in the US stems in part from a desire to reduce the chances for left-turn accidents.

7. See Polanyi 1967; Polanyi 1958; Nonaka and Takeuchi 1995.

8. Ryle 1949.

9. I am not going to get caught up in the philosophical debates about forms of tacit knowledge, about the similarities and differences between Polanyi's notion of tacit knowledge and Gilbert Ryle's distinction between knowing-how and knowing-that, or about the difference between tacit knowledge (noun) and tacit knowing (verb). How I distinguish tacit knowledge from explicit knowledge should be clear from my examples.

10. The character of Jack Aubrey is based on a real British naval officer, Thomas Cochrane, who was nicknamed "le loup de mer" ("the sea wolf") by the French who fought against him during the Napoleonic Wars.

11. O'Brian 1972. p. 141.

12. O'Brian 1983. p. 327.

13. O'Brian 1973. p. 312.

14. O'Brian 1977. p. 298.

15. This example is adapted from Gawande 2007a.

16. Harris-Thompson and Wiggins 2007.

17. Klein 2004.

18. Klein 1998.

19. Staszewski 2008.

20. Ford and Kraiger (1995) compiled a set of synonyms for mental models: knowledge structures, cognitive maps, and task schemata.

21. Doyle and Ford 1998.

22. Crandall et al. 2006.

Chapter 4

1. Heuristics are informal methods that can be used to rapidly solve problems, form judgments, and perform other mental activities. Although I am treating them as reasoning strategies, they can take other forms, such as a memory strategy to use mnemonics.

2. See Plous 1993; Gilovich 1991; Kahneman, Slovic, and Tversky 1982; Gilovich, Griffin, and Kahneman 2002; Dawes 2001.

3. On how the research on heuristics has gotten transformed into a hunt for biases, see Lopes 1991.

4. Gerd Gigerenzer (1991) has been a leading critic of the heuristics-and-biases approach. He argues that the concept of *heuristic* was used by the artificial intelligence community as a way to make computers smart, whereas for decision researchers in the heuristics-and-biases tradition the concept is used to explain why people aren't smart.

5. Kahneman and Tversky 1982.

6. Gilovich et al. 2002.

7. This example is described in LuperFoy (1995).

8. This problem is illustrated in Jorge Luis Borges's story *Funes the Memorius*. In describing a person with photographic memory, Borges writes: "Without effort he had learned English, French, Portuguese, Latin. I suspect, nevertheless, that he was not very capable of thought. To think is to forget a difference, to generalize, to abstract. In the overly replete world of Funes there were nothing but details, almost contiguous details" (1962, p. 115).

9. I am usually skeptical of attempts to explain real-world errors in terms of laboratory demonstrations of biases. See Klein 1989.

10. Smith and Kida 1991.

11. Phelps and Shanteau 1978

12. For more general criticisms of claims of judgment and decision biases, see Cosmides and Tooby 1996; Cohen 1993; Cohen 1981.

13. Saxberg 1987.

14. Babler and Dannemiller (1993) and Saxberg (1987) shot baseballs onto fields and found that outfielders did a poor job of estimating where the balls would land.

15. The angle of gaze is the angle between the eye and the ball, relative to the ground. McLeod and Dienes (1996) performed the research demonstrating the gaze heuristic.

16. Also, players run slowly while they are trying to establish the gaze angle. Their coaches sometimes reprimand them for getting off to a slow start, not understanding that this is part of the strategy.

17. Gigerenzer 2005.

18. Klein 2004. See also Klein 2007a.

19. While I was developing the PreMortem method, Mitchell et al. (1989) published an article on prospective hindsight, showing that we do a better job of imagining reasons if we have a mindset of being certain—for example, being certain that a project failed.

20. Gigerenzer et al. 1998.

21. Cosmides and Tooby (1996) have shown that when frequency representations were presented instead of probability representations, 76 percent of subjects—and sometimes as high as 92 percent—showed Bayesian reasoning, and overconfidence, the conjunction fallacy, and neglect of the base rate disappeared.

Chapter 5

1. This is the way Herbert Simon defined it. See Chase and Simon 1973; Simon 1992.

2. Westin and Weinberger 2004.

3. These arguments are based on Westen and Weinberger 2004. Meehl (1954) has also stated that his concerns about human judgment focus on data integration, and not on the clinical observations that provide data in the first place.

4. He could account for 81% of the variance in chess ratings merely by using their performance in the blitz chess tournament when they had 5% of the usual time available.

5. Burns 2004.

6. Calderwood et al. (1988) also found that highly skilled chess players rely more heavily on rapid recognition than less-skilled players.

7. This metaphor is from Woods and Wreathall 2008.

8. By "complex" they meant the amount of information the choice required—basically, the number of attributes that had to be considered.

9. The participants got write-ups for the four cars. The write-up for one car had 75% positive attributes and 25% negative attributes. Two of the cars got 50% positive and 50% negative; one car had 75% negative attributes.

10. Similarly, Johnson, Driskell, and Salas (1997) showed that subjects instructed to rationally generate different options and contrast them did worse than subjects left to their own intuitive reasoning.

11. For a good review, see Wilson 2002.

12. In *Sources of Power* (1998), I referred to overthinking as "hyperrationality."

13. Potchen 2006.

14. Damasio 1994; Bechara et al. 1997.

15. Lowenstein 2000, p. 235.

16. Nocera 2009, p. 50.

Chapter 6

1. The formal term for this approach is *multi-attribute utility analysis.*

2. For example, Beach and Mitchell (1978) had trouble identifying any non-analytical decision strategies. The best they could do was refer to gut feel or emotion or random counting rules. Beach (1993) later broadened his definition of decision making beyond simply making a choice.

3. Zakay and Wooler 1984.

4. Slovic 1995.

5. Decision analysts now suggest that the value of these methods is to help people understand the situation better.

6. Minsky (1986) called this phenomenon "Fredkin's paradox." Another term for it is "the flat maximum."

7. Much of this research showing that giving people more choices interferes with their decision making is described in Schwartz 2004.

8. Klein 1998.

9. I describe this research in *Sources of Power* (1998).

10. The RPD model is related to three of the heuristics studied by Kahneman and Tversky: availability, representativeness, and the simulation heuristic. Traditional decision researchers could have seen the potential of these heuristics and formulated a version of the RPD model for skilled decision makers. I think that didn't happen because the researchers focused on the limitations of these heuristics—their capacity for bias—and not on their advantages.

11. Galdi et al. (2008) reported that even when people believe they are undecided, their mental associations, and presumably their pattern repertoire, predicted their future choices.

12. Johnson and Raab (2003) replicated these findings using sports judges.

13. See Epstein 1994; Sloman 1996; Evans 2008.

14. Evans (2008) suggests that we need to further elaborate the two systems that have been proposed.

15. The formal terms for these are *System 1* and *System 2*. Here I am using the terms suggested by Thaler and Sunstein (2008).

16. Lipshitz 1997.

17. deGroot 1978.

18. Raiffa 1968. See also Bazerman 2006.

19. This strategy dates back to Benjamin Franklin.

20. Ross et al. 2004.

21. Wallsten 2000.

Chapter 7

1. On how seeing connections relates to creativity, see Duggan 2007.

2. On the strengths and weaknesses of experts, see Chi 2006.

3. See Reason's 1990 book *Human Error*.

4. The CIA review group identified some weaknesses in the tradecraft used to assess the threat of Iraqi WMD. Nevertheless, the review group did not conclude that by following highest standards for analysis the agency would have come to the correct conclusion. An unclassified CIA report concludes that Saddam Hussein ordered the destruction of Iraq's WMD in the early 1990s, but deliberately left the issue ambiguous to preserve some deterrence against Iran and to avoid admitting earlier lies. Better CIA tradecraft might have listed that among several possibilities, but would not have pushed that possibility to the top of the list.

5. Manos 2004.

6. Anderson and Smith 2005.

7. H. A. Klein and Meininger 2004; H. A. Klein and Lippa 2008; Lippa and H. A. Klein 2008.

8. I thank Katherine Lippa for this anecdote about a friend of hers.

9. Kahneman and Klein, in press. We took advantage of research by Jim Shanteau (1992), who had contrasted domains in which expertise did or did not develop.

10. Gigerenzer (2005) has suggested some criteria for good errors: We are better off making the error than not making it, the error helps us reach goals more efficiently and learn more effectively. Rasmussen (1990) has argued that some errors may be necessary in order to maintain expertise because people have to cross the tolerance limits and use errors or near errors to clarify where these limits are and how they operate.

11. Is it better to reflect on mistakes, or on successes? My speculation is that when we are skilled, we can learn more from failures than successes. When we are beginning to acquire skills, positive examples that we can model may be more helpful. That is because

when we are starting out we have no shortage of failures but lack the sophisticated mental models to learn from them. When we are skilled, failures are less frequent and highly instructive. They let us find the remaining flaws in our mental models.

Chapter 8

1. On how smart technology makes us stupid, see chapter 16 of my 2004 book *The Power of Intuition*.

2. Skitka et al. (2000) labeled this passivity "automation bias."

3. Personal communication, June 7, 2008.

4. This example is from pp. 81 and 82 of Klein 2007b.

5. Sills 2009.

6. Garg et al. 2005. See also O'Conner et al. 1999.

Chapter 9

1. Lipshitz and Strauss (1997) also talk about response uncertainty—having the information but not knowing which option to select. And Paul Schoemaker (personal communication) takes a very different perspective. He describes our situation when we don't know which variables to consider as "ambiguity," and our situation when we don't know the state of the variables once we figure out what they are as "uncertainty."

2. Schmitt and Klein 1996.

3. Gregory Treverton (2001) distinguished between puzzles and mysteries. His distinction was popularized by Malcolm Gladwell (2007).

4. It is possible that intelligence analysts do know his location but that our government doesn't know what to do about it. That moves it into the realm of mystery.

5. Goldstein and Gigerenzer (1999) and Hall et al. (2007) have made this claim, but their demonstrations involve limited context situations that don't concern us.

6. David Woods, a professor at Ohio State University, suggested this term.

7. This description of the surprise attack on Pearl Harbor (adapted from Klein 2006) is based on accounts by Wohlstetter (1962) and Prange (1981). Kahn (1991–92) argued the opposite: that there wasn't enough information to anticipate the Pearl Harbor attack, even if the noise had been removed and the mindsets cleared.

8. The 9/11 material presented herein is primarily from the report of the "9/11 Commission" (National Commission on Terrorist Attacks Upon the United States), from Wright 2006, and from Hersh 2002.

9. Also see Gladwell 2007.

10. Martin wasn't the only observer warning about the pending economic collapse. I have highlighted him because he made his comments at a conference about spotting early danger signs.

11. For more about managing uncertainty, see Lipshitz and Strauss 1997; Klein 2004.

Chapter 10

1. When I wrote this chapter, a good demonstration was available at http://www.ahs .uwaterloo.ca/~kin356/bpdemo.htm.

2. Yergin 1991, p. 335.

3. Was Stalin really that oblivious? One speculation is that Stalin explained away these signs, expecting that Hitler was preparing to threaten him, and would make some strong demands that Stalin would simply have to accept because of his military weakness relative to Germany. That made more sense to Stalin than a military attack that would divert Hitler's resources from Western Europe. However, I have heard the opposite explanation—that Stalin had lots and lots of tanks and other equipment—Hitler was astonished by the amount of armament the Germans captured—and may have been overconfident in his own abilities. Whatever the reason, Stalin tenaciously held onto his belief that Hitler wasn't going to attack him.

4. If we really wanted people to keep an open mind, we wouldn't have graduate students begin their dissertation topics by doing literature reviews. Instead, we'd encourage them to collect some data and see for themselves what appears to be happening.

5. See also Rudolph, Morrison, and Carroll, in press.

6. This notion of fallible speculation owes a great deal to Karl Popper's (1959) idea of fallibilism. Where we part company is that Popper encourages scientists to search for ways in which their theories might be wrong, whereas fallible speculation merely tries to reduce the chance that people will fixate on their initial speculations.

7. The sources here are Watson 1968 and Olby 1974. Watson's book is easier to read, but Olby's is more useful.

8. Watson 1968, p. 114.

9. Anticipation isn't the same as prediction. For example, if I'm playing chess with you I'm not trying to predict your next move, because if I guess wrong I can get into trouble. Instead, I want to anticipate the kinds of moves you might make. I want to understand your possibilities well enough to counter any serious attacks. If I fail, I say "I should have anticipated that you might make that move." Hawkins and Blakeslee (2004) see prediction as shaping the evolution of intelligence. Their assertions apply equally well to anticipatory thinking.

10. Source: Pradhan et al. 2005.

11. Ordinarily, the F-15s would have known that the Black Hawks were friendly because the helicopters would have emitted a coded Identify Friend or Foe (IFF) signal to that effect. However, another of the many glitches that contributed to the accident was that the security officials had imposed different IFF signals for Turkey and Iraq. Aircraft crossing the border had to change the frequency of the signal. Even worse, no one had ever told the Army helicopter community that they were supposed to shift their IFF frequency. Therefore, the F-15s found that the Black Hawks were emitting the wrong IFF signal, making them even more suspicious. So many things had to go wrong for this shoot down to occur.

Chapter 11

1. Although 164 people took my survey, not all of them responded to every question. The number of respondents varied between 160 and 164 for each statement.

2. Balzer et al. 1989; Early et al. 1990; Johnson et al. 1993.

3. Feltovich, Spiro, and Coulson (1993) described these oversimplifications as "the reductive tendency."

4. Pradhan et al. 2005.

5. On the importance of learner's taking initiative rather than passively being instructed, see Chi et al. 2001.

6. Here are some of the major types of learning: Recognizing and applying analogies, reinforcing responses, classical conditioning to create associations, deduction, induction, imitation learning, episodic learning, and implicit learning. And here are some of the things we learn: Skills, connections (e.g., perceptual-motor), mental models, patterns, typicality, habituation, sensitization, categories, concepts, object recognition, language, metacognition (learning about oneself), instances (episodic learning), facts (declarative knowledge), attention management, spatial mapping, generalization and discrimination, tool learning, decentering (taking the perspective of someone else), emotional control, statistical and analytical methods, and sequencing of tasks. Thus, the term "learning" covers a lot of ground. People trying to create learning organizations might want to pin down what kind of learning they want to foster.

7. I described this incident on p. 224 of Klein 2004.

8. See chapter 14 of Klein 2004.

Chapter 12

1. Endsley's (1995) model of situation awareness reflects this information processing view. Level 1 situation awareness is perceiving the patterns. Level 2 is performing inferences. Level 3 is making projections about future states.

2. The problem here is the notion of atomism—that the world comes ready-made for us in natural units. Few people believe in atomism today.

3. Source: Silberberg and Suen 2001, pp. 9–10.

4. Cox et al. 2006.

5. Gladwell (2008) has described additional ways in which Gates and Allen had a privileged position for seeing connections that were invisible to others at the time.

6. Source: Klein et al. 2007.

7. Crandall and Gamblian 1991.

8. Source: Hoffman 1999.

9. For a further discussion of these issues, see chapter 16 of Klein 2004. Also see Waldmann's (1996) discussion of the top-down mode that people use to apply their beliefs about causality on the data they are viewing.

10. Kauffmann 2005. Rochefort misunderstood Yamamoto's intent. which was to lure the few remaining US aircraft carriers to Midway Atoll in order to destroy them and gain unquestioned supremacy in the Pacific. Midway wasn't intended to be the Japanese launching pad; it was going to be a lure.

11. This example comes from Lia DiBello, whose work in this mold factory I described in chapter 12 of Klein 2004.

12. Medin et al. 1997.

Chapter 13

1. The source of these illustrations of the Traveling Salesman Problem is Wikipedia.

2. Pizlo et al. (1995) have described a computer program that does a good job of approximating human performance by abandoning the notion of exhaustive search and modeling the human—solving first for a blurred version and then adding more detail. The rationale is that our visual system is designed for the blurriness of walking around, followed by a detailing of areas of relevance.

3. This argument was made forcefully by Dreyfus (1972).

4. We developed an initial version of the cognitive decathlon, but the BICA program was ended after its first year because of DARPA budget problems. The cognitive decathlon in its current state is described in Mueller and Minnery 2008.

Chapter 14

1. Greenwood (1981) has traced the early development of Management by Objectives.

2. This decision-making exercise is slightly adapted from one I used in Klein 2004.

3. Several of the examples in this chapter are from Klein 2007b and Klein 2007c.

4. See Jacobson and Hillkirk 1986; Ellis 2006.

5. For a fuller discussion of these issues, see the critique of the Critical Path Method posted by Hal Macomber in his weblog Reforming Project Management (http://weblog .halmacomber.com).

6. Thunholm described the research project to me. I haven't read his report, which is in Swedish.

7. Rothman 2006. For more about this effort, see www.ariagroup.com.

8. The actual legal maneuvers were much more complicated than I have described.

9. This approach is consistent with the "garbage can model" that disconnects problems, solutions, and decision makers. Solutions have their own momentum, waiting for the right problem in order to be activated (Cohen et al. 1972).

Chapter 15

1. Aven 2003.

2. The coaches here were John Schmitt and Keith Holcomb, who also designed the scenarios.

3. George and Stern 2002.

4. The solution quality was judged by raters who reviewed each solution that was generated.

5. Klein 2007a.

6. Taleb 2007, pp. 129–130.

7. These observations about the problems of decomposing systems into parts whose failure probabilities can be independently calculated were made by Erik Hollnagel (personal communication, 2004).

8. Feynman 1988.

9. Source: Routley et al., undated.

10. See, e.g., Wu et al. 2004.

11. Baruch Fischhoff has taken the lead in studying ways to improve risk communication. For a good overview of his work, see Fischhoff 2005.

12. In the first stage, Shapira (1995) conducted in-depth interviews with 50 top executives. In the second stage he administrated a questionnaire to 656 executives.

13. This book was published in Hebrew. My source was an unpublished English version.

14. See also Woods and Wreathall 2008; Woods 2006; Weick and Sutcliffe 2007.

Chapter 16

1. Klein et al. (2004) discuss relay races and other examples of joint activity that depend on common ground.

2. The essential work on common ground is a set of analyses presented in Clark 1996. Clark's account of common ground focused on ordinary conversations but his ideas seem to apply to coordination in general.

3. Klein 2001.

4. The correlation was negative because the best teams got the lowest ranks in the tournament. For example, the top team was rated number 1.

5. This incident was reported in Smith et al. 1998. The description here is from Klein, Feltovich, Bradshaw, and Woods 2004.

6. The analysis of what actually happened is from Euler et al. 2001. See also Sawyer 1999.

7. I have referred to this problem as the Fundamental Common Ground Breakdown (Klein et al. 2004).

8. I appreciate Karl Weick's suggestion that poor perspective taking is responsible for many common ground breakdowns (personal communication, August 4, 2007).

9. This incident, described in Klein et al. 2004, was originally reported in Klein et al. 2000.

10. The formal term for defining by example is "ostensive definition."

11. The transformation of words is referred to as *polysemy*. For more on polysemy, see D. Klein and Murphy 2001.

12. Contranyms are words that can have opposing senses. Lambe (2007) provides these examples: cleave (to cut in two, to join), buckle (to bend and break, to fasten together), clip (to attach, to cut off), fast (not moving, moving rapidly). Here is another: "oversight" which can mean monitoring the operations and being in charge, or missing something because you didn't monitor it carefully enough.

13. Flin and Maran (2004) distinguish "constituted" teams and ad hoc or temporary teams. Commercial aircrews are temporary teams—the captain and the first officer usually don't know each other prior to the flight legs they'll be flying together.

14. One of the most moving accounts of a common ground Breakdown is Scott Snook's 2000 book *Friendly Fire*, about the incident in which US F-15 pilots shot down two US helicopters in northern Iraq. I discussed this incident in chapter 10, in the discussion of anticipatory thinking. Snook shows the confusions that affected the F-15 pilots, the helicopter pilots, and the AWACS weapons directors. Another good book on this topic is Charles Perrow's *Normal Accidents* (1984).

15. Brennan 1998.

16. Weick et al. 1999.

17. Orasanu 1994; Patterson et al. 1999.

18. The nurses might be using a situational script, such as (1) What is the most important issue to you to know about this patient? (2) What have I been watching and what should you watch out for? (3) Any questions? A situational script such as this differs from a routine script that covers specific information items in a fixed order. The advantage of a routine script—assurance that all topics will be covered and predictability of what comes next—is replaced by the flexibility of a situational script.

Chapter 17

1. On the basis for fixation, see DeKeyser and Woods 1993.

2. For these reasons the process of acquiring cognitive skills and building comprehension is not smooth. At each point, at each succeeding improvement in mental models, learners anchor on their current beliefs and use these beliefs to explain events and to explain away anomalies. Learners are not seeking to fixate. Nor are they trying to confirm their hypotheses. They are using their beliefs to shape what counts as data. The result is fixation.

3. The process of being too quick to discard hypotheses in the face of contradictory evidence is called vagabonding. See Dörner 1996.

4. Chapter 10 referred to their study to show what can happen if physicians fail to keep an open mind.

5. These ideas about unlearning and cognitive transformation are taken from Klein and Baxter 2009.

6. See also Bransford et al. 2000.

7. The training program focused on the judgments underlying safe flight at low altitudes. The assumption was that pilots who knew what information to look for, when to look for it, where to find it, and how to use it would be able to recognize potential dangers and execute the appropriate task management and flying skills. The training program also included practice in a flight simulator and classroom instruction on topics such as optical flow patterns.

8. Lovallo and Kahneman 2003; Klein and Weitzenfeld 1982.

9. This example is from Brown and Clement 1989. See also Brown and Clement 1992.

10. Heuer (1999) has made the same suggestion by advocating that intelligence analysts use a method called the analysis of competing hypotheses.

11. This example is from Parker 2007.

Chapter 18

1. *Webster's Third New International Dictionary of the English Language, Unabridged* (1986), p. 1497.

2. For Norman and Kuras, a system is complex if you can't infer the structure and behavior of the overall system from its component parts and if its "elements" change depending on the context.

3. The work of Dave Snowden (e.g., Kurtz and Snowden 2003) has helped me appreciate how the ten claims in table 18.1 would hold in well-ordered situations rather than complex ones, rather than debating whether the claims are right or wrong. Snowden makes additional distinctions between complicated, complex, and chaotic situations, in contrast to simple and well-ordered situations.

Chapter 19

1. See Klein and Hoffman 1993.

2. For a fuller description of problem detection, see Klein, Pliske, and Crandall et al. 2005.

3. Faragher 1992, p. 65.

4. For a description of a set of navigation incidents that require sensemaking, see Klein 2007d.

Bibliography

Anderson, R., and Smith, B. 2005. *Deaths: Leading Causes for 2002*. National Vital Statistics Reports 53, no. 17.

Ariely, D. 2008. *Predictably Irrational: The Hidden Forces That Shape Our Decisions*. HarperCollins.

Aven, T. 2003. *Foundations of Risk Analysis: A Knowledge and Decision-Oriented Perspective*. Wiley.

Babler, T., and Dannemiller, J. 1993. Role of Image Acceleration in Judging Landing Location of Free-Falling Projectiles. *Journal of Experimental Psychology: Human Perception and Performance* 19: 15–31.

Bach, P., Jett, J., Pastorino, U., Tockman, M., Swensen, S., and Begg, C. 2007. Computed Tomography Screening and Lung Cancer Outcomes. *JAMA* 297: 953–961.

Baker, N., Green, S., and Bean, A. 1986. Why R&D Projects Succeed or Fail. *Research Management* 29, no. 6: 29–34.

Balzer, W., Doherty, M., and O'Connor, R. 1989. The Effects of Cognitive Feedback on Performance. *Psychological Bulletin* 106: 410–433.

Baxter, H., Harris-Thompson, D., and Phillips, J. 2004. Evaluating a Scenario-Based Training Approach for Enhancing Situation Awareness Skills. In Proceedings of Interservice/Industry Training, Simulation, and Education Conference, Orlando.

Bazerman, M. 2006. *Judgment in Managerial Decision Making*, sixth edition. Wiley.

Beach, L. 1993. Broadening the Definition of Decision Making: The Role of Prechoice Screening of Options. *Psychological Science* 4, no. 4: 215–220.

Beach, L., and Mitchell, T. 1978. A Contingency Model for the Selection of Decision Strategies. *Academy of Management Review* 3: 439–449.

Bechara, A., Damasio, H., Tranel, D., and Damasio, A. 1997. Deciding Advantageously before Knowing the Advantageous Strategy. *Science* 275: 1293–1295.

Bernstein, N. 1996. On Dexterity and Its Development. In *Dexterity and Its Development*, ed. M. Latash and M. Turvey. Erlbaum.

Berri, D., Schmidt, M., and Brook, S. 2006. *The Wages of Wins: Taking Measure of the Many Myths in Modern Sport*. Stanford University Press.

Blickensderfer, E., Cannon-Bowers, J., and Salas, E. 1998. Assessing Team Shared Knowledge: A Field Test and Implications for Team Training. Presented at 42nd Annual Meeting of Human Factors and Ergonomics Society, Chicago.

Bonabeau, E. 2003. Don't Trust Your Gut. *Harvard Business Review*, May: 116–123.

Borges, J. 1962. Funes the Memorius. In *Ficciones*. Grove.

Brafman, O., and Brafman, R. 2008. *Sway: The Irresistible Pull of Irrational Behavior*. Doubleday.

Bransford, J., Brown, A., and Cocking, R. 2000. *How People Learn: Brain, Mind, Experience, and School*. National Academy Press.

Brennan, S. 1998. The Grounding Problem in Conversations With and Through Computers. In *Social and Cognitive Psychological Approaches to Interpersonal Communication*, ed. S. Fussel and R. Kreuz. Erlbaum.

Brown, D., and Clement, J. 1989. Overcoming Misconceptions via Analogical Reasoning: Abstract Transfer Versus Explanatory Model Construction. *Instructional Science* 18: 237–261.

Brown, D., and Clement, J. 1992. Classroom Teaching Experiments in Mechanics. In *Research in Physics Learning: Theoretical Issues and Empirical Studies*, ed. R. Duit et al. Institut für die Pädagogik der Naturwissenschaftern an der Universitatät Kiel.

Bruner, J., and Potter, M. 1964. Interference in Visual Recognition. *Science* 144: 424–425.

Burns, B. 2004. The Effects of Speed on Skilled Chess Performance. *Psychological Science* 15: 442–447.

Calderwood, R., Klein, G., and Crandall, B. 1988. *American Journal of Psychology* 101: 481–493.

Campitelli, G., and Gobet, R. 2004. Adaptive Expert Decision Making: Skilled Chess Players Search More and Deeper. *ICGA Journal* 27, no. 4: 209–216.

Canham, M., Hegarty, M., and Smallman, H. 2007. Using Complex Visual Displays: When Users Want More Than Is Good for Them. Paper presented at 8th International Conference on Naturalistic Decision Making, Pacific Grove, California.

Ceci, S., and Liker, J. 1986. Academic and Nonacademic Intelligence: An Experimental Separation. In *Everyday Intelligence: Origins of Competence*, ed. R. Sternberg and R. Wagner. Cambridge University Press.

Cesna, M., and Mosier, K. 2005. Using a Prediction Paradigm to Compare Levels of Expertise and Decision Making Among Critical Care Nurses. In *How Professionals Make Decisions*, ed. H. Montgomery et al. Erlbaum.

Chase, W., and Simon, H. 1973. The Mind's Eye in Chess. In *Visual Information Processing*, ed. W. Chase. Academic.

Chi, M. 2006. Two Approaches to the Study of Experts' Characteristics. In *The Cambridge Handbook of Expertise and Expert Performance*, ed. K. Ericsson et al. Cambridge University Press.

Chi, M., Siler, S., Jeong, H., Yamauchi, T., and Hausmann, R. 2001. Learning from Human Tutoring. *Cognitive Science* 18: 439–477.

Chinn, C., and Brewer, W. 1993. The Role of Anomalous Data in Knowledge Acquisition: A Theoretical Framework and Implications for Science Instruction. *Review of Educational Research* 63: 1–49.

Clark, H. 1996. *Using Language*. Cambridge University Press.

Cohen, L. 1981. Can Human Irrationality Be Experimentally Demonstrated? *Behavioral and Brain Sciences* 4: 317–370.

Cohen, M. 1993. The Naturalistic Basis for Decision Biases. In *Decision Making in Action: Models and Methods*, ed. G. Klein et al. Ablex.

Cohen, M., Freeman, J., and Thompson, B. 1997. Training the Naturalistic Decision Maker. In *Naturalistic Decision Making*, ed. C. Zsambok and G. Klein. Erlbaum.

Cohen, M., Freeman, J. and Thompson, B. 1998. Critical Thinking Skills in Tactical Decision Making: A Model and a Training Method. In *Decision-Making Under Stress: Implications for Training and Simulation*, ed. J. Cannon-Bowers and E. Salas. American Psychological Association.

Cohen, M., March, J., and Olsen, J. 1972. A Garbage Can Model of Organizational Choice. *Administrative Science Quarterly* 17, no. 1: 1–25.

Cooke, N., and Durso, F. 2008. *Stories of Modern Technology Failures and Cognitive Engineering Successes*. Taylor and Francis.

Cosmides, L., and Tooby, J. 1996. Are Humans Good Intuitive Statisticians After All? Rethinking Some Conclusions from the Literature on Judgment under Uncertainty. *Cognition* 58: 1–73.

Cox, D., Long, W., Wiggins, S., Miller, T., and Stevens, L. 2006. Cognitive Evaluation of NWS FSI Prototype. Constraints on the Cognitive Performance of the Warning Weather Forecaster. Evaluation Report prepared for National Weather Service, Norman, Oklahoma. Klein Associates Division, Applied Research Associates.

Crandall, B., and Gamblian, V. 1991. Guide to Early Sepsis Assessment in the NICU. Instruction manual prepared for Ohio Department of Development. Klein Associates.

Crandall, B., Klein, G., and Hoffman, R. 2006. *Working Minds: A Practitioner's Guide to Cognitive Task Analysis*. MIT Press.

Damasio, A. 1994. *Descartes' Error*. Putnam.

Dawes, R. 2001. *Everyday Irrationality: How Pseudo-Scientists, Lunatics, and the Rest of Us Systematically Fail to Think Rationally*. Westview.

deGroot, A. D. 1978. *Thought and Choice in Chess*. Mouton. Originally published in 1946.

De Keyser, V., and Woods, D. 1993. Fixation Errors: Failures to Revise Situation Assessment in Dynamic and Risky Systems. In *Advanced Systems in Reliability Modeling*, ed. A. Colombo and A. Saiz de Bustamante. Kluwer.

Dekker, S. 2003. When Human Error Becomes a Crime. *Human Factors and Aerospace Safety* 3, no. 1: 83–92.

DiBello, L. 2001. Solving the Problem of Employee Resistance to Technology by Reframing the Problem as One of Experts and Their Tools. In *Linking Expertise and Naturalistic Decision Making*, ed. E. Salas and G. Klein. Erlbaum.

Dijksterhuis, A., Bos, M., Nordgren, L., and van Baaren, R. 2006. On Making the Right Choice: The Deliberation-Without-Attention Effect. *Science* 311: 1005–1007.

Dobbs, M. 2008. *One Minute to Midnight: Kennedy, Khrushchev, and Castro on the Brink of Nuclear War*. Knopf.

Dörner, D. 1996. *The Logic of Failure*. Perseus.

Doyle, J., and Ford, D. 1998. Mental Models Concepts for System Dynamics Research. *System Dynamics Review* 14, no. 1: 3–29.

Dreyfus, H. 1972. *What Computers Can't Do: A Critique of Artificial Intelligence*. MIT Press.

Dreyfus, H. 1997. Intuitive, Deliberative, and Calculative Models of Expert Performance. In *Naturalistic Decision Making*, ed. C. Zsambok and G. Klein. Erlbaum.

Dreyfus, H., and Dreyfus, S. 1986. *Mind over Machine: The Powers of Human Intuition and Expertise in the Era of the Computer*. Free Press.

Duggan, W. 2007. *Strategic Intuition: The Creative Spark in Human Achievement*. Columbia Business School Publishing.

Early, C., Northcraft, G., Lee, C., and Lituchy, T. 1990. Impact of Process and Outcome Feedback on the Relation of Goal Setting to Task Performance. *Academy of Management Journal* 33: 87–105.

Edwards, W., and Fasolo, B. 2001. Decision Technology. *Annual Review of Psychology* 52: 581–606.

Ellis, C. 2006. *Joe Wilson and the Creation of Xerox*. Wiley.

Elstein, A., Shulman, L., and Sprafka, S. 1978. *Medical Problem Solving: An Analysis of Clinical Reasoning*. Harvard University Press.

Endsley, M. 1995. Toward a Theory of Situation Awareness in Dynamic Systems. *Human Factors* 37, no. 1: 32–64.

Endsley, M., Bolte, B., and Jones, D. 2003. *Designing for Situation Awareness: An Approach to Human-Centered Design*. Taylor and Francis.

Epstein, S. 1994. Integration of the Cognitive and Psychodynamic Unconscious. *American Psychologist* 49: 709–724.

Ettenson, R., Shanteau, J., and Krogstad, J. 1987. Expert Judgment: Is More Information Better? *Psychological Reports* 60: 227–238.

Euler, E., Jolly, S., and Curtis, H. 2001. The Failures of the Mars Climate Orbiter and Mars Polar Lander: A Perspective from the People Involved. In Proceedings of Guidance and Control 2001, American Astronautical Society.

Evans, J. 2008. Dual-Processing Accounts of Reasoning, Judgment and Social Cognition. *Annual Review of Psychology* 59: 255–278.

Faragher, J. 1992. *Daniel Boone: The Life and Legend of an American Pioneer*. Holt.

Feltovich, P., Coulson, R., and Spiro, R. 2001. Learners' (Mis)Understanding of Important and Difficult Concepts: A Challenge to Smart Machines in Education. In *Smart Machines in Education*, ed. K. Forbus and P. Feltovich. AAAI/MIT Press.

Feltovich, P., Johnson, P., Moller, J., and Swanson, D. 1984. LCS: The Role and Development of Medical Knowledge in Diagnostic Expertise. In *Readings in Medical Artificial Intelligence: The First Decade*, ed. W. Clancey and E. Shortliffe. Addison-Wesley.

Feltovich, P., Spiro, R., and Coulson, R. 1993. The Nature of Conceptual Understanding in Biomedicine: The Deep Structure of Complex Ideas and the Development of Misconceptions. In *Cognitive Science in Medicine: Biomedical Modeling*, ed. D. Evans and V. Patel. MIT Press.

Feynman, R. 1988. An Outsider's Inside View of the *Challenger* Inquiry. *Physics Today*, February: 26–37.

Fischhoff, B. 1982. Debiasing. In *Judgment under Uncertainty: Heuristics and Biases*, ed. D. Kahneman et al. Cambridge University Press.

Fischhoff, B. 2005. Risk Perception and Communication. In *McGraw-Hill Handbook of Terrorism and Counter-Terrorism*, ed. D. Kamien. McGraw-Hill.

Flin, R., and Maran, N. 2004. Identifying and Training Non-Technical Skills for Teams in Acute Medicine. *Quality and Safety in Health Care* 13: 80–84.

Ford, J., and Kraiger, K. 1995. The Application of Cognitive Constructs to the Instructional Systems Model of Training: Implications for Needs Assessment, Design, and Transfer. *International Review of Industrial and Organizational Psychology* 10: 1–48.

Foushee, H., and Helmreich, R. 1988. Group Interaction and Flight Crew Performance. In *Human Factors in Aviation*, ed. E. Wiener and D. Nagel. Academic.

Frederick, S. 2005. Cognitive Reflection and Decision Making. *Journal of Economic Perspectives* 19: 25–42.

Friedman, E., Treadwell, M., and Beal, E. 2007. *A Failure of Nerve: Leadership in the Age of the Quick Fix*. Seabury.

Galdi, S., Arcuri, L., and Gawronski, B. 2008. Automatic Mental Associates Predict Future Choices of Undecided Decision-Makers. *Science* 321: 1100–1102.

Gallwey, W. 1974. *The Inner Game of Tennis*. Random House.

Garg, A., Adhikari, N., McDonald, H., Rosas-Arellano, M., Devereaux, P., Beyene, J., Sam, J., and Haynes, R. 2005. Effects of Computerized Clinical Decision Support Systems on Practitioner Performance and Patient Outcomes: A Systematic review. *JAMA* 293: 1197–1203.

Gawande, A. 2007a. The Way We Age Now. *The New Yorker*, April 30: 50–59.

Gawande, A. 2007b. The Checklist. *The New Yorker*, December 10: 86–95.

Gawande, A. 2007c. A Lifesaving Checklist. *New York Times*, December 30, 2007.

George, A., and Stern, E. 2002. Harnessing Conflict in Foreign Policy Making: From Devil's to Multiple Advocacy. *Presidential Studies Quarterly*, September: 484–508.

Gigerenzer, G. 1991. How to Make Cognitive Illusions Disappear: Beyond "Heuristics and Biases." In *European Review of Social Psychology*, volume 2, ed. W. Stroebe and M. Hewstone. Wiley.

Gigerenzer, G. 2005. I Think, Therefore I Err. *Social Research* 72: 195–218.

Gigerenzer, G., Hoffrage, U., and Ebert, A. 1998. AIDS Counseling for Low Risk Clients. *AIDS Care* 10, no. 2: 197–211.

Gilovich, T. 1991. *How We Know What Isn't So: The Fallibility of Human Reasoning in Everyday Life*. Free Press.

Gilovich, T., Griffin, D., and Kahneman, D. 2002. *Heuristics and Biases: The Psychology of Intuitive Judgment*. Cambridge University Press.

Gladwell, M. 2005. *Blink*. Little, Brown.

Gladwell, M. 2007. Open secrets: Enron, Intelligence, and the Perils of Too Much Information. *The New Yorker*, January 8: 44–53.

Gladwell, M. 2008. *Outliers*. Little, Brown.

Goldstein, D., and Gigerenzer, G. 1999. The Recognition Heuristic: How Ignorance Makes Us Smart. In *Simple Heuristics That Make Us Smart*, ed. G. Gigerenzer et al. Oxford University Press.

Greenwood, R. 1981. Management by Objectives: As Developed by Peter Drucker, Assisted by Harold Smiddy. *Academy of Management Review* 6, no. 2: 225–230.

Grove, W., Zald, D., Lebvow, B., Snitz, B., and Nelson, C. 2000. Clinical versus Mechanical Prediction: A Meta-Analysis. *Psychological Assessment* 12: 19–30.

Halberda, J., Mazzocco, M., and Feigenson, L. 2008. Individual Differences in Non-Verbal Number Acuity Correlate with Maths Achievement. *Nature* 455, no. 2: 665–669.

Hall, C., Ariss, L., and Todorov, A. 2007. The Illusion of Knowledge: When More Information Reduces Accuracy and Increases Confidence. *Organizational Behavior and Human Decision Processes* 103: 277–290.

Harris-Thompson, D., and Wiggins, S. 2007 When SOP Is Not Enough. *Law Officer Magazine*, May: 24–26.

Hawkins, J., and Blakeslee, S. 2004. *On Intelligence*. Henry Holt.

Haynes, A., Weiser, T., Berry, W., Lipsitz, S., Breizat, A., Dellinger, E., Herbosa, T., Joseph, S., Kibatala, P., Lapitan, M., Merry, A., Moorthy, K., Reznick, R., Taylor, B., and Gawande, A. 2009. A Surgical Safety Checklist to Reduce Morbidity and Mortality in a Global Population. *New England Journal of Medicine* 360, no. 5: 491–499.

Hersh, S. 2002. Missed Messages: Why the Government Didn't Know What It Knew. *The New Yorker*, June 3: 40–48.

Hertwig, R., and Gigerenzer, G. 1999. The "Conjunction Fallacy" Revisited: How Intelligent Inferences Look Like Reasoning Errors. *Journal of Behavioral Decision Making* 12, no. 4: 275–305.

Heuer, R. 1999. *Psychology of Intelligence Analysis*. Central Intelligence Agency.

Hockey, G., Sauer, J., and Wastell, D. 2007. Adaptability of Training in Simulated Process Control: Knowledge Versus Rule-Based Guidance under Task Changes and Environmental Stress. *Human Factors* 49: 158–174.

Hoffer, W., and Hoffer, M. 1989. *Freefall: 41,000 Feet and Out of Fuel—A True Story*. St. Martin's.

Hoffman, D. 1999. I Had a Funny Feeling in My Gut. *Washington Post Foreign Service*, February 10.

Hoffman, R., and Nead, J. 1983. General Contextualism, Ecological Science and Cognitive Research. *Journal of Mind and Behavior* 4: 507–560.

Hoffrage, U., Lindsey, S., Hertwig, R., and Gigerenzer, G. 2000. Communicating Statistical Information. *Science* 290: 2261–2262.

Jacobson, G., and Hillkirk, J. 1986. *Xerox: American Samurai*. MacMillan

James, W. 1936. *The Varieties of Religious Experience*. First Modern Library edition. Original copyright 1902.

Jamieson, G., and Miller, C. 2000. Exploring the "Culture of Procedures." In Proceedings of 5th International Conference on Human Interaction with Complex Systems, Urbana, Illinois.

Johnson, D., Perlow, R., and Piper, K. 1993. Differences in Team Performance as a Function of Type of Feedback: Learning Oriented Versus Performance Oriented Feedback. *Journal of Applied Psychology* 23: 303–320.

Johnson, J., Driskell, J., and Salas, E. 1997. Vigilant and Hypervigilant Decision Making. *Journal of Applied Psychology* 82, no. 4: 614–622.

Johnson, J., and Raab, M. 2003. Take the First: Option-Generation and Resulting Choices. *Organizational Behavior and Human Decision Processes* 91, no. 2: 215–229.

Johnston, N. The Paradox of Rules: Procedural Drift in Commercial aviation. Unpublished manuscript.

Kahn, D. 1991–92. The Intelligence Failure of Pearl Harbor. *Foreign Affairs*, winter: 138–152.

Kahneman, D., and Klein, G. In press. Conditions for Intuitive Expertise: A Failure to Disagree. *American Psychologist*.

Kahneman, D., Slovic, P., and Tversky, A. 1982. *Judgment under Uncertainty: Heuristics and Biases*. Cambridge University Press.

Kahneman, D., and Tversky, A. 1982. On the Study of Statistical Intuitions. *Cognition* 11: 123–141.

Kaiser, R., Hogan, R., and Craig, S. 2008. Leadership and the Fate of Organizations. *American Psychologist* 63: 96–110.

Kauffmann, B. 2005. Unsung Hero Saves the Day at Midway. *Dayton Daily News*, June 4.

Kelley, T., and Littman, J. 2005. *The Ten Faces of Innovation: IDEO's Strategies for Defeating the Devil's Advocate and Driving Creativity Throughout Your Organization*. Doubleday Currency.

Klein, D., and Murphy, G. 2001. The Representation of Polysemous Words. *Journal of Memory and Language* 45, no. 2: 259–282.

Klein, G. 1979. User Guides: Theoretical Guidelines for their Use. Paper presented at American Psychological Association Meeting, New York.

Klein, G. 1989. Do Decision Biases Explain Too Much? *Human Factors Society Bulletin* 23, no. 5: 1–3.

Klein, G. 1998. *Sources of Power: How People Make Decisions*. MIT Press.

Klein, G. 2001. Features of Team Coordination. In *New Trends in Cooperative Activities*, ed. M. McNeese et al. Human Factors and Ergonomics Society.

Klein, G. 2004. *The Power of Intuition*. Doubleday/Currency.

Klein, G. 2007a. Performing a Project Premortem. *Harvard Business Review*, September: 18–19.

Klein, G. 2007b. Flexecution as a Paradigm for Replanning, Part 1. *IEEE Intelligent Systems* 22, no. 5: 79–83.

Klein, G. 2007c. Flexecution, Part 2: Understanding and Supporting Flexible Execution. *IEEE Intelligent Systems* 22, no. 6: 108–112.

Klein, G. 2007d. Corruption and Recovery of Sensemaking During Navigation. In *Decision Making in Complex Environments*, ed. M. Cook et al. Ashgate.

Klein, G., Armstrong, A., Woods, D., Gokulachandra, M., and Klein, H. A. 2000. Cognitive Wavelength: The Role of Common Ground in Distributed Replanning. Technical Report AFRL-HE-WP-TR-2001-0029, US Air Force Research Laboratory, Wright-Patterson Air Force Base, Ohio.

Klein, G., and Baxter, H. 2009. Cognitive Transformation Theory: Contrasting Cognitive and Behavioral Learning. In *The PSI Handbook of Virtual Environments for Training and Education*, volume 1, ed. D. Schmorrow et al. Praeger Security International.

Klein, G., Calderwood, R., and Clinton-Cirocco, A. 1986. Rapid Decision Making on the Fireground. In *Proceedings of the Human Factors and Ergonomics Society 30th Annual Meeting*.

Klein, G., Feltovich, P., Bradshaw, J., and Woods, D. 2004. Common Ground and Coordination in Joint Activity. In *Organizational Simulation*, ed. W. Rouse and K. Boff. Wiley.

Klein, G., and Hoffman, R. 1993. Seeing the Invisible: Perceptual/Cognitive Aspects of Expertise. In *Cognitive Science Foundations of Instruction*, ed. M. Rabinowitz. Erlbaum.

Klein, G., Phillips, J., Rall, E., and Peluso, D. 2007. A Data/Frame Theory of Sensemaking. In *Expertise Out of Context*, ed. R. Hoffman. Erlbaum.

Klein, G., Pliske, R., Crandall, B., and Woods, D. 2005. Problem Detection. *Cognition, Technology & Work* 7: 14–28.

Klein, G., Ross, K., Moon, B., Klein, D. E., Hoffman, R., and Hollnagel, E. 2003. Macrocognition. *IEEE Intelligent Systems* 18, no. 3: 81–85.

Klein, G., and Rothman, J. 2008. Staying on Course When Your Destination Keeps Changing. *Conference Board Review*, November-December: 24–27.

Klein, G., and Weitzenfeld, J. 1978. Improvement of Skills for Solving Ill-Defined Problems. *Educational Psychologist* 13: 31–41.

Klein, G., and Weitzenfeld, J. 1982. The Use of Analogues in Comparability Analysis. *Applied Ergonomics* 13: 99–104.

Klein, H. A., and Lippa, K. 2008. Type II Diabetes Self-Management: Controlling a Dynamic System. *Journal of Cognitive Engineering and Decision Making* 2: 48–62.

Klein, H. A., and McHugh, A. 2005. National Differences in Teamwork. In *Organizational Simulation*, ed. W. Rouse and K. Boff. Wiley.

Klein, H. A., and Meininger, A. 2004. Self Management of Medication and Diabetes: Cognitive Control. *IEEE Transactions on Systems, Man and Cybernetics, Part A: Systems and Humans* 34: 718–725.

Kontogiannis, T. 2000. The Effect of Training Systemic Information on the Acquisition and Transfer of Fault-Finding Skills. *International Journal of Cognitive Ergonomics* 4: 243–267.

Kruger, J., Wirtz, D., and Miller, D. 2005. Counterfactual Thinking and the First Instinct Fallacy. *Journal of Personality and Social Psychology* 88: 725–735.

Kurtz, C. F., and Snowden, D. J. 2003. The New Dynamics of Strategy: Sensemaking in a Complex and Complicated World. *e-Business Management* 42, no. 3.

Lambe, P. 2007. *Organising Knowledge: Taxonomies, Knowledge and Organizational Effectiveness*. Chandos.

Langer, E. 1989. *Mindfulness*. Addison-Wesley.

Lanir, Z. 1983. *Fundamental Surprise: The National Intelligence Crisis*. Center for Strategic Studies, Tel Aviv University.

Latash, M. 1996. The Bernstein Problem: How Does the Central Nervous System Make Its Choices? In *Dexterity and Its Development*, ed. M. Latash and M. Turvey. Erlbaum.

Laufer, A. 2009. *Breaking the Code of Project Management*. Palgrave Macmillan.

Lewis, M. 2003. *Moneyball: The Art of Winning an Unfair Game*. Norton.

Lippa, K., and Klein, H. 2008. Portraits of Patient Cognition: How Patients Understand Diabetes Self-Care. *Canadian Journal of Nursing Research* 40: 80–95.

Lipshitz, R. 1997. Coping with Uncertainty: Beyond the Reduce, Quantify and Plug Heuristic. In *Decision Making under Stress: Emerging Themes and Applications*, ed. R. Flin et al. Ashgate.

Lipshitz, R., and Ben Shaul, O. 1997. Schemata and Mental Models in Recognition-Primed Decision Making. In *Naturalistic Decision Making*, ed. C. Zsambok and G. Klein. Erlbaum.

Lipshitz, R., and Strauss, O. 1997. Coping with Uncertainty: A Naturalistic Decision-Making Analysis. *Organizational Behavior and Human Decision Processes* 69: 149–163.

Lopes, L. 1991. The Rhetoric of Irrationality. *Theory and Psychology* 1, no. 1: 65–82.

Lovallo, D., and Kahneman, D. 2003. Delusions of Success: How Optimism Undermines Executives' Decisions. *Harvard Business Review* 81, no. 7: 56–63.

Lowenstein, R. 2000. *When Genius Failed: The Rise and Fall of Long-Term Capital Management*. Random House.

LuperFoy, S. 1995. Naturalistic Dialogs with Artificial Agents: Why I Lie to My Toaster. Paper presented at MIT Language, Cognition, and Computation Seminar.

Macey, J. 2003. A Pox on Both Your Houses: Enron, Sarbanes-Oxley and the Debate Concerning the Relative Efficiency of Mandatory Versus Enabling Rules. *Washington University Law Quarterly* 81: 329–355.

MacGregor, J., Ormerod, T., and Chronicle, E. 2000. A Model of Human Performance on the Traveling Salesperson Problem. *Memory and Cognition* 28: 1183–1190.

Manos, D. 2004. Majority of Diabetics Do Not Follow Guidelines for Maintaining Health, Despite a Decade of Warning, Study Shows. *Medical Guidelines and Outcomes Research* 15: 1–6.

Mauboussin, M. 2007. *More Than You Know: Finding Financial Wisdom in Unconventional Places*. Columbia University Press.

McCarthy, P., Ball, D., and Purcell, W. 2007. Project Phoenix—Optimizing the Machine-Person Mix in High-Impact Weather Forecasting. Presented at 22nd American Meteorological Society Conference on Weather Analysis and Forecasting, Park City, Utah.

McLeod, P., and Dienes, Z. 1996. Do Fielders Know Where to Go to Catch the Ball or Only How to Get There? *Journal of Experimental Psychology: Human Perception and Performance* 22: 531–543.

McNeil, B., Pauker, S., Sox, H., and Tversky, A. 1982. On the Elicitation of Preferences for Alternative Therapies. *New England Journal of Medicine* 306, no. 21: 1259–1262.

Medin, D., Lynch, E., Coley, J., and Atran, S. 1997. Categorization and Reasoning Among Tree Experts: Do All Roads Lead to Rome? *Cognitive Psychology* 32: 49–96.

Meehl, P. 1954. *Clinical vs. Statistical Prediction: A Theoretical Analysis and a Review of the Evidence*. University of Minnesota Press.

Minsky, M. 1986. *The Society of Mind*. Simon and Schuster.

Mintzberg, H. 1994. *The Rise and Fall of Strategic Planning*. Free Press.

Mitchell, D., Russo, J., and Pennington, N. 1989. Back to the Future: Temporal Perspective in the Explanation of Events. *Journal of Behavioral Decision Making* 2: 25–38.

Mlodinow, L. 2008. *The Drunkard's Walk: How Randomness Rules Our Lives*. Pantheon.

Morris, N., and Rouse, W. 1985. Review and Evaluation of Empirical Research in Troubleshooting. *Human Factors* 27: 503–530.

Mueller, S., and Minnery, B. 2008. Adapting the Turing Test for Embodied Neurocognitive Evaluation of Biologically Inspired Cognitive Agents. Presented at AAAI symposium.

National Commission on Terrorist Attacks Upon the United States. 2004. *The 9/11 Commission Report*.

Neace, W., Michaud, S., Bolling, L., Deer, K., and Zecevic, L. 2008. Frequency Formats, Probability Formats, or Problem Structure? A Test of the Nest-Sets Hypothesis in an Extensional Reasoning Task. *Judgment and Decision Making* 3, no. 2: 140–152.

Nemeth, C., Brown, K., and Rogers, J. 2001. Devil's Advocate Versus Authentic Dissent: Stimulating Quantity and Quality. *European Journal of Social Psychology* 31: 707–720.

Nemeth, C., Connell, J., Rogers, J., and Brown, K. 2001. Improving Decision Making by Means of Dissent. *Journal of Applied Social Psychology* 31: 48–58.

Newell, B., Wong, K., Cheung, J., and Rakow, T. 2009. Think, Blink or Sleep on It? The Impact of Modes of Thought on Complex Decision Making. *Quarterly Journal of Experimental Psychology* 62, no. 4: 707–732.

Nocera, J. 2009. Risk Mismanagement. *New York Times Magazine*, January 4.

Nonaka, I., and Takeuchi, H. 1995. *The Knowledge Creating Company*. Oxford University Press.

Norman, D. 1988. *The Design of Everyday Things*. Doubleday.

Norman, D. 1993. *Things That Make Us Smart: Defending Human Attributes in the Age of the Machine*. Addison-Wesley.

Norman, D., and Kuras, M. 2006. Engineering Complex Systems. In *Complex Engineered Systems: Science Meets Technology*, ed. D. Braha et al. Springer.

Northcraft, G., and Neale, M. 1987. Experts, Amateurs, and Real Estate: An Anchoring-and-Adjustment Perspective on Property Pricing Decisions. *Organizational Behavior and Human Decision Processes* 39: 84–97.

Nygren, T., and White, R. 2002. Assessing Individual Differences in Decision Making Styles: Analytical vs. Intuitive. In Proceedings of 46th Annual Meeting of Human Factors and Ergonomics Society.

O'Brian, P. 1970. *Master and Commander*. William Collins.

O'Brian, P. 1972. *Post Captain*. William Collins.

O'Brian, P. 1973. *H.M.S. Surprise*. William Collins.

O'Brian, P. 1977. *The Mauritius Command*. William Collins.

O'Brian, P. 1983. *Treason's Harbour*. William Collins.

O'Conner, A., Rostom, A., Fiset, V., Tetroe, J., Entwistle, V., Llewellyn-Thomas, H., Holmes-Rovner, M., Barry, M., and Jones, J. 1999. Decision Aids for Patients Facing Health Treatment or Screening Decisions: Systematic Review. *British Medical Journal* 319: 731–734.

Olby, R. 1974. *The Path to the Double Helix: The Discovery of DNA*. University of Washington Press.

Omodei, M., McLennan, J., Elliott, G., Wearing, A., and Clancy, J. 2005. "More Is Better?": A Bias toward Overuse of Resources in Naturalistic Decision-Making Settings. In *How Professionals Make Decisions*, ed. H. Montgomery et al. Erlbaum.

Orasanu, J. 1994. Shared Problem Models and Flight Crew Performance. In *Aviation Psychology in Practice*, ed. N. Johnston et al. Ashgate.

Orasanu, J., and Connolly, T. 1993. The Reinvention of Decision Making. In *Decision Making in Action: Models and Methods*, ed. G. Klein et al. Ablex.

Orr, J. 1990. Sharing Knowledge, Celebrating Identity: Community Memory in a Service Culture. In *Collective Remembering*, ed. D. Middleston and D. Edwards. Sage.

Oskamp, S. 1965. Overconfidence in Case Study Judgments. *Journal of Consulting Psychology* 29: 61–265.

Parker, M. 2007. *Panama Fever*. Doubleday.

Patrick, J., and Haines, B. 1988. Training and Transfer of Fault-Finding Skill. *Ergonomics* 31: 193–210.

Patterson, E. 2008. Editorial: Structuring flexibility: The Potential Good, Bad, and Ugly in Standardisation of Handovers. *Quality and Safety in Healthcare* 17, no. 1: 4–5.

Patterson, E., Watts-Perotti, J., and Woods, D. 1999. Voice Loops as Coordination Aids in Space Shuttle Mission Control. *Computer Supported Cooperative Work* 8, no. 4: 3535–371.

Patton, M. 1978. *Utilization-Focused Evaluation*. Sage.

Perrow, C. 1984. *Normal Accidents*. Basic Books.

Phelps, R., and Shanteau, J. 1978. Livestock Judges: How Much Information Can an Expert Use? *Organizational Behavior and Human Performance* 21: 209–219.

Pizlo, Z., Rosenfeld, A., and Epelboim, J. 1995. An Exponential Pyramid Model of the Time-Course of Size Processing. *Vision Research* 35: 1089–1107.

Plous, S. 1993. *The Psychology of Judgment and Decision Making*. McGraw-Hill.

Polanyi, M. 1958. *Personal Knowledge*. University of Chicago Press.

Polanyi, M. 1967. *The Tacit Dimension*. Doubleday.

Popper, K. 1959. *The Logic of Scientific Discovery*. Basic Books.

Potchen, E. 2006. Measuring Observer Performance in Chest Radiology: Some Experiences. *Journal of the American College of Radiology* 3: 423–432.

Pradhan, A., Hammel, K., DeRamus, R., Pollatsek, A., Noyce, D., and Fisher, D. 2005. Using Eye Movements to Evaluate Effects of Driver Age on Risk Perception in a Driving Simulator. *Human Factors* 47: 840–852.

Prange, G. 1981. *At Dawn We Slept: The Untold Story of Pearl Harbor*. Penguin.

Pronovost, P., Needham, D., Berenholtz, S., Sinopoli, D., Chu, H., Cosgrove, S., Sexton, B., Hyzy, R., Welsh, R., Roth, G., Bander, J., Kepros, J., and Goeschel, C. 2006. An Intervention to Decrease Catheter-Related Bloodstream Infections in the ICU. *New England Journal of Medicine* 355, no. 26: 2725–2732.

Raiffa, H. 1968. *Decision Analysis: Introductory Lectures on Choices under Uncertainty*. Addison-Wesley.

Rasmussen, J. 1990. The Role of Error in Organizing Behavior. *Ergonomics* 33: 1185–1199.

Reason, J. 1990. *Human Error*. Cambridge University Press.

Rickenbacker, E. 1919. *Fighting the Flying Circus*. Lippincott.

Rittel, H., and Webber, M. 1973. Dilemmas in a General Theory of Planning. *Policy Sciences* 4: 155–169.

Rittel, H., and Webber, M. 1984. Planning Problems Are Wicked Problems. In *Developments in Design Methodology*, ed. N. Cross. Wiley.

Ross, K., Klein, G., Thunholm, P., Schmitt, J., and Baxter, H. 2004. The Recognition-Primed Decision Model. *Military Review* 74, no. 4: 6–10.

Rothman, J. 2006. Identity and Conflict: Collaboratively Addressing Police-Community Conflict in Cincinnati, Ohio. *Ohio State Journal on Dispute Resolution* 22, no. 1: 105–132.

Routley, J., Jennings, C., and Chubb, M. Undated. High-Rise Office Building Fire: One Meridian Plaza, Philadelphia, Pennsylvania. National Fire Data Center, Federal Emergency Management Agency.

Rudolph, J. 2003. Into the Big Muddy and Out Again: Error Persistence and Crisis Management in the Operating Room. Dissertation, Boston College.

Rudolph, J., Morrison, J., and Carroll, J. In press. The Dynamics of Action-Oriented Problem Solving: Linking Interpretation and Choice. *Academy of Management Review.*

Russo, J., and Schoemaker, P. 1989. *Decision Traps: The Ten Barriers to Brilliant Decision-Making and How to Overcome Them.* Doubleday.

Ryle, G. 1949. *The Concept of Mind.* University of Chicago Press, 1984.

Sauer, J., Hockey, G., and Wastell, D. 2000. Effects of Training on Short- and Long-Term Skill Retention in a Complex Multi-Task Environment. *Ergonomics* 43: 2043–2064.

Sawyer, K. 1999. Mystery of Orbiter Crash Solved. *Washington Post*, October 1.

Saxberg, B. 1987. Projected Free Fall Trajectories: I. Theory and Simulation. *Biological Cybernetics* 56: 159–175.

Schacter, D. 2001. *The Seven Sins of Memory: How the Mind Forgets and Remembers.* Houghton Mifflin.

Schmidt, R., and Wulf, G. 1997. Continuous Concurrent Feedback Degrades Skill Learning: Implications for Training and Simulation. *Human Factors* 39: 509–525.

Schmitt, J., and Klein, G. 1996. Fighting in the Fog: Dealing with Battlefield Uncertainty. *Marine Corps Gazette*, August: 62–69.

Schwartz, B. 2004. *The Paradox of Choice: Why More Is Less.* HarperCollins.

Self, N. 2008. *Two Wars: One Hero's Flight on Two Fronts—Abroad and Within.* Tyndale House.

Seligman, M. 2002. *Authentic Happiness: Using the New Positive Psychology to Realize Your Potential for Lasting Fulfillment.* Simon and Schuster.

Sengupta, K., Abdel-Hamed, T., and Van Wassenhove, L. 2007. The Experience Trap. *Harvard Business Review*, February: 94–101.

Shafir, E. 1993. Choosing and Rejecting: Why Some Options Are Both Better and Worse. *Memory and Cognition* 21: 546–556.

Shalin, V., and Verdile, C. 2003. The Identification of Knowledge Content and Function in Manual Labor. *Ergonomics* 46, no. 7: 695–713.

Shanteau, J. 1992. Competence in Experts: The Role of Task Characteristics. *Organizational Behavior and Human Decision Processes* 53: 252–262.

Shapira, Z. 1995. *Risk Taking: A Managerial Perspective.* Russell Sage Foundation.

Silberberg, E., and Suen, W. 2001. *The Structure of Economics: A Mathematical Analysis,* third edition. Irwin/McGraw-Hill.

Sills, D. 2009. On the MSC Forecaster Forums and the Future Role of the Human Forecaster. *Bulletin of the American Meteoreological Society.*

Simon, H. A. 1957. *Models of Man: Social and Rational.* Wiley.

Simon, H. 1992. What Is an Explanation of Behavior? *Psychological Science* 3: 150–161.

Skinner, B. F. 1948. *Walden Two.* Macmillan.

Skitka, L., Mosier, K., and Burdick, M. 2000. Accountability and Automation Bias. *International Journal of Human-Computer Studies* 52: 701–717.

Sloman, S. 1996. The Empirical Case for Two Systems of Reasoning. *Psychological Bulletin* 119: 3–22.

Sloman, S., Over, D., Slovak, L., and Stibel, J. 2003. Frequency Illusions and Other Fallacies. *Organizational Behavior and Human Decision Processes* 91: 296–309.

Slovic, P. 1995. The Construction of Preference. *American Psychologist* 50, no. 5: 364–371.

Smallman, H., and Hegarty, M. 2007. Expertise, Spatial Ability and Intuition in the Use of Complex Displays. Paper presented at 51st Annual Conference of Human Factors and Ergonomics Society, Baltimore.

Smith, J., and Kida, T. 1991. Heuristics and Biases: Expertise and Task Realism in Auditing. *Psychological Bulletin* 109: 472–489.

Smith, P., Woods, D., McCoy, E., Billings, C., Sarter, N., and Dekker, S. 1998. Using Forecasts of Future Incidents to Evaluate Future ATM System Designs. *Air Traffic Control Quarterly* 6, no. 1: 71–85.

Snellman, L. 1977. Operational Forecasting Using Automated Guidance. *Bulletin of the American Meteorological Society* 58: 1036–1044.

Snook, S. 2000. *Friendly Fire: The Accidental Shootdown of US Black Hawks over Northern Iraq*. Princeton University Press.

Snowden, D., Klein, G., Chew, L., and Teh, C. 2007. A Sensemaking Experiment: Techniques to Achieve Cognitive Precision. In Proceedings of 12th International Command and Control Research and Technology Symposium.

Staszewski, J. 2008. Cognitive Engineering Based on Expert Skill: Notes on Success and Surprises. In *Naturalistic Decision Making and Macrocognition*, ed. J. Schraagen et al. Ashgate.

Stewart, S. 1992. *Emergency: Crisis on the Flight Deck*. Airlife.

Stewart, T., Moninger, W., Heideman, K., and Reagan-Cirincione, P. 1993. Effects of Improved Information on the Components of Skill in Weather Forecasting. *Organizational Behavior and Human Decision Processes* 53: 107–134.

Stewart, T., Roebber, P., and Bosart, L. 1997. The Importance of the Task in Analyzing Expert Judgment. *Organizational Behavior and Human Decision Processes* 69: 205–219.

Strack, F., and Mussweiler, T. 1997. Explaining the Enigmatic Anchoring Effect: Mechanisms of Selective Accessibility. *Journal of Personality and Social Psychology* 73: 437–446.

Sutcliffe, K., and Weick, K. 2008. Information Overload Revisited. In *The Oxford Handbook of Organizational Decision Making*, ed. G. Hodgkinson and W. Starbuck. Oxford University Press.

Syrotuck, W. 1976. *Analysis of Lost Person Behavior: An Aid to Search Planning*. Barkleigh Productions.

Taleb, N. N. 2007. *The Black Swan: The Impact of the Highly Improbable*. Random House.

Tetlock, P. 2005. *Expert Political Judgment: How Good Is It? How Can We Know?* Princeton University Press.

Thaler, R., and Sunstein, C. 2008. *Nudge: Improving Decisions about Health, Wealth, and Happiness.* Yale University Press.

Thunholm, P. 2005. Planning Under Time Pressure: An Attempt Toward a Prescriptive Model of Military Tactical Decision Making. In *How Professionals Make Decisions*, ed. H. Montgomery et al.. Erlbaum.

Thunholm, P. 2007. Militär genomförandeledning—Vad händer när det oväntade inträffar? [Commanding Execution—What happens when the unexpected occurs?]. Publication 1525/7:1, Swedish National Defence College.

Treverton, G. 2001. *Reshaping National Intelligence for an Age of Information.* Cambridge University Press.

Tversky, A., and Kahneman, D. 1974. Judgment under Uncertainty: Heuristics and Biases. *Science* 185: 1124–1130.

Tversky, A., and Kahneman, D. 1982. Judgments of and by Representativeness. In *Judgment under Uncertainty: Heuristics and Biases*, ed. D. Kahneman et al. Cambridge University Press.

Tversky, A., and Kahneman, D. 1983. Extensional versus Intuitive Reasoning: The Conjunction Fallacy in Probability Judgment. *Psychological Review* 90: 293–315.

Tversky, A., and Shafir, E. 1992. Decision under Conflict: An Analysis of Choice Aversion. *Psychological Science* 6: 358–361.

Vanderbilt, T. 2008. *Traffic: Why We Drive the Way We Do (and What It Says about Us).* Knopf.

Van Hecke, M. 2007. *Blind Spots: Why Smart People Do Dumb Things.* Prometheus.

Vicente, K. 1999. *Cognitive Work Analysis: Toward Safe, Productive, and Healthy Computer-Based Work.* Erlbaum.

Vicente, K. 2002. Work Domain Analysis and Task Analysis: A Difference That Matters. In *Cognitive Task Analysis*, ed. J. Schraagen et al. Erlbaum.

Vos Savant, M. 1990. Ask Marilyn. *Parade*, September 9.

Waldmann, M.R. 1996. Knowledge-Based Causal Induction. In *The Psychology of Learning and Motivation*, volume 34: *Causal Learning*, ed. D. Shanks et al. Academic.

Wallsten, T. 2000. A Letter from the President. *Society for Judgment and Decision Making Newsletter*, June: 4–5.

Watson, J. 1968. *The Double Helix.* Atheneum

Wears, R., and Berg, M. 2005. Computer Technology and Clinical Work: Still Waiting for Godot. *JAMA* 293: 1261–1263.

Weick, K., and Sutcliffe, K. 2001. *Managing the Unexpected: Assuring High Performance in an Age of Complexity.* Jossey-Bass.

Weick, K., and Sutcliffe, K. 2006. Mindfulness and the Quality of Attention. *Organization Science* 17, no. 4: 514–525.

Weick, K., Sutcliffe, K., and Obstfeld, D. 1999. Organizing for High Reliability: Processes of Collective Mindfulness. *Research in Organizational Behavior* 21: 81–123.

Westin, D., and Weinberger, J. 2004. When Clinical Description Becomes Statistical Prediction. *American Psychologist* 59: 595–613.

Wilson, T. 2002. *Strangers to Ourselves: Discovering the Adaptive Unconscious*. Harvard University Press.

Wohlstetter, R. 1962. *Pearl Harbor: Warning and Decision*. Stanford University Press.

Woods, D. 2006. Essential Characteristics of Resilience for Organizations. In *Resilience Engineering: Concepts and Precepts*, ed. E. Hollnagel et al. Ashgate.

Woods, D. 2007. Creating Safety by Engineering Resilience. Invited talk, Almaden Institute, IBM Almaden Research Center.

Woods, D. 2009. Escaping Failures of Foresight. *Safety Science* 47: 498–501.

Woods, D., and Hollnagel, E. 2006. *Joint Cognitive Systems: Patterns in Cognitive Systems Engineering*. Taylor and Francis.

Woods, D., Patterson, E., and Roth, E. 2002. Can We Ever Escape from Data Overload? A Cognitive Systems Diagnosis. *Cognition, Technology and Work* 4: 22–36.

Woods, D., and Wreathall, J. 2008. Stress-Strain Plot as a Basis for Assessing System Resilience. In *Resilience Engineering: Remaining Sensitive to the Possibility of Failure*, ed. E. Hollnagel et al. Ashgate.

Wright, L. 2006. The Agent: Did the CIA Stop an FBI Detective from Preventing 9/11? *The New Yorker*, July 10 and 17.

Wu, G., Zhang, J., and Gonzalez, R. 2004. Decision under Risk. In *Blackwell Handbook of Judgment and Decision Making*, ed. D. Koehler and N. Harvey. Blackwell.

Xiao, Y., Seagull, F., Nieves-Khouw, F., Barczak, N., and Perkins, S. 2004. Organizational-Historical Analysis of the "Failure to Respond to Alarm" Problems. *IEEE Transactions on Systems, Man, and Cybernetics, Part A* 34, no. 6: 772–778.

Yamagishi, K. 2003. Facilitating Normative Judgments of Conditional Probability: Frequency or Nested Sets? *Experimental Psychology* 50: 97–106.

Yates, J., Veinott, E., and Patalano, A. 2003. Hard Decisions, Bad Decisions: On Decision Quality and Decision Aiding. In *Emerging Perspectives on Judgment and Decision Research*, ed. S. Schneider and J. Shanteau. Cambridge University Press.

Yergin, D. 1991. *The Prize: The Epic Quest for Oil, Money, and Power*. Free Press.

Zakay, D., and Wooler, S. 1984. Time Pressure, Training, and Decision Effectiveness. *Ergonomics* 27: 273–284.

Zhu, L., and Gigerenzer, G. 2006. Children Can Solve Bayesian Problems: The Role of in Mental Computation. *Cognition* 98: 287–308.

Index